Ten Commandments
for today

Brian H Edwards

DayOne

© Day One Publications 2002
First printed 1996
Revised edition 2002

Scripture quotations are from The New International Version unless otherwise stated.
© 1973, 1978, 1984, International Bible Society. Published by Hodder and Stoughton.

British Library Cataloguing in Publication Data available
ISBN 1 903087

Published by Day One Publications
3 Epsom Business Park, Kiln Lane, Epsom, Surrey KT17 1JF.
t 01372 728 300 FAX 01372 722 400
email—sales@dayone.co.uk
www.dayone.co.uk

Designed by Steve Devane and printed by CPD

Dedication

This book is dedicated to my granddaughters,
Susanna, Adele, and Cara, and to all the young people of
their generation, that they may discover the joy and
freedom of obeying the Commandments of God.

Contents

'**D**on't tell me they've found another Commandment,' said a worried school-boy when he heard about the discovery of the Dead Sea Scrolls! Perhaps he was reflecting the difficulty we all have with those ten all-inclusive laws that God gave to Moses.

This book unpacks the crammed meaning of these terse commands, applies them pointedly to life in a deregulated age, and directs us to Christ who gives pardon and righteousness to those who turn to him from their habitual law-breaking.

But do we really need another book on the Ten Commandments? I think we do. First, eternal truth needs regular restatement; otherwise the shifting sands of time may drift over and obliterate the ancient landmarks. Secondly, in a fast-changing world, each generation needs to have great abiding principles applied to it in a contemporary and specific way. Thirdly, in our generation the very status of the Ten Commandments in the life of Christian people has been called into question.

My friend Brian Edwards wrote this substantial treatment of *The Ten Commandments for Today* in 1996. I am glad that it has been much in demand and that re-publication is now called for. But *today* for us is in 2002 and an awful lot happens in six years! Of course God's word endures for ever, but our world is changing all the time. So, some of the illustrations and examples had to be updated and some of the applications had to be addressed to new situations. And this revision gave the opportunity of developing the exposition here and there.

All this makes an excellent book even better! May God use it more and more!

Andrew Anderson
International Baptist Church of Brussels, Belgium
April 2002

Whose law?

God spoke all these words. Exodus 20:1

Dunblane is a quiet rural town near Stirling just where the M9 motorway comes to an end in Scotland. Even those who do not easily cry must have wept silently at the horrific events of Wednesday 13th March 1996. Shortly after 9.15, as the children were settling into their classes, Thomas Watt Hamilton walked into the local primary school and shot dead a teacher, and sixteen of her children all under the age of six. I was travelling on the M4 motorway when I switched on the radio half-way through a news bulletin. At first I assumed the unfolding story had happened somewhere across the world: South America perhaps, or Africa, the Middle East—yes, it must be Jerusalem. Things like that happen in places like those. Then the reality hit me: Dunblane—Stirling—Scotland—here in the United Kingdom!

My mind ran back thirty years when, at 9.15 on an October morning in 1966 a spoil-tip slid onto the local primary school in the small South Wales mining village of Aberfan and engulfed five teachers and one hundred and nine children in black choking mud: the result, according to the official enquiry, of 'bungling ineptitude' by the Coal Board.

At 11.35 a.m. on Tuesday April 20 1999 two teenagers, Eric Harris and Dylan Klebold walked into the cafeteria of Columbine High School in Littleton, Colorado and began a deadly shooting spree resulting in a final toll of fifteen people dead—most of them their own classmates. Harris and Klebold left video tapes in their rooms in which they filmed themselves gloating over the cruel carnage that they were about to achieve.

In January 2000 the medical career of Dr Harold Shipman, a family doctor in Hyde, Greater Manchester, came to an end after twenty four years during which time he may have killed more than two hundred and fifty of his patients. Shipman's name will go down in history as possibly the most destructive serial killer on record.

Dunblane, Aberfan, Littleton, Hyde, places which, like Lockerbie, few of us could locate on the map until a tragedy shot them into prominence.

And each disaster was man-made: a callous gunman, a careless and greedy Coal Board, two power-crazy teenagers and a medical doctor so sinister and evil that even the tabloids could hardly describe him. And these incidents are not as isolated or exceptional as we would wish them to be. The names of Myra Hindley, Mary Bell and Fred and Rosemary West are just a few of the most prominent in a notorious line-up of brutal and sadistic murderers.

And then–to quote the *Daily Mail* cover headline—'Apocalypse—NY Sept.11th 2001'. Such a disaster could never happen, but it did; no one could ever carry out such callously vile acts, but they could. The world went numb with shock.

In the wake of such terrible events, editorials, leader-writers and articles all focus on the state of our nation and offer criticism of the government, the church, the educational system and society generally. The pollsters get busy with their interviews and statistics. One writer drew the conclusion from a Gallup poll that 'It should be possible to build on an existing moral consensus' to produce part of the school curriculum. The ground of this optimism lay in the fact that ninety percent of those interviewed favoured 'respect for people in authority' and 'tolerance for the opinions of others'. That was our consensus; our 'shared moral values'. But must we build our hope for a safe society on such a minimum?

During the last week of November 1993 two ten-year old boys abducted and battered to death three-year old James Bulger, leaving his savagely shattered body on a railway line. In the aftermath of this unimaginable brutality John Major, the British Prime Minister, desperate to lead a morally bankrupt society somewhere, spoke of the need to 'get back to basics'. He offered no suggestion as to what the 'basics' were, or where they were to be found, and, not surprisingly, the whole crusade collapsed untidily under the 'revelations' of the private lives of government ministers. There had been no reference to the Commandments of the Creator and, on Monday 29th November 1993, less than a week after the murder of Jamie Bulger, the Government brought before Parliament a Bill to deregulate Sunday trading. So, an appeal to get 'back to basics' was accompanied by a law to destroy the relevance of one of the Ten Commandments! Clearly the Commandments were not considered to be 'basic'.

Two years later, after another wave of violence including the murder of headmaster Philip Lawrence outside his north London school, the nation went through its customary soul searching. However, having forgotten where its soul came from, the nearest one Member of Parliament could get was to suggest that what we needed was 'something like the Ten Commandments'. Notice that: only something *like* the Ten Commandments'. Perhaps he thought that we could improve on them?

Today, we have a morality defined by consensus and experiment. Right and wrong is what the majority wants—or more generally what the loudest or most powerful minority wants. Occasionally the consensus will change when the experiment goes wrong. But not always. Over the next thirty years two hundred million people across the world will die from AIDS. In the United Kingdom alone there are nearly thirty thousand reported cases of HIV infection and between eight and nine thousand AIDS victims. Yet if everyone obeyed the seventh Commandment, AIDS would be eradicated from the entire world within three decades. Will we give up our immoral lifestyles of adultery, promiscuity and homosexual behaviour so that innocent victims are not infected? By contrast in the Spring of 1996 when a few tragic deaths from Creutzfeldt-Jakob Disease (CJD) were recorded with a 'possible' link with Bovine Spongiform Encephalopathy (BSE or 'Mad Cow Disease'), the whole world gave up eating British beef!

Only when we are prepared to teach our children absolutes and to model those absolutes by our own lives, will there be any arrest to the downward spiral of moral decline. There is an almost total loss of respect in our society. We have no respect for authority, for leadership, for women, for laws, for property. Just about the only respect left is for animals and trees!

The Ten Commandments insist upon respect for God, for parents, for life, for marriage, for property and for truth. Therefore few things should be more important today than a return to understanding and to teaching them.

One of the greatest tragedies of our modern age is that confidence in moral absolutes, belief in God who is holy, and an awareness of the reality of judgement to come, are all out of fashion. Supported by a welfare state, pension schemes and advancing medical science, life for most in western civilization is not too bad. People cannot imagine why God should be so bothered with them, least of all why he should be angry with them. If we talk to modern men and women about hell and judgement, they wonder what the fuss is all about. After all, even large sections of the so-called Christian church don't believe in that sort of thing any more. Civilization has moved on, we are told: this is not the eighteenth century but the third millennium!

In fact, the only reason why our society is marginally safer than that of the eighteenth century is due to the introduction of street lights and a more efficient and significantly larger police force. If we turned off the lights and reverted our 'Bobbies' to the eighteenth century 'Charlies', imagine what would happen: no one would venture out after dark unless they were a fool or well-armed; that would be Georgian England all over again. However, in spite of electricity and the modern Bobby, many parts of our nation from concrete estates to urban sprawl to rural communities are terrorised by the equivalent of the eighteenth century buffers, smashers, nosers, sharpers, bustlers, footpads, highwaymen and pickpockets. In 1752 Sir Horace Mann complained bitterly: 'One is forced to travel, even at noon, as if one were going to battle.' Ladies were escorted to their card parties by young boys armed with clubs. All that cruelty, violence, callous greed and selfish ambition of eighteenth century England is exceeded, blow for blow, by our society in the new millennium.

Listening to the wrong voice

Today we have violent criminals often too young to stand in the dock, and crimes of such horrific brutality that a shocked nation has begun to ask fundamental questions like: 'What is wrong with our generation?' At the risk of sounding simplistic, we may respond with a serious answer: What is wrong with this generation is that we are dealing with children who are the third generation to be brought up in almost total ignorance of the rules that their Creator has given them—and the personal implications of these rules.

Put another way, society is doing what it has always been doing ever since the tragedy in the Garden of Eden: it is listening to the wrong voice. Our first parents had been daily listening to the voice of God. His was the only voice they heard, and the only voice they wanted to hear; he spoke with both authority and kindness, and Adam and Eve saw no contradiction between those two. They knew that the authority was kind because it was for their good. Then another voice broke in and whispered the insinuation that God was cheating them out of something better, and that if they broke free from his 'petty' rules, they could really be free to find their fulfilment, satisfaction and purpose in life.

In the event they lost everything. But above all they lost an awareness of the wholeness of God; they saw him now as the one who intended their harm, and instead of loving him for his laws they feared him (Genesis 3:10). Indeed, they hated his authority and so they hid from him in the garden. Ever since then, the world has been listening to the wrong voice. True there is a cacophony of voices hammering conflicting ideas into the mind of mankind, but in reality it is only one voice. Through a multitude of religions and social philosophies there is just one message coming through loud and clear: 'Did God really say?' (Genesis 3:1). Chief among the casualties from the Fall was mankind's unwillingness to listen any more to the voice of God. And chief among the casualties of that is God's rule of law.

Certainly the Apostle Paul in the New Testament understood this. Writing to the Christians at Rome he commented, 'What shall we say, then? Is the law sin? Certainly not! Indeed I would not have known what sin was except through the law. For I would not have known what coveting really was if the law had not said, "Do not covet"'. Paul concluded, 'So then, the law is holy, and the commandment is holy, righteous and good' (Romans 7:7,12).

Nearly two hundred years ago Henry Martyn, a brilliant Cambridge mathematician, went to India with the good news of Christ. On 23rd March 1809 he wrote in his diary: 'Having been reading the law and the prophets to my servants for three quarters of the year I thought them sufficiently prepared for hearing the gospel. So I began reading Matthew to them.' Perhaps that was a little too rigid! Nine months of bad news before sharing the good news leaves open the possibility that some of his servants may have passed into eternity before Henry Martyn ever reached the gospel. But Martyn got his order of priorities right; and we are decidedly wrong if we think of the Ten Commandments only as 'bad news'. Today especially, they are some of the best news we can ever receive from God.

Henry Martyn was right to begin by reminding his servants of what God expected of them. Only then could they measure themselves by the proper standard and realise how far short they had fallen. Two hundred years on from Henry Martyn, little has changed. Nineteenth century or twenty-first, East or West, people are the same.

Alongside the majority in the world at large who are hardly aware of the existence of the law of God, there are many in the church who choose to ignore it. The law in general, and the Ten Commandments in particular, are an embarrassment. Freedom and joy are preached to the exclusion of law and judgement. We are told that a modern age will not be attracted by the thundering of Sinai; the Christian life must be presented as an exciting adventure with peace and happiness in full measure. This, we are assured, is 'fullness of life'. We are more interested in finding ourselves than in finding our God, and the gospel is presented in terms of purpose and meaningfulness rather than in terms of reconciliation and forgiveness. But the New Testament emphasis is clearly directed towards reconciliation and forgiveness.

Outside the church, and often even within it, the psychotherapist is more important than the law of God. Self-awareness and self-worth are big in today's values. How we feel is often considered more important than what we do. This is a disastrous philosophy.

The day after Thomas Hamilton gunned down sixteen children and their teacher in that Dunblane primary school, Anthony Daniels, a practising family doctor, wrote an article in the *Daily Mail*. In it he attacked this modern view that how a person feels is more important that what he does, with the result that anger is seen as a noble emotion and its outcome becomes self-justifying. Daniels wisely commented, 'We need to recognise once again what our ancestors knew instinctively: that hypocrisy, outward conformity and insincerity are not always vices, but on the contrary are essential social virtues. As long as we continue to believe that a man's feelings count for more than his actions, then we may expect further psychotherapy by mass murder of the innocent, such as that which took place so tragically in Dunblane.' Dr Daniels was absolutely right in all but one essential: the 'instinct' of our ancestors was never ultimately reliable.

It is the law of the Creator that should govern our actions and keep us in check. It is God's law that will tell everyone, plainly and without compromise, what is right and what is wrong; and it is never wrong to do the right—however much we really would love to do the opposite. This may not be what the nation wants to hear, but it is without question what a rising generation misled into the non-conformity of free expression and hedonism needs to hear.

Has the law of God ever been popular? One of the criticisms levelled by the media against the churches today is that they are so vague in answering the question: 'Where is morality to be found?' The church is apologetic and hesitant, as if it too believes that we need something only '*like* the Ten Commandments'.

At the very time when the world is becoming ever more desperate to find answers, and may just be ready to listen to the God who 'spoke all these words', much of the Christian 'church' appears to have lost its message. At this very window of opportunity many Christians seem to be busy downgrading the law and denying its relevance for today. But before we come to that, we must define our terms.

What do we mean by the 'law of God'?

That may seem an unnecessary question with a straightforward answer. Surely the law is the Old Testament moral code that sets out what is required of God's people. But there is much more to it than that. In order to make clear the different kinds of law recorded in the Old Testament I am going to divide the various laws into five categories. This is a purely artificial division because the people of Israel never 'carved up' the law into these neat segments; for them, every part of their life, and therefore their law, was to do with their relationship with God. We make the following distinctions merely for the sake of describing the law. It may be useful to have a 'flavour' of their diversity.

Ceremonial law

Why all the ceremonies, sacrifices, festivals, and priests? Every detail of the Old Testament law was pointing like a signpost towards Christ. Whatever the detail, it was intended to prepare the people to respect the holy God who was sending his holy Son into a sinful world to bring us total salvation.

All the rules for religious ceremony are fulfilled in Christ. He is our sacrifice and our priest; he is our altar and offering for sin. When we place our trust in Christ for salvation we are fulfilling all of this part of the law, because it was wholly completed in Christ.

For this reason there can be no significant place in true Christian worship for religious buildings, clothes, ceremonies, festivals and actions that carry salvation significance—with the sole exception of the Lord's Supper and baptism, both of which Christ himself instituted and which primarily look back to what has taken place (the cross and conversion) rather than to what will take place. We need no other signposts. Sacerdotalism is the name given to the priestly ritual and sacrifices offered under the name of 'Christianity'. Sacerdotalism is an anachronism—it has no place in New Testament Christianity.

For more than fifty years the Worldwide Church of God, through its magazine Plain Truth, had impressed upon its members the necessity of following the Old Testament laws to the letter. Among other things they celebrated the Feast of Tabernacles, the Feast of Unleavened Bread, the Feast of Trumpets, and the Passover (see Leviticus 23). That was a misunderstanding, and therefore a misuse, of the old covenant ceremonial law. After an agony of searching and the loss of half its members, the WCG published an apology by its pastor general, Joseph Tkach, Jr. in the March/April 1996 issue of Plain Truth. It included this admission: 'We imposed on our members a works-orientated approach to Christian living. We required adherence to burdensome regulations of the Old Testament code... Our former old covenant approach fostered attitudes of exclusivism and superiority rather than the new covenant teaching of brotherhood and unity.' And so, with considerable courage, the Worldwide Church of God moved into the New Testament and the gospel.

There are two great values of the Old Testament ceremonial law for us today. First, it helps us to appreciate that worship is a holy thing. God made the ceremonial law so detailed because he was saying to his people: 'I am a holy God and you must not come to me carelessly.' There are awesome examples in the Old Testament of men who did break that command. Nadab and Abihu offered an unholy sacrifice to God and fire fell from heaven and killed them (Leviticus 10); Uzzah touched the ark of God as it was brought into Jerusalem on an ox cart and was struck dead in an instant (2 Samuel 6). God is no less holy now than he was then. How we worship is not a matter of pleasing ourselves but of pleasing God. The Jews were forbidden to worship God in the way of the world around them: 'You must not worship the LORD your God in their way' (Deuteronomy 12:4), and they were also warned not to worship in just any way they wanted: 'You are not to do as…everyone sees fit' (12:8). The ceremonial law teaches us how holy God is. The way we worship God does matter, not only because it brings honour to the Sovereign Creator, but because our understanding and appreciation of God is revealed in the way we worship—and, of course, the way we worship governs how we live.

Secondly, the ceremonial law reveals how seriously God takes sin, and yet at the same time how ready he is to forgive. Whenever a sacrifice was brought to the priest, the person offering it would place his hand on the animal as a sign that his sin was transferred and the animal's life would be taken instead of his own; that was a vivid reminder of the enormity of his own sin. It was a picture of the one true sacrifice of Christ for sin. As the offerer went away leaving the sacrificed animal behind he knew he was free.

When we place our faith in Christ all that the ceremonial law pictures is fulfilled for us. Paul makes it clear that 'The law was put in charge to lead us to Christ' (Galatians 3:24). It is very important to understand this. When we trust in Christ for salvation we are not putting the ceremonial law on one side and saying that it is irrelevant. On the contrary we are acknowledging that Christ perfectly fulfilled it.

Civil law

'There's nowt so queer as folks'! And for this reason every society needs rules to keep their 'folks' in check. Israel was no exception, but their rules were given by God. We live in a non-Christian culture and therefore many of our laws are made without any reference to the Scriptures. However, there is nothing in the Old Testament civil law that is entirely irrelevant for us today. Let me give just one illustration.

Restitution is a significant part of the Old Testament civil law. There are no instructions for building prisons because the idea that most criminals will become penitent (hence the 'penitentiary') and change their ways after a spell in prison is foreign to God's plan. We all know that the prison system has failed. Basically there were only two ways of dealing with the criminal in the Old Testament. If he had committed what we call a capital offence, he was put to death. For other offences he was required to put right what he had done wrong. Exodus 22 establishes this principle of restitution; for example a man caught stealing an ox would have to pay back five in place of the one (v 1).

In the United States an interesting experiment has been set up in at least two states. It is referred to as 'innovative justice', but there is nothing 'innovative' about it at all; it is as old as the Old Testament. Instead of certain offenders being sent to prison they are made to pay back what they have stolen. More than this, the authorities try to reconcile the criminal to his victim. In 1983 Florida established what they call a 'Community Control Programme' with restitution as its basis. By the turn of the century they could claim that more than 14,000 offenders had been put through their community control programme. Four-fifths of them were heading for prison sentences, but after going through this Community Control Programme fewer than seven percent have been re-arrested for further crimes, whereas normally nearly three-quarters of the men who leave prison are re-arrested within four years. Incidentally Florida maintains that this system has saved them seven and a half new prisons! The same is being tried in the United Kingdom by setting certain offenders Community Service instead of a custodial sentence. We have actually passed laws recently so that, in the case of particular offences, courts can confiscate property in order to deprive the criminal of the benefits of his crime. But it is taking us a long time to catch up with the Old Testament.

Christ is sometimes accused of doing away with the Old Testament civil punishment; for example, by his treatment of the woman taken in adultery. The Old Testament ordered death for that particular sin. By protecting the woman our Lord was demonstrating that the penalty for breaking the law could always be tempered with mercy. God had done exactly the same a thousand years before in the case of King David (2 Samuel 12:13). These laws helped the nation to understand that their God was a God of justice, and that justice could also be merciful.

Food and hygiene laws

The order that goes out in millions of households every day: 'Wash your hands before dinner', is in line with some of the rules that God gave to his people in the Old Testament.

The complaint of the Pharisees and teachers recorded in Mark 7:1–5 was not that the disciples broke the Old Testament rules—we have no reason to assume they did not wash dirty hands before eating—but that they broke the 'tradition of the elders' (v 5); Our Lord's quotation from Isaiah 29:13 proves this: '… their teachings are rules taught by men.' The law is for the wise to guard their physical and spiritual health: it is the fool who either ignores it altogether or adds to it the traditions of man.

In Matthew 5 Christ implies that the whole law is relevant. The list of clean and unclean food recorded in Leviticus 11 closely parallels the meat we eat or avoid even today. It may be true that we can eat pig's flesh because there is less danger now than there was then. In fact Peter learnt in Acts 11 that he was allowed to do just that, but Christ had already dealt with this subject according to Mark 7:14–23. In this passage our Lord 'declared all foods "clean"' (v 19). He was not suggesting that the food laws of the Old Testament were, or had ever been, irrelevant, but rather that a misuse of them had always been spiritually flawed. God never intended his people to believe that true religion was a matter simply of what we eat or how we wash our hands before meals. God had given his people stringent food and hygiene laws in order to protect their health, but more importantly to show them up as a very different people in the ancient world. When Christ releases his disciples from strict adherence to the food laws, the principles behind them remain unaltered. They are to be a 'clean' people in their habits and in their whole lives. When Christ releases us from the letter of the law he does not release us from its spirit.

Two hundred years ago many households in London threw their rubbish into the street and hoped the rain would wash it all away. In the summer, when it did not rain, cholera often spread. And when it did rain the filth was washed into dykes, streams and rivers. Early in the eighteenth century a writer claimed Fleet Street, Fleet Lane and Holborn in London was 'heaped with filth' and that the Fleet River was a gently flowing canal of filth. The River Thames was referred to as a slow moving cesspool. Today we actually take for granted many of the Old Testament laws of sanitation and hygiene. More than three thousand years ago God had established sanitation rules for his people when, among other regulations, he commanded latrines to be dug outside the encampment (Deuteronomy 23:12–14).

God also commanded that if a housewife came down one morning and found her baking pot occupied by a dead lizard, she must break the pot (Leviticus 11:32–33). That may sound a drastic response to a relatively minor mortality, but it would soon teach the people to leave pots upside down overnight and therefore less likely to be contaminated! Such hygiene may seem obvious to us, but today we are sending medical teams around the world to teach people such basic rules. In the Middle Ages one third of the population of Europe died by the Plague largely because simple hygiene rules were ignored.

In the early 1840s a young doctor named Ignaz Semmelweis was given responsibility for one of the obstetrical wards in the famous Allegemeine Krakenhaus teaching hospital in Vienna, Austria. He was alarmed at the high mortality rate of women in these wards: on average one in six. Observing that the highest mortality was among those women who had been examined by the teachers and students who had been dissecting bodies in the mortuary, he established a rule that in his ward every physician and student coming from the dissecting room must carefully wash his hands before examining a new patient. The mortality rate dropped dramatically to one in eighty-four! Later, against howls of protest at the inconvenience, Dr Semmelweis demanded that they wash their hands between the examination of living patients also. The mortality rate plummeted even further. Sadly, professional jealousy blocked the renewal of his contract, his successor threw out the wash basins and the death rate shot up. Eventually Semmelweis died a broken man, but not before he had committed his research to writing. The use of running water for washing soiled clothes and infected bodies is laid down in Leviticus 15 where it is translated as 'fresh' water (v 13). Significantly the context refers to precautions during infectious illness.

I came across a small book called *None of These Diseases* (S I McMillen, Marshall, Morgan and Scott, 1963). The author was a medical doctor and the book demonstrated how many modern diseases could be avoided if we simply followed the biblical rules. So before we dismiss Old Testament hygiene laws, we should surely ask the question: 'What do they mean?' They are all relevant. Jesus said none of them have passed away. There are principles to learn from them. These laws also teach us the nature of our God who is clean in every way, and who expects the same of those people who represent him.

Some argue that these food and hygiene laws have little or nothing to do with the physical well-being of the nation but were part of the ceremonial rules to ensure that Israel remained wholly different from the other nations. One writer goes so far as to assert that the list of allowed and forbidden animals had 'nothing to do with hygiene and health' (*Pig Out?* Jordan, Transfiguration Press, 1992). But that is incredibly short-sighted. Of course everything Israel did had religious implications since it was to be an example to the nations, but the laws were not set by an arbitrary and capricious God. His wise rules ensured that the people were clean both morally and physically. The promise in Deuteronomy 7:15 is directly related to Israel's observance of the food and hygiene laws: 'The LORD will keep you free from every disease. He will not inflict on you the horrible diseases you knew in Egypt....' All the Lord's commands were given to Israel 'for your own good' (Deuteronomy 10:13), and it is nonsense to suggest that this promise has nothing to do with physical well-being.

General laws

When I was a boy, I collected birds' eggs. The hobby is called 'oology'; although I didn't know the word at the time, and the practice is illegal today. In the Old Testament egg-collecting for food was a necessity, so God regulated it with a law that you will find in Deuteronomy 22:6. God's command was that the hen bird on a nest must not be harmed, although the eggs could be taken. Obviously the reason is that she will have another clutch in the same season. That is not oology but ecology. It is looking after the world in which we live and managing our resources wisely. Everybody today seems interested in environmental science, ecology and all matters 'green', but it is hardly novel; there are many instructions on this issue in the Old Testament law. We should never dismiss these laws as irrelevant, but should ask, 'What do they mean and how do they apply?'

In this same chapter in Deuteronomy God commands his people that they were to be sure that they built a parapet round the edge of the flat roof of their houses. God gives a reason for this: it would prevent anyone falling off the roof and the householder becoming guilty of manslaughter (22:8). It is only in recent times that we have tightened our laws on such issues, and the Health and Safety Executive is a relatively new addition to society. God legislated for such things long ago. It was all part of Israel's relationship with him. As a holy nation they revealed a deep concern for the value of human life—something significantly absent from other ancient law codes.

Moral laws

In the course of a sermon on Matthew 5, Dr Martyn Lloyd-Jones, the outstanding preacher at Westminister Chapel in London for thirty years from the 1930s, commented, 'There is nothing more fatal than to regard holiness and sanctification as experiences to be received. No, holiness means being righteous, and being righteous means keeping the law. Therefore if your so-called grace (which you say you have received) does not make you keep the law, you have not received grace. You may have received a psychological experience, but you have never received the grace of God. What is grace? It is that marvellous gift of God which, having delivered a man from the curse of the law, enables him to keep it and to be righteous as Christ was righteous, for he kept the law perfectly' (*Studies in the Sermon on the Mount*, Inter Varsity Press 1959, Vol. 1 p. 197). But we must return to this theme in the next chapter.

The New Testament is our infallible guide as to how to apply Old Testament law. These various laws are not irrelevant since they teach us about the character of God and what he expects of his people; in the Sermon on the Mount our Lord showed how many of these laws can be summarised by wide-ranging principles.

Christ taught obedience to all the Ten Commandments. Compare Matthew 22:37 with the first two commandments, and Matthew 5:33–37 with the third. Mark 2:27 is a clear commentary on the fourth commandment. This verse does not mean that the Sabbath was made for man to do what he liked with, but that it was made for man's benefit.

Compare Matthew 10:21 with the fifth commandment, Matthew 5:21–30 with the next two, Mark 10:19 with the command against stealing, Matthew 5:11 against the ninth command and Matthew 6:19–24 with the last one. Our Lord actually warns us that there is no place in the Kingdom of God for those who teach that the law is irrelevant. When he spoke about righteousness in Matthew 5:20 he was talking about law-righteousness.

What kind of God gave these laws?

To speak of 'God' in our 'pluralistic' society is virtually a word without meaning. We have dozens of religions worshipping in our cities and scores of redundant church buildings used for unfamiliar rituals and 'mixed-faith' services. The gods of New Age, Hinduism, Islam, Buddhism, Sikhism, and the perversions of the Christian God produced by the cults create a confusion that is compounded by the politically correct assertion that they all lead us to the truth. We can too easily forget the kind of God who is revealed as the author of the Ten Commandments. He is unique.

1. A communicating God to be heard

'A lull *after* the storm'. That is sadly typical of many homes in our nation. Days, weeks or months of arguments and rows are followed by gloomy and moody silence. Neither party is speaking. No one will break through the barrier and re-establish communications. Often each longs for the other to make a move and say something, but meanwhile meaningful relationship has broken down—sometimes irretrievably.

'The LORD called to Moses and said...' (Exodus 19:3) are significant words. When Adam and Eve fell into sin their instinctive reaction was to run away and hide from God. But the sovereign and holy Creator did not simply turn the other way and leave men and women to wallow in their own misery. Our God is a communicating God and the initiative is always from him. The great difference between Christianity and every religion of the world is that in religion humanity is left to crawl upwards to its god; in true Christianity, God reaches down. The first word of hope after the Fall came in the words to Adam found in Genesis 3:9, 'Where are you?' That was grace; the undeserved love of God. In fact anything God ever says to mankind is grace; even his words of judgement, and especially his words of warning. But those first words after the Fall were God's appeal to Adam and Eve to stop and think where their sin had landed them.

Here, at Mount Sinai, is the same God speaking again. The people were not pleading with him to speak; they were not asking, 'Oh why is heaven silent? Will God please say something? Can we have some laws to tell us how to work and live together? Can you say something that will give us a pattern for life?' They cried for freedom (Exodus 2:23–24), but little realised that freedom involved rules—it always does. Mankind has never asked for God's laws; it is the one thing we do not want. So God spoke. The phrase 'God said' is the most significant statement in the history of the human race. It occurs fifteen times in the first three chapters of Genesis. But since the Fall the human race has been preoccupied with at least four desperate avoidance measures.

First, we deny that God has spoken at all: 'The serpent... said to the woman: "Did God really say?"' (Genesis 3:1). That is perhaps the most common contemporary response to any claim that God has given us his laws.

Secondly, we doubt the truthfulness of God's words: 'You will not surely die' (Genesis 3:4). That has been the busy response of critics of the Bible's authority particularly over the past two centuries.

Thirdly, we manipulate the meaning of God's words to suit our own agenda: 'Ignorant and unstable people distort (them) to their own destruction' (2 Peter 3:16). A whole world of false teachers have become tools in the hand of the enemy.

Fourthly, we write our own script. Paul warned the church at Thessalonica about prophecies, reports and letters: 'supposed to have come from us' (2 Thessalonians 2:2). All the 'holy' writings of the religious world, from the book of Mormon to the book of Mohammed, are counterfeit. There is only one God who speaks—all else is Satan's lie. It is not coincidental that in the context of the giving of the law Moses warned, 'Do not add to what I command you and do not subtract from it, but keep the commands of the LORD your God that I give you' (Deuteronomy 4:2). It is not that there are no good or wise things said in all the religious literature around the world, but the voice of God is not to be heard in them. They cannot offer the hope of salvation or the authentic laws of the Creator.

Diluted poison is still poison—it just kills more slowly. An illustration of this is found in a set of laws written a little before the time of Moses.

HAMMURABI'S LAW

One of the oldest law codes on record is that of Hammurabi, the sixth of eleven kings in the Old Babylonian Dynasty. He is generally reckoned to have reigned around seventeen hundred years before Christ which, if the date is correct, would place him a little later than Abraham and a little earlier than Moses. Among his 282 laws recorded in what has become known as the 'Hammurabi Code' some bear a striking resemblance to the detailed laws found in Exodus and Deuteronomy. Inevitably critics have suggested that Moses must have copied some of his laws from Hammurabi. Leaving aside the fact that the dating of these early dynasties is by no means settled and that it is likely we may yet discover that Moses long predates Hammurabi, to conclude that Moses copied the laws of this Babylonian king is to read the laws with only half an eye.

In the Hammurabi Code there is nothing remotely equivalent to the laws Moses received as a revelation from God; on the contrary the prologue of Hammurabi's Code runs to almost ninety lines extolling the virtues, achievements and piety of the king himself. The word 'god' and the name 'Marduk' occur only thirteen times in the entire law list—although a dozen or more gods are recorded in the prologue.

More significantly, whereas the laws given to Moses are concerned chiefly with respect for people, Hammurabi's are predominantly concerned with property. Added to this, some of Hammurabi's penalties are excessive: a thief is ordered to repay thirty-fold and if he cannot pay he is to be put to death (8); if a man is found looting at a fire 'that man shall be thrown into that fire' (25). Certainly some high moral standards are required by Hammurabi, and a few laws are at least interesting: for example doctors' fees are graded according to the patient's ability to pay (215–217) and if the doctor is unsuccessful he is to be punished (218)!

No ancient laws remotely touch the wisdom and clarity of those revealed by God to Moses. Even the Islamic *Koran* with the benefit of hindsight (being written in the seventh century AD—more than two thousand years after the law of Moses), has nothing to compare with the Ten

Commandments or the Sermon on the Mount. Although the *Koran* claims to confirm the book of Moses which is 'a guide and a blessing to all men' (46:12), it has little in common with it, and clearly Mohammed was poorly acquainted with Old Testament narratives, many of which are totally muddled in the *Koran*—especially those concerning Joseph and Moses.

Israel was unique as a people in that they worshipped the only true God, who communicated his laws for their good.

2. A holy God to be feared

Exodus 19 contains some of the most terrifying preparations for the Commandments of chapter 20. Let me take you through them.

Washday on this occasion was serious business; it wasn't the neighbour who would check out the results, but God himself (v 10–11). Even outwardly they had to be ready for him. Then the people were told not to come near the mountain (v 12). A line was to be drawn around the foot of the mountain that they must not cross. They must not touch the mountain, not because that mound of earth and rock contained magical powers, but because it represented the holy presence of God among them. One thing that the people had to learn was that they would never understand God's words until they had learned to appreciate his holiness. When someone complains that these ten great laws are intended to spoil our freedom and our life, you can be sure that they have no idea of the nature of the one true God.

Many people are afraid of thunderstorms, and not without some good reason: a lightning flash up to thirty centimetres wide, two miles long and packing a billion or more volts can be scary! Suddenly Sinai became alive with thunder and lightning such as the people had never seen before. A thick cloud covered the mountain and it began to shake violently. Thunder, lightning and a thick cloud are all perfectly natural. But this was exceptional. Something was happening on that mountain that forced the people to say, 'We've heard thunder and seen lightning before but never like this.' Israel was expected not simply to be excited, curious or mystified, they were to learn what the thunder, lightning and cloud meant. Here was a God whose power and authority are 'beyond tracing out' (Romans 11:33).

As Israel watched and heard the lightning crackling across the sky, the thunder rumbling through the clouds, and the thickening cloud settling upon Mount Sinai, suddenly they heard something that was both unnatural and exceptional: a loud trumpet blast from heaven (Exodus 19:16,19). The people trembled—and so they might. There are only two occasions in the Bible where we read of the trumpet sounding from heaven. One was on Mount Sinai and the other we are still waiting to hear. According to 1 Thessalonians 4:16 the trumpet will sound again at the coming of Christ. And then, as at Sinai, those who hear will tremble. At the coming of the Lord on Sinai, and the coming of the Saviour in glory, the trumpets of God sound an alarm. According to Exodus 19:17–18 the people were afraid even to stand at the foot of the mountain because the smoke and the fire became so great and so powerful and the whole mountain shook so violently. The trumpet became louder and louder until there was a mighty crescendo of noise. Then Moses spoke.

That is incredible: 'Moses spoke and the voice of God answered him' (v 19). I have to read it again and say to myself: 'Is something wrong here? The sound of the trumpet grew louder and louder. Surely now God is going to speak.' But *Moses* spoke. What did he say? We don't know. I wish we did. Perhaps Moses cried out, 'Oh LORD, enough. If you come any closer you will destroy us by your burning holiness and awesome power.' And when God answered, what did *he* say? We don't know. Perhaps he said, 'Moses, before they hear my laws the people must understand the kind of God they are dealing with. I'm not just tossing down a few ideas for you to take or leave, I'm not going to give you a few laws and regulations which you can pin up on the camp notice board so that people can look down the list and decide which ones they like or which ones are inconvenient. Moses, I want these people to realise the character of the God that stands behind these laws.' The activity of God on the mountain was to encourage the people to fear him. It is no surprise that they did (Exodus 20:18). This God of power, might and purity who is far too clean and holy for a sinful man to approach was to be approached with 'fear'. That God is our God.

Phrases that refer to fearing God occur more than one hundred and fifty times in the Old Testament and around thirty in the New Testament. It is arguably the clearest summary of true worship. The phrase, 'Stand in awe of God' (Ecclesiastes 5:7) is translated powerfully in the *Authorised*

Version 'Fear thou God'. The psalmist promised, 'Blessed is the man who fears the LORD, who finds great delight in his commands' (Psalm 112:1). To these people at Sinai the warning was given, 'If you do not carefully follow all the words of this law, which are written in this book, and do not revere (fear) this glorious and awesome name—the LORD your God—then...'— and judgement follows (Deuteronomy 28:58). Notice in these verses the link between fear and obedience. Paul makes the same connection in 2 Corinthians 7:1, 'Perfecting holiness out of reverence (fear) for God.' A proper understanding of the character of God should always issue in obedience to his commands.

But what does 'fear' mean in this context? Both the Hebrew and Greek words come from a root that means 'alarm' or 'terror', and both move through stages of development until they carry the meaning of 'awe, wonder, reverence or respect'. Perhaps we can best define the fear that God wants from his people as living and worshipping in the light of the awesome and holy character of God. This kind of fear stems from both the character and the actions of God.

God is terrifyingly holy. He is the God who rules in the heavens (Job 26:7), and among the host of angels (Daniel 4:35); he rules over the events of the universe (Ephesians 1:11) and in the lives of all men and women (Acts 17:25,28); he controls the destiny of every member of the human race (Proverbs 16:4,33) and is sovereign in both history and geography (Acts 17:26); he provides for the earth (Matthew 5:45), controls even the natural disasters (Isaiah 45:7), and cares for his people (Psalm 121); he has written every chapter of the story of this earth and the universe—including the last one (1 Corinthians 15:24–25). God is uncreated and self-existing (John 5:26), eternal and unlimited (Revelation 21:6), unchanging and immense (Malachi 3:6 and Jeremiah 23:24), he is all light (1 John 1:5), all knowing (1 Samuel 2:3), all powerful (Luke 1:37), all present (Psalm 139:7–12), all holy (Exodus 15:11), and all love (1 John 4:8). To this we can only respond, 'Great is the LORD and most worthy of praise; his greatness no one can fathom' (Psalm 145:3).

But he is also a God whose actions are terrifyingly holy. Here at Sinai the physical effect of his presence was awesome (Exodus 19:16–25). Later, two sons of Aaron 'fell dead before the LORD' when they offered unholy worship

(Numbers 3:4). When David tried to bring the Ark of the Covenant into Jerusalem, Uzzah died for a single act of unholy disobedience (2 Samuel 6). Our Lord warned of the fearful God 'who has power to throw you into hell' (Luke 12:5), Hebrews warns that 'our God is a consuming fire' (Hebrews 12:29), and the vivid pictures in Revelation 6:12–17 and 14:9–12 speak for themselves. Above all, the awesome death of Christ reveals the holy anger of a God who made his Son 'become a curse for us' so that we might be rescued from the curse of broken Commandments (Galatians 3:13); or, as Isaiah describes it: 'The punishment that brought us peace was upon him' (53:5).

God expects a holy worship and an obedient response to both his character and his actions.

3. A moral God to be obeyed

What if God allowed us to rearrange the Ten Commandments, or better still, to write out our own list! It would be interesting to see how we would re-shape the priority order of the Commandments, or what our modern society would propose as the top ten, if none had been given to us by the Creator. Whatever we would invent, the following is not too far from the reality of today's society:

1   There are many gods worshipped in the world and none is to be considered more significant than the others.

2   The worship of idols is to be seen as a healthy acknowledgement of the deity in all its forms.

3   People should never speak disparagingly of any religion or offend the sensitivities of its devotees; with the exception of Christianity and Christians.

4   Productivity and profit are all important and dividends to shareholders are more significant than fair wages, reasonable working hours and the stability of our families.

5   Parents should honour their children by refraining from any form of physical discipline and dogmatic instruction that is likely to influence them significantly to believe in moral absolutes and a Creator God; this is likely to cause grave emotional instability in later life.

6   No one should forfeit their life for murder, however callous or vile; and the rights of a murderer are to be guarded at all costs. Exceptionally, children in the womb have no rights and their destruction is a matter of the personal preference of the mother.

7   Marriage between one man and one woman is only one of many options, and not necessarily the best. It should never be allowed to limit the freedom of one partner to enjoy whatever additional relationships they consider will bring pleasure and self-fulfilment.

8   It is expected that private enterprise will mislead and exploit in favour of shareholders and that the work force will engage in petty theft in order to remain satisfied in their work.

9   Politicians may spin to their own advantage, however far from the truth it may be, and small lies in society generally will be overlooked as necessary to maintain good relationships.

10 Grasping ambition, self-esteem and the National Lottery are good for the economy of the nation and are the best motivation for personal achievement.

We might have commandments dealing with social injustice, racial and sexual inequality, international relationships, commercial exploitation and ecology—because these are the sins of other people and governments. Yet the Creator, whose wisdom invented the whole complex universe, has omitted any direct reference to such issues in his foundational requirements for human relationships. Our society wants commandments that are totally non-personal. We want to be able to excuse ourselves and point the finger at governments and institutions as the guilty parties. We would prefer comfortable problems that are sufficiently distant so that we can either throw charity at them or blame others for them.

On the other hand every one of the Ten Commandments points very close to home—literally. They all raise issues that affect the way I and my family live every day: in my home, factory, office, classroom or workshop. God starts with people not institutions, with families and not with governments. He begins with us, and that is very uncomfortable.

The Bible is often criticised for appearing to say little to governments; we are told that there is no political philosophy in the Bible, no economic mandate, no charter for a league of nations and only passing references to ecology. This is not true. The Bible does speak to institutions, to families and governments, and it does address 'green' issues. But it is primarily concerned with people. What is wrong with our world, and what always has been wrong, is not governments or institutions, but people—ordinary people like all of us—because people are foundational to society. Governments and institutions will never be more moral than the people who form them.

The politician of a century ago said it all when he left a church service muttering, 'Things have come to a pretty pass when religion is allowed to interfere in one's private life'! The Ten Commandments are unpopular precisely because they are personal and because our philosophy today refuses to accept an objective standard of right and wrong that 'interferes' in the life of the individual. If a religion does not interfere in one's private life then that religion is not worth a straw.

It is one of the greatest failures of modern Western society that social morality has taken the place of personal morality. The man in the street howls with rage at government sleaze, boardroom fraud, football 'bungs', and the drug barons. But he wants the freedom to keep his soft-porn, petty fiddling, back-handers and betting. We want 'society' to reform without any upset to our own life-style. To reverse God's order in that way spells tragedy.

When the Jewish leaders tried to establish their innocence in the eyes of the law, Christ brought them all back under its judgement by a closer application than they wanted to hear. He reminded them that the breach of Sabbath law, dishonour to parents, murder, adultery and covetousness were all sins of the mind and heart before ever they turned into action (Matthew 15:18–20). Governments are a macrocosm of each level of society down to the family which is the fundamental unit. True religion, whether Old Testament Judaism or New Testament Christianity, is concerned primarily with people and families. God knows that when these obey his Commandments they will influence others around them, and if sufficient people are changed then governments will change.

Thank God for the Ten Commandments

The greatest thing about the Ten Commandments is that they are there at all. Even the very law that condemns me as a sinner and reveals how far short I fall is a massive token of God's grace. Because in revealing this law, God reveals himself. The kindest thing God does for me is to show me himself, and the second kindest thing is to show me myself. But I understand the second clearly only when I understand the first. The magnificent part of God's grace is not that he first reveals the disobedience of my spirit, but that he reveals the holiness of himself. If only we could understand that. Of course the cross is grace; the gospel of salvation is grace. But grace began long before then. Grace starts when God speaks into our sin and then tells us the kind of God he is. He could have kept that a secret from fallen humanity. There is nothing in the Code of Hammurabi to compare with the assurance to Israel that God has spoken or with the confidence that it is God and not Moses who gives the laws and expects obedience.

This awesome, powerful, good and pure God could have left in place the roadblock caused by sin. And it could have remained that way until the day the whole world stands before him in judgement and awakens to the horrifying realisation of God and of how holy he is. It is grace that he has told us beforehand. Everything that happened in Exodus 19 is grace, and everything God said in chapter 20 is grace also. This is why the apostle Paul in the New Testament can say that the law is good (Romans 7:12). Of course it is, because it drives us to God. It is the law that tells us that we have fallen far short of God, and it is the law that reminds us that we can do nothing to make up the gap. The law tells us how much we need salvation.

Eager though we may be to go right into the commands themselves, this chapter has already raised too many questions and avoided too many issues. Before we can reap the harvest there is a field to be ploughed, weeds to be destroyed and seeds to be sown. Never has the law of God been so attacked as it is today, and not by the world—that we expect—but by those who ought to be its friends. We must now turn to the fundamental issue of how we can be certain that the law is relevant today, and of how far we can apply it.

The value of the law

'We will do everything the LORD has said'. Exodus 19:8

A few years ago I had to work my way through the 1989 Children Act. I knew some of it was especially applicable to the life of Christian churches but for this purpose only a few pages were directly relevant. So what did I do with the rest? I was tempted to tear it out and bin it! In fact I carefully read the whole law in order to understand the 'big picture' that the government wanted to convey, and also because I knew that the entire Act was relevant to every citizen in the United Kingdom even though I was especially concerned about only one part of it at that particular time.

Christians are often undecided as to how they ought to use the Old Testament law. Should they bin large parts of it, or just hope that sooner or later they will find it useful? It is undeniable that the moral code contained in Exodus 20 is good, but even a superficial read further into the book presents some serious problems of application. How far can these laws really be relevant today? Do they have something, or nothing, to say? Can we take them as a moral code for the Christian? Are the Ten Commandments simply a title page to the laws of God for his people three and a half thousand years ago, or could we base Christian laws on them?

So, before we begin our study of the Commandments in detail we will try to answer some of these questions and begin by looking at them in their context.

In the silence of a desert

Three and a half thousand years ago God brought a poor nation of some two million people out of Egyptian slavery. Through a series of miracles he led them to the foot of a barren, rugged mountain in the desert called Sinai, in what is today known as the Sinai peninsula at the northern end of the Red Sea.

We must not lose the significance of the fact that they came to a desert (Exodus 19:1). God deliberately brought the Israelites to a place of total dependence upon him. In a desert, such a large company of people had to depend upon God for both food and water. They also had to depend upon him for their health and safety. So, by leading the people into the desert God was effectively saying, 'You are totally dependent upon me and in spiritual and moral relationships you are equally to be dependent upon me. As you scoop up the water that flows miraculously from the rock, and as you gather up the manna that falls miraculously around you, you will learn to trust me. As you trust me for health and strength, and as you look to me for safety among the surrounding nations, I want you to realise that I have brought you into a desert place to remind you that in yourselves you are helpless. There is nothing you can do but to trust me wholly. You are to trust me for your spiritual well-being and for your moral welfare just as much as for your food and safety.'

Today we are too confident in our own ability. We are no longer aware that we depend upon God for our food and water, our health and strength, our safety and security. We have our supermarkets, our giant utilities, and our social welfare. God warned Israel: 'You may say to yourself, "My power and the strength of my hands have produced this wealth for me." But remember the LORD your God, for it is he who gives you the ability to produce wealth' (Deuteronomy 8:17–18). In exactly the same way we do not think we need God for our moral or spiritual laws either. The achievements of science—in physics, medicine and space—have created in us the conviction that we are master of our own fate and captain of our own soul. This, together with an evolutionary philosophy that has persuaded us that 'every day in every way we're getting better and better', has led to the fearful prospect that in virtually every area of life the creature thinks it knows better than its Creator.

Someone has said that our present generation is losing the ability to wonder. That may be so, but we have certainly lost the sense of dependence. Our pride knows few limits. We think that we are on the verge of creating life *ex nihilo*, of manipulating genes omnipotently, of calculating the incalculable, and of discovering life on Mars! Anyone who dares to suggest the need for moral absolutes has clearly forgotten that we are three and a half thousand years ahead of Sinai.

I live in a London suburb. From our back garden the outlook is pleasant enough with trees and playing-fields stretching right up to the A3 just three hundred metres away. But the rush of traffic noise never ceases—except early on Christmas day morning. Sometimes on holiday we enjoy simply listening to the quietness around us. A desert was a place without distractions. It was a silent place; a place to listen. Today there is no time to listen to what God has to say, and if ever we do stop, the voice of God is obliterated by the cacophony of noise that is our life-style. Many in our nation are never quiet for more than a few seconds at a time. From breakfast to bedtime, noise is on the menu. On the building site, in the factory, at the supermarket, through the radio, the personal CD/radio, and the piped mind-control, we are bathed in noise. Silence is feared above all by the generation hurtling through the third millennium. Our politicians, educators, industrialists and church leaders have allowed the confusion of voices clamouring for our attention to squeeze out the voice of God.

Lying on my desk is the glossy advertisement for an extravagant praise day at Wembley Conference Centre in London; it promises to include: 'dramatic technomedia presentation' and the key attractions will be, 'Cinema-style, large-screen projections, intelligent lighting, 10 kilowatt surround sound and total ultra violet coverage'. That is the modern definition of 'the Spirit's revival dynamics'—10 kw surround sound! It would seem that even in worship, silence is unpopular. We dare not be silent for a moment. The more noise we can make, the less chance there will be that God's word, or even our own conscience, will get through to us. An apt description of some of our worship today is found in the words of the preacher in Ecclesiastes: 'as the crackling of thorns under the pot, so is the laughter of fools' (7:6). It is not without significance that a short while after Moses went up the mountain to receive the law of God, the people were partying in the valley; it was the old ploy of the devil that they should not hear the voice of God.

God brought these people to the foot of a great mountain in a silent desert so that they would listen to what he had to say. It was in the 'gentle whisper' that Elijah heard the word of God (1 Kings 19:12). In the buzz of life God encourages his people to 'Be still (the word can be correctly translated 'be quiet') and know that I am God' (Psalm 46:10). Silence is one of the greatest needs of today's mega-decibel world; but it is the thing we are most afraid of. Perhaps it is for this reason that the preacher encourages us to believe the seemingly ridiculous notion that 'It is better to go to a house of mourning than to go to a house of feasting' (Ecclesiastes 7:2).

Who believes for one moment that a funeral is better than a party? God does! Because the noise of a party is deliberately calculated to stifle the whispering conscience of the law, whereas the quiet reflection of a funeral may cause the living 'to take this to heart'. More things are done—and regretted—at a party than ever at a funeral.

For Israel only?

God first addressed his laws to his chosen people: 'This is what you are to tell the people of Israel' (Exodus 19:3). Their roots go back to a man called Abraham whose family grew into a tribe and the tribe into a nation. The family, the tribe and the nation were chosen by God not for any attraction in themselves, but simply because God loved them: 'The LORD did not set his affection on you and choose you because you were more numerous than other peoples, for you were the fewest of all peoples. But it was because the LORD loved you' (Deuteronomy 7:7–8).

But God also had a greater purpose; he told Israel that through them he would reveal himself to the world and millions would be blessed because of them. In fact God told Israel that he would reveal himself in two ways: By his *words* he would reveal his holy character through the obedience that he expected of his own special people, and by his *actions* demonstrating his hatred of sin and his compassion for the sinner. God was speaking to the people he had chosen, to those he had called out of the world to be his own treasured possession (Deuteronomy 7:6).

Because God was speaking to the Jews in this great list of laws, there are many who say that these laws can have nothing to do with non-Jews today, not even to Christians. This was the law for the Jews, and that's where it must end. But look again at Exodus 19:5–6, 'If you obey me fully and keep my covenant, then out of all nations you will be my treasured possession. Although the whole earth is mine, you will be for me a kingdom of priests and a holy nation. These are the words you are to speak to the Israelites.'

Notice those phrases: 'my treasured possession', 'a kingdom of priests', 'a holy nation'. Those words are significant because they are exactly echoed in 1 Peter 2:9 and 10. God, through Peter, is not writing to the Jews but to the church when he says, 'You are a chosen people, a royal priesthood, a holy nation, a people belonging to God, that you may declare the praises of him who called you out of darkness into his wonderful light. Once you were not a people, but now you are the people of God; once you had not received mercy, but now you have received mercy.' So, God speaks in the same way to the Christian church as he did to the Jews. In other words, these Commandments are what is expected of the people who belong to God, whoever they are and wherever they are.

But even more important than this, God does not have one law for his people and another law for the world. What government makes one set of laws for the law-keepers and an easier set of laws for the law-breakers? So why should we expect the holy Sovereign of the universe to have one set of laws for his chosen people, and a lower standard of laws, or no standard at all, for everyone else?

I passed my driving test in a four-by-four Landrover. It was old, battered, had no mechanical signalling, and I had to double declutch both up and down the gears. Even in those far-off days there were some smart cars on the road with winking signals and automatic transmission. It was hard driving that Landrover, and it seemed unfair that I was expected to meet the same exacting standard as the fellow taking his test in a gleaming new model of the early sixties. But my examiner made no allowance. I had to learn the same highway code as the other guy, obey the same rules, and drive with the same accuracy. Apparently no one even considered lowering the standard for drivers of bone-shakers!

Here is an example from the New Testament. Paul (Ephesians 5) and Peter (1 Peter 3) both describe relationships within the family; clearly they have in mind the Christian family, but has this nothing to say to all families? Of course it has. If the Christian family should be the model for all families, then the law of the Old Testament for Israel was equally the model for the pagan and idolatrous world around. This is precisely God's reasoning in Deuteronomy 4:5–8; when the nations hear the laws of God they will conclude, 'This nation is a wise and understanding people', and they will envy the 'righteous decrees and laws' of Israel. Are we to assume that, having revealed such good laws to the nations through Israel, God had no interest in whether or not those nations obeyed the laws? These are not simply the best laws God revealed, they are the *only* laws he revealed. It would be remarkably strange if the Creator was indifferent as to whether or not the larger part of humanity obeyed the only laws he has given.

John the Baptist condemned Herod Antipas for his adultery (Matthew 14:4) and Paul reasoned with the Governor Felix about 'righteousness, self-control and the judgement to come' (Acts 24:25), because the Jewish king and the Roman governor were both men under the moral law of a holy God. Where did Paul get his 'reasoning' from? He certainly could not rely on the good nature of Felix or the infallibility of Roman law. For Paul, righteousness was defined by God's law.

There really should be no doubt that God's purpose in these Commandments is for the whole world and not just for Israel. These are the Maker's instructions. The more complicated the equipment, the more detailed the instructions will be—and there is nothing in the known universe more incredibly complex than a human life: physically, mentally, emotionally and spiritually.

It is sometimes claimed that the Commandments are simply part of the exclusive covenant with Israel and therefore they are primarily ceremonial laws which, as we have seen, ended with the coming of Christ. That sounds all right until you read Deuteronomy 31:12–13. Moses gave the laws to the priests and the elders of Israel and ordered that every seven years during the Feast of Tabernacles the law should be read to 'all Israel'. However, Moses then added, 'Assemble the people—men, women and children, *and the aliens living in your towns*—so that they can listen and learn to fear the LORD your God and follow carefully all the words of this law.' The next sentence is even more significant: '*Their children, who do not know this law, must hear it and learn to fear the* LORD *your God as long as you live in the land....*' 'Their children' refers to the 'aliens living in your towns'. Nothing is said about them becoming Jews or entering the covenant. They presumably remained foreigners, but they must learn to fear the only true God. And how? By learning the Commandments of the God of Israel.

This passage in Deuteronomy 31 is significant against the argument that the Commandments are exclusively for Israel. It reveals God's care for the nations, and that care begins with the expectation that some of them will hear the law. To deny a knowledge of God's law to the nations is as bad as denying the gospel. It may be understandable that we begin Bible translation for newly reached people-groups with the New Testament, but it is indefensible that we often stop there.

God therefore sets these laws in place for the Christian and the non-Christian to keep. But with this difference: he expects the Christian to keep them and provides all the help needed to do so. He has given the Christian new life and has put the Holy Spirit within the Christian. On the other hand, God commands the world to keep these Ten Commandments, but he knows that they will not.

You do not expect a goat to sing Handel's *Messiah!* It is incapable of doing so. Neither does God expect the non-Christian to be able to obey these laws. But whereas the goat was never created to be a solo soprano, mankind *was* created to be a law-keeper. We do not blame the goat because it makes a poor rendering of *The Messiah*, but God will judge men and women for their disobedience to his law. We were created capable of being law-keepers, but by our wilful disobedience we became law-breakers.

Clearly then, these Ten Commandments are God's standard for both Christian and non-Christian.

Jesus and the law

What did Jesus mean when he said, 'Do not think that I have come to abolish the Law or the Prophets. I have not come to abolish them but to fulfil them' (Matthew 5:17)?

The word 'fulfil' has two basic meanings. It can either mean that he has come to fill up what is lacking—in the sense of completing an unfinished job; or it can mean that he will carry out the law perfectly—in the sense both of obeying it and of fulfilling its purpose. Our Lord uses the same word in Matthew 3:15 at his baptism: 'It is proper for us to do this to fulfil all righteousness.' His reply to John the Baptist meant: 'I must carry out everything perfectly, and baptism is one of those things.'

Some maintain that the word simply means that he came to bring all the laws to completion in himself so that when we believe in Christ for salvation we are released from all the obligations of the law. But that would make the rest of his statement unnecessary: 'I tell you the truth, until heaven and earth disappear, not the smallest letter, not the least stroke of a pen, will by any means disappear from the law until everything is accomplished. Anyone who breaks one of the least of these commandments and teaches others to do the same will be called least in the kingdom of heaven, but whoever practices and teaches these commands will be called great in the kingdom of heaven' (Matthew 5:18–19). How could he say that none of it will disappear if in fact that is exactly what he came to achieve? And how must we keep every part of it and teach others to do the same if in fact we have nothing to keep?

Look again at that word 'fulfil'. In Romans 13:9 Paul offers us a summary of the law of God and then tells us that it is all 'fulfilled' in the word love. He makes the same point in Galatians 5:14, 'The entire law is summed up in a single command "love your neighbour as yourself."' Significantly the word translated 'fulfilled' in Romans 13 and 'summed up' in Galatians 5 is the same word that is used by our Lord in Matthew 5:17.

The most natural understanding of this verse is that the whole life of Christ is a summary of obedience to the law of God. We watch him to see what obedience to the law means. When we come to some difficult application in our modern society we must ask, 'How would Christ have obeyed the law at this point?' This is the sense in which our Lord uses the word here in Matthew 5:17. He came to carry out the law perfectly in his life so that the law had no claim upon him. He lived it perfectly, and he taught the people to obey it. Dr Martyn Lloyd-Jones said of this passage in Matthew 5, 'Notice how very careful our Lord was to observe the law; he obeyed it down to the minutest detail. Not only that, he taught others to love the law and he explained it to them, confirming it constantly and asserting the absolute necessity of obedience to it' (*Studies in the Sermon on the Mount*, IVP 1959, Vol. 1, p. 191).

That is exactly what Christ did. But when people failed, he taught them to repent and accept forgiveness. This is why he dealt with the woman taken in adultery in the way he did. He did not say to her, 'It doesn't matter how you live'; on the contrary he said, 'Go and sin no more.' When our Lord concluded, 'Neither do I condemn you', he was not detracting from the law; by referring to sin he was saying that it does matter. She was condemned and under the judgement of God, but Christ offered her free forgiveness.

God had done exactly the same for King David after his double sin of adultery and murder (2 Samuel 12). Christ did not soften the demands of the law, but he tempered its penalty with mercy.

We must be very clear about all this. The righteousness of the law is essential to gain heaven! So, when a young man asked Christ what he had to do to inherit eternal life, our Lord replied, 'You know the commandments, obey them' (Luke 18:18–20). On this basis we all fail, and that is exactly why Christ came. He obeyed the law perfectly, and salvation is offered on the basis of Christ's perfect law-righteousness. The purpose of his death was to pay the penalty for our sinful failure to keep the law.

A few years ago someone generously paid for the post office franking machines to carry this message into hundreds of thousands of homes: 'Christ died paying for our sins'. I have no doubt it was well-intentioned, but it was badly worded. The present participle 'paying' made it sound like a tragic accident. When we read, 'The winch-man died taking a line to the drowning seaman' we know that death was never the intention of the would-be rescuer. That is not what happened in the case of our Saviour. His purpose was to die. The message should have read, 'Christ died in order to pay for our sins'. It was the only way.

However, the fact that Christ came to set us free from the penalty of the law does not mean that he came to set us free from its righteous demands. He kept the law, and so must we. The whole law is ours; every part of it. It is actually a great privilege to be under the law, not for salvation, because that can never be possible, but for a righteousness that pleases God. God's law will never pass away, because it is now written on the hearts of Christians (Jeremiah 31:33). Or, as the psalmist expressed it, 'I will walk about in freedom for I have sought out your precepts' (Psalm 119:45). The prophet Isaiah put into the mouth of the righteous in Israel this relationship between obedience to the law and love for God: 'Yes, LORD, walking in the ways of your laws, we wait for you; your name and renown are the desire of our hearts' (Isaiah 26:8).

A bridge too far—Theonomy and Christian Reconstruction

'Theonomy' is Greek for 'God's Law', and it is the word used for the study of applying God's law today. It starts with the conviction that all the Old

Testament laws have something to say to Christians in every age. Theonomy does not insist on the detailed application of every law without reference to a changed world and culture, but it does recognise that 'everything that was written in the past was written to teach us...' (Romans 15:4). We were actually applying theonomy in chapter one when we considered the subject of birds' nesting!

'Christian Reconstruction' is a particular approach to theonomy. Some Christians believe that as we get nearer to the Second Coming of Christ there will be an increasing influence of the gospel upon the nations until the majority of people, or at least a significant minority, will want to be governed by the just laws of the Old Testament. They believe we should start the process now by reminding governments of God's laws, and that we are under an obligation to keep the Old Testament moral laws (that is, everything except the ceremonial laws). These laws are still the standard by which all national laws should be modelled. Sometimes this is referred to as 'Dominion Theology', but the more popular term used to describe this position is 'Christian Reconstruction'.

The leaders in Christian Reconstruction today come from the United States of America and the notable names are Rousas John Rushdoony, Gary North, Greg Bahnsen and David Chilton. Their books are both exhaustive and exhausting. Gary North, for example, produced a four volume *An Economic Commentary on the Bible*, and the volumes covering Genesis to Leviticus alone reach around 4,000 pages! These writers point to passages like Deuteronomy 4:5–8, Proverbs 14:34 and Isaiah 2:2–4 to show that the laws of God are always the best laws for the nations.

Christian Reconstruction is not a heresy and its leading writers are mostly sincere evangelical men who firmly believe that the Bible is both relevant and without error from the beginning to the end. They are making a serious attempt to understand the Old Testament and to apply it to today's world; in doing this they take the Old Testament law very seriously. This can prove valuable to the Christian church and we should not react thoughtlessly.

Reconstruction is wedded to a post-millennial theology. This view maintains that through the persistent witness of the church and a powerful Holy Spirit revival, there will come a time when the gospel will triumph across the world and the authority of Christ and his word will be accepted by at least a significant minority of people. Whether or not this is a correct understanding of Bible prophecy is not our concern here, although it has to be said that there is no plain evidence from Scripture that there will ever be a time when the laws of God will be generally adopted by the governments of the world.

However, a more significant criticism of Reconstruction is that it was certainly not on the agenda of either our Lord or the apostle Paul. When Christ responded to the challenge of Pilate: 'My kingdom is not of this world… But now my kingdom is from another place' (John 18:36), he was referring not to the location but to the character of his kingdom. He meant that his rule and authority, unlike earthly empires, is essentially spiritual; apparently Christ never envisaged a time when he would rule by means of earthly laws and governors. Similarly, when Paul wrote about the duty of those who govern and those who are governed in Romans 13, he made no reference to Old Testament law. We might expect the apostle to have taken this opportunity to set out his agenda for Reconstruction as a model for Rome, but in 1 Corinthians 5:12 he specifically asks the Corinthians: 'What business is it of mine to judge those outside the church?' Although Christians may be politicians, and the Christian church may remind politicians of their obligations, active politics was not on the church's programme in the first century.

Perhaps the reason why reconstructive theonomy was not on Paul's agenda is because it runs too close to the danger of legalism. We will look at the meaning of this word shortly, but law books that are based upon the detailed interpretation and application of Old Testament laws must at the very least run the risk of falling into the trap of the Teachers of the Law (the Scribes) in the time of Christ. They believed that God had given Moses both the written law and the oral tradition—the *Halakhah*; in course of time the law took second place to the authoritative interpretation of it in the *Halakhah*. In the anticipated post-millennial kingdom of the Reconstructionists what safeguard is there that the same would not happen with their own writings?

In his superb analysis of Judaism in the time of Christ, Alfred Edersheim comments on the traditions of the Jews which were intended to protect the law of God: 'They provided for every possible and impossible case, entered into every detail of private, family, and public life; and with iron logic, unbending rigour, and most minute analysis pursued and dominated man, turn whither he might, laying on him a yoke which was truly unbearable' (*The Life and Times of Jesus the Messiah* Vol. 1 p. 98). That may be a timely warning to those involved in Christian Reconstruction.

However, the chief problem today lies not with those who over-use the law of God, but with those who object to almost any use of it. There is a growing number of evangelical people who question the relevance of the law for today.

Is the law only about Christ?

An opt-out among some Christians today is that as all of Scripture is about Christ, the law is therefore all about him. So, we must find Christ in every passage of Scripture, and having found him that is all we need. To use the law for moralising, regulations, ordering of societies or for any other reason than to reveal Christ is to misuse it. Those who follow this approach conclude that the Ten Commandments are not descriptive of the nature of God, only Christ can be that. After all, Christ explained to his disciples what was said about himself 'in all the Scriptures' (Luke 24:27). To handle the law as instructions for modern man, or for that matter to use Old Testament narratives to point up lessons in morality, is to come to the Scriptures in a dry and sterile way. I believe this approach to be significantly flawed.

In the first place, when Christ explained to the disciples how they would find him in all the Scriptures he did not mean in every word and verse of Scripture; that is a nice idea and it may seem very spiritual, but it is contrary to the truth. Nor does it mean that that is the only purpose of Scripture. All Scripture will eventually lead us to Christ, but it may have many other purposes along the way. A signpost may reveal our final destination, but its immediate purpose is to show us the correct turn at this particular junction.

Secondly, the New Testament does not use the Old Testament solely to show us Christ. Again and again Christ turned his hearers back to the law as a moral guide, and Paul did the same. The apostle was unashamed to use Deuteronomy 25:4 as a model for the financial support of those who minister the word of God. Deuteronomy gives instructions for the care of the ox grinding corn, but in 1 Corinthians 9:9–10 Paul applies the same principles to preachers! Eventually this will bring us to Christ no doubt, but not immediately.

Besides, what did Paul mean when he claimed that the Scriptures are profitable for: 'teaching, rebuking, correcting and training in righteousness, so that the man of God may be thoroughly equipped for every good work' (2 Timothy 3:16–17)? It is absurd to suggest that it is dry and sterile to read Old Testament narratives in general, and the law in particular, as teaching material for moral welfare. On the contrary, not to use it this way allows us to draw the most fanciful and ridiculous spiritual applications from the Old Testament, and in so doing to miss the primary meaning. If the law was not dry and sterile in the time of Moses or David, why should it be so now?

There should be no contrast between Christ and the law. It is Christ's law that we read in the Old Testament and it must therefore reveal to us the character of the author.

We live in a world that is careering out of control. Do we stand by and watch the inevitable pile-up at the bottom without at least pointing to the escape lane? Whilst we are busy enjoying spiritual 'I-spy' from the Old Testament pages of our Bible, are we not at least prepared to inform the reckless drivers of our confused generation where the brakes are? Are we content to watch a world running wild without sounding a clear, strident and robust voice for unchanging truth and morality?

Has the New Testament released us from the law?

It is true that there are Scriptures that, on a first reading, seem to imply that the Christian has nothing more to do with the law. Here are some of them: Romans 6:14, 'We are not under law but under grace'; Galatians 3:25 claims that the Christian is, 'no longer under the supervision of the Law', and Galatians 5:18 reads, 'If you are led by the Spirit you are not under law'. In 2 Corinthians 3:11 Paul tells us that the law 'was fading away' whereas the gospel lasts.

But equally there are passages that appear to teach the opposite: Romans 3:31 asks, 'Do we, then, nullify the law by this faith? Not at all! Rather, we uphold the law'; and 1 Timothy 1:8 advises us, 'We know that the law is good if one uses it properly'; 2 Timothy 3:16–17 reminds us that 'All Scripture is God-breathed and is useful for teaching, rebuking, correcting and training in righteousness, so that the man of God may be thoroughly equipped for every good work.' This is primarily a reference to the Old Testament and it is hard to understand what Paul meant by 'all Scripture' if the Old Testament law has no relevance for the Christian.

Imagine the church at Rome receiving a letter from Paul. Some of those in the congregation are converted Jews and others come from a pagan background. At the moment they have no New Testament, perhaps not even the complete Gospel record. Where will they go to find standards for the Christian? They could rely upon the inner witness of the Holy Spirit in their lives, but the converted pagans had very little for the Spirit to build on! Perhaps the Jewish Christians encouraged a careful study of the Old Testament law. Of course there was always the danger that some would fail to see the essential difference between those parts that had been fulfilled in Christ (the ceremonial) and those that still had value (the moral). Anyway, the debate got underway: do we need only the Spirit to teach us? Has the Jewish law—so good for so long and so different from anything else known in the world—now been firmly set aside? Some say 'Yes' and others say 'No'. Then Paul's letter arrives and in it they hear an Elder read, 'Everything that was written in the past was written to teach us, so that through endurance and the encouragement of the Scriptures we might have hope' (Romans 15:4). Do you think that would settle the debate for them?

These passages of Scripture that *appear* to be contradictory cannot really be so—if only because they all come from the pen of Paul! So what is the relationship of the law to the life of the Christian? In Galatians 3:25 Paul has a particular problem in mind when he writes, 'Now that faith has come, we are no longer under the supervision of the law.' Someone had been telling the Christians in Galatia that in addition to trusting in Christ for salvation they must keep the Old Testament ceremonial law as well—especially the law relating to circumcision. Therefore Paul sets out to prove that in order to be a Christian we must trust in Christ alone because we do not earn salvation by obeying the Old Testament ceremonial law. He makes that absolutely clear in 2:16, 'By observing the law no-one will be justified'.

But in case someone thinks Paul is dismissing the law altogether, he tells us about its value. In 3:23 he says that the law was like a guard to ensure that we didn't break free from God altogether and make up our own rules. Then in verses 24–25 he says it was like a supervisor or schoolteacher to prepare the way for the coming of Christ. Now that we are justified by faith in Christ we no longer need the law as a prison guard or as a supervisor because, as Paul makes clear in Galatians 3:26 and 5:1, we are children of God and we are therefore free.

In the same way, in Romans 10:4 Paul claims that Christ is 'the end of the law', but he doesn't mean Christ puts an end to the law, he means that Christ is the goal to which the law has been moving. Just as we say to someone: 'What end have you in mind by doing that?' As the moral law points to the necessity for Christ as the one who would keep it perfectly, so the ceremonial law points to the sacrifice of Christ. That's why I said earlier that when Christ 'fulfilled' the law it means that he both kept it (by obeying the moral law) and carried it out (by fulfilling the ceremonial law). According to Paul in Romans 7:12, 'the commandment is holy, righteous and good.'

There are some things that the law cannot do. It cannot save us or even add anything to our salvation. We need only to read Romans 3:28 to have this proved to us: 'We maintain that a man is justified by faith apart from observing the law.' That much is clear to every true Christian. However, breaking the law of God is still a description of sin because according to 1 John 3:4, 'Everyone who sins breaks the law; in fact sin is lawlessness.' Obedience to the Ten Commandments is therefore one test of a desire to please God in everything. This is clear from the way our Lord used the Old Testament law. He frequently challenged the people: 'Have you not read in the law?' or 'What is written in the law?'—in other words, far from dismissing the value of the law, he wanted them to learn how to use it correctly. The New Testament writers often refer back to the law to support their argument. In 1 Corinthians 9:8 Paul writes, 'Doesn't the law say the same thing?' and in the following verse he adds, 'It is written in the law of Moses…' Later in 14:21 and 34 Paul supports his arguments with: 'In the law it is written' and, 'as the law says'.

If you service your own car, the workshop manual gives a general summary such as: 'On re-assembly do not overtighten any bolts.' But each bolt has its own individual torque—the amount of twist or tightness relevant to that particular bolt. You have to refer to the handbook to know the torque for each bolt. That is like Paul summarising in Galatians 5:14 and 16 by saying that love is a summary of the law, and that if we live by the Spirit we will not gratify the desire of the sinful nature. But sometimes we need to know what God expects on a particular matter so that we can obey the law of love and keep in step with the Spirit. The law of God is like the torque for a particular situation. Take for example the subject of giving our money to God. In 1 Corinthians 16:2 Paul encourages us to give regularly and proportionately to our income, but because he doesn't tell us what proportion to give we cannot make this a matter of law for Christians. However, the value of the Old Testament law is that it lays down an obligation on the Israelite to tithe, which means giving one tenth, and therefore provides us with the pattern that pleases God. In other words we have used the Old Testament as our torque.

Jeremiah 31:33 says the same thing when the prophet speaks of the gospel as a time when God will put his laws in our minds and write them on our hearts. And Psalm 40:8 is similar: 'To do your will, O God, is my desire; your law is within my heart.' We need God's law available to guide us at all times.

The law is still vital for our Christian life because it helps us to see how holy God is, it helps to define sin, and it helps to keep us in check when we step out of line. For the Christian the law is not an enemy, but a friend whose directions we love; and it brings freedom, not slavery, because the royal law of love now controls us. Remember, the whole of the Old Testament is for *our* instruction.

Has the law of love dispensed with the law of words?

It is often assumed that in Romans 13:9 Paul releases us from an obligation to the law of God on the basis that all the commandments are summed up in the one rule 'Love your neighbour as yourself.' But this actually proves the value of the law, because a summary includes all the things it summarises. You may describe a well polished mahogany cabinet, a strong iron framework, a collection of black and white ivory pads, many metres of high tension wire and an amount of felt. Those are the parts. A summary would call it all a 'piano'.

It is the same with God's law. In Matthew 22:37–40 Jesus answered the question: 'Which is the greatest commandment in the Law?' by stating the importance of love for God and our neighbour; but he then added, 'All the Law and the Prophets hang on these two commandments.' That was another way of saying these two sum up all the others. When Paul tells us in Romans 13:9 that love is a 'summary' of the law, and in Galatians 5:14 that love 'fulfils' the law, he is saying the same thing. He means that love, far from dispensing with the law, actually includes it. This is Paul's point in Romans 13:8–10, 'Let no debt remain outstanding, except the continuing debt to love one another, for he who loves his fellow-man has fulfilled the law. The commandments, "Do not commit adultery," "Do not murder," "Do not steal," "Do not covet," and whatever other commandment there may be, are summed up in this one rule: "Love your neighbour as yourself." Love does no harm to its neighbour. Therefore love is the fulfilment of the law.' Here Paul is saying, 'If you want to describe love, you will find it best of all in the Commandments.'

When you are learning to play the piano there is a lot of hard work and attention to detail; but once you have mastered the rules they become, as it were, part of you, and you obey them without thinking. You are not free from the rules but you have freedom in obeying them. When you make a mistake it's those rules of music that show you where you went wrong. This is surely the psalmist's experience when he declares, 'I will walk about in freedom, for I have sought out your precepts' (Psalm 119:45). True freedom is not freedom to do what I like, but freedom to do what I was meant to do and freedom to be what I was meant to be. Paul considers that all the commandments are valid for the life of the Christian, but if we follow the summary of love we will not need them as law. On the other hand if we step out of line then the law is there to remind us of what God declares is right and wrong.

In John 13:34 Jesus told his disciples that he was giving them a *new* commandment' that they should love one another. He did not mean that he was giving them a rule that no-one had ever heard before, because the phrase 'love your neighbour as yourself' is found as far back as Leviticus 19:18. Our Lord was describing the kind of love that he expected from his disciples and then he continued with the *new* part: 'Even as I have loved you, so you must love one another.' In other words, what was new was not love, but the standard and quality of love: 'as I have loved you'. We might call that the New Testament 'plus factor'.

Two young people may justify sex before marriage because of love; a husband may defend his adultery on the basis of love; the murder of a cruel husband may be prompted by love for the wife and children; two men may enjoy a close bond of loving friendship—such as David and Jonathan experienced—but what will hold them back from allowing it to degenerate into a sexual relationship? Who is to say whether any of these actions are right or wrong? In each case it is the law that regulates love. Law and love were never intended to be divorced, as Deuteronomy 6:5–6 makes clear.

Far from law and love being opposites, the law actually defines and describes love. If love is our only test of whether an action is right or wrong that leaves us with a very subjective and uncertain basis. Which is precisely the confusion in our society today.

Are grace and law incompatible?

A man attempting to smuggle weapons on board an aircraft with the intent of hi-jacking the flight knows that there are powerful laws condemning his activity, backed by severe penalties. He fears the laws and the penalties so he approaches the airport security with a pounding heart and sweating palms. The law is a tyrant to him. By contrast a law-abiding passenger passes through the security checks without a second thought. He is under an obligation to the same laws and penalties as the first man, but he has no fear; in fact he delights in those laws which are there to protect the passengers' life and liberty. That was exactly the psalmist's attitude to the law in Psalm 119:44–45,47, 'I will always obey your law, for ever and ever. I will walk about in freedom, for I have sought out your precepts... I delight in your commandments because I love them.' Law is only a tyrant to the law-breaker. This is surely what Paul meant when he told Timothy that 'the law is made not for good men but for lawbreakers and rebels' (1 Timothy 1:9).

The past few years have seen a significant debate over whether or not we can accept Christ as Saviour without at the same time accepting him as Lord. On the one hand Zane Hodges maintained that there was no necessary relationship between faith and works and that to insist upon good works as the evidence of salvation is actually to deny the free and unconditional offer of the gospel. Hodges claimed that conversion requires 'No spiritual commitment whatsoever' (*The Gospel Under Siege* 1981). He was supporting Charles Ryrie who, in his book *Balancing the Christian Life* (1969) had concluded that to make repentance a condition of salvation is 'a false addition to faith.' Ryrie created some significant ripples in the evangelical pool by claiming that you can take Christ as Saviour without having him as your Lord. He may have been only affirming that a true Christian may not always live like one, but the die was cast. Comparisons were made with Robert Sandeman who, in the mid-eighteenth century, taught that a mental assent to the facts of the gospel is sufficient for salvation. This purely intellectual response to Christ is known as 'Sandemanianism'.

Against the background of this seemingly low view of salvation, the Christian life, evangelism and of Christ himself, John MacArthur responded in 1988 with his book *The Gospel According to Jesus.* (*You Call me Lord* is the title of the U.K. edition). MacArthur is committed to a gospel that radically changes lives, so that saving faith inevitably leads to a life under the lordship of Christ. After all, the watchword of the Reformers was *Sola fides justificat, sed non fides quae est sola*—Faith alone justifies, but not the faith that is alone. As Martin Luther wisely commented in sixteenth century Germany: 'Works are not taken into consideration when the question respects justification. But true faith will no more fail to produce them than the sun can cease to give light.' Or, as James comments in the New Testament: 'You *see* that a person is justified by what he does and not by faith alone' (James 2:24).

There can be no doubt that faith and works are bound together inextricably in New Testament thinking. Paul refers to those who 'Claim to know God, but by their actions they deny him' (Titus 1:16) and he asserts in Romans 8:14 that it is only those who are led by the Spirit of God who are the sons of God. John is equally clear that 'Whoever claims to live in Christ must walk as Jesus did' (1 John 2:6). Of course a Christian can fall into sin without losing salvation, and some Christians live in this way for a long time. However, we must not forget that in the New Testament there are some things that are possible but not permissible. The proof of sonship is to be owned by the Holy Spirit, and the proof of that ownership is to be led by the Spirit (Galatians 5:25). But the Spirit only leads us through the Scriptures he has revealed. Keeping in step with the Spirit is not listening to extra-terrestrial voices or to inner impressions, but being obedient to the clear revelation of the Spirit given in the whole of the Bible.

Think again of that conspirator boarding a passenger jet with his concealed weapons. Grace and law are only opposites for those who are on the outside of grace. Once we are on the receiving end of grace, the law itself is seen to be grace. It is no longer a tyrant condemning us, but a friendly force to keep us, and others, in check. This may be hard for some to understand but it is vital to grasp. The psalmist loved God's law for it brought him freedom not slavery. He thought about it often and delighted in it (Psalm 1:2; 119:70,77,97,113,163,174). He wanted nothing better than to have the perfect law of God in his heart (37:31; 40:8).

Does law lead to legalism?

Not necessarily. Legalism is the word used to describe a salvation that is obtained and maintained by conformity to law as opposed to salvation being by God's free offer of forgiveness. Practically, legalism is a demand that we observe the letter of the law and, in a misguided attempt to 'protect' the law of God, it invents additional man-made rules. The Pharisees had written 613 rules to hedge around the laws of God.

Legalism is not what constraints I place myself under but the demands I place upon others. Paul was ready to forgo eating meat if that was an offence to others (1 Corinthians 8:13) but that was not legalism; on the other hand, had he made the same demand of others, that would be legalism (Romans 14:2). Legalism is what Alfred Edersheim called 'legalised customs'—turning tradition and culture into law. One thing is certain: Obeying the Ten Commandments, and insisting that others do the same, is not legalism, since the Commandments are not tradition from men but revelation from God.

Legalism is very understandable. It often grows out of a desire to avoid excess; we may ban something that in itself is harmless because of the fear of others going too far. But when we invent rules to guard God's laws we have set ourselves up as wiser than God himself. Legalism may sincerely attempt to control human passions but it is bound to fail. Paul handled this approach in Colossians 2:20–23. All the rules man can invent, however wise and well-intentioned, 'lack any value in restraining sensual indulgence'. The monastic movement discovered this to its hurt. The early monastics were God-fearing and sincere Christians. In the second century Tertullian boasted that those who stayed in the world to fight would be defeated whilst those who ran away to the monastery would be victorious. They had to learn the hard way that the monk took his sinful nature with him!

Sometimes legalism is the way leaders will exercise authority over their followers. In 1 Peter 5:3 Peter urges spiritual leaders not to throw their weight around. Legalism is often the result of wanting to have an answer for everything; we are afraid of questions that do not have clear answers, or of issues that do not have firm legislation. But Paul reminded the Romans that there are what he called 'disputable matters' (14:1). It is precisely because God does not treat his people as little children, but encourages them to use their mind, influenced and controlled by the Bible, that he leaves us to apply the law to particular cases.

In Romans 14 Paul tackles the subject head on. On those 'disputable matters' he allows the Christian's conscience to dictate. But we must not become each other's conscience. First century Christians differed in their willingness to eat meat that had been offered to idols (v 2, 14–17), in their observance of Christian festivals (v 5–6), and in their attitude to alcohol (v 21). This is not Paul's 'grand slam' against the law of God but his warning against an enthusiastic legalism. Our insistence upon the abiding value of the law of God is not legalism. It will only become legalistic when we add new rules to God's laws. When Amish leaders spend hours debating the permitted width of a girl's hair bow, that is legalism.

A few years ago I was discussing with a group of young people the whole matter of Christian giving. Before long we were ransacking the Old Testament to discover the details of the law of the tithe. It was a little disconcerting to discover that the Jews actually spent some of their tithe on the sacrifice, part of which they ate. We wondered whether the Christian could therefore count an evening at MacDonald's within the tithe! The problem was that we had started from the wrong end. As Christians we had started from law instead of from grace. So, we began again and searched for information in the New Testament. From 2 Corinthians 8 and 9, and 1 Corinthians 16, and from Matthew 6 we gathered a list of words to describe Christian giving: sacrificially, joyfully, willingly, spontaneously, proportionately, abundantly, secretly, humbly, regularly, trustfully—that was all the result of grace. At this point the young people asked for a biblical pattern, a rule by which to measure our giving. We then returned to the tithe. Legalism started with the tithe and would make it mandatory, even a high mark of spirituality, but grace led us there willingly.

To avoid legalism there is one simple rule that is not a contradiction of anything we have already said. The rule is this: The Old Testament law is no longer binding unless grace leads us to it. Legalism is going where grace does not lead.

Does law kill peace and joy?

I drive many thousands of miles on our motorways, and at high speeds the margin for error is very small. There are hundreds of laws that govern each vehicle and the way it is driven. They range from laws that ensure that the car in front of me—and its driver—are in a fit condition to be on the road, to laws that ensure that the road itself is maintained to a high standard of safety. I am well aware of drivers who are reckless in their speed and thoughtless in their lane-changing, but I have a peace of mind that, by and large, my fellow motorists are obeying the same laws as I am. In fact, without that knowledge I doubt whether I would venture on to the roads at all—unless I was driving a tank! The law, far from killing peace, may well save me from being killed.

The seventeenth century Puritan, Thomas Watson, wisely commented, 'They who will not have the law to rule them, shall have the law to judge them.' Or as an old Methodist preacher is reported to have observed, 'We either keep the Ten Commandments or we illustrate them.' Christians, as all men and women, are under an obligation to keep the law of God. They were written, remember, not on sheets of paper or rolls of leather so that we can bend them, but on tablets of stone so that we either keep them or break them. The law for the Christian does not condemn but it does command.

To read the law simply as a narrow check-list is to misread it entirely. It may prove conveniently comfortable to take the plain statement: 'You shall not commit adultery', and claim a one hundred per cent success rate because you have been physically faithful to your wife, but clearly that is not all that is intended by God, as Christ's Sermon on the Mount explained. Similarly in Romans 2:22 Paul chides the Jews for self-confident arrogance: 'You who abhor idols, do you rob temples?' Perhaps he has in mind Malachi and the tithe. Every generation must learn to apply the Commandments to itself.

The confusion in society today over what is right and wrong—and even whether there is such a thing as right or wrong—is a direct result of our ignorance of the law of God. The biblical Proverb that 'Those who forsake the law praise the wicked, but those who keep the law resist them' (28:4) is right on! It should never be a mystery to the Christian why standards are turned on their head and the most degrading and godless behaviour is applauded in our society. That is the inevitable outcome of a society that has relegated the Ten Commandments to obscure antiquity as the ancient rules of a primitive Semitic race. The greater tragedy is that many professing Christians appear to be in agreement.

When the psalmist of Israel read the laws of his God he did not spend his time disputing them; on the contrary he once wrote, 'I delight in your commandments because I love them' (Psalm 119:47).

In the history of the Christian church there have been three main uses of the law of God. First, it is seen as a hammer to convict the sinner—laws to convince us how far we have fallen from God's standard; secondly it is seen as a shackle to keep an unruly society in check—laws that tell us what is right and wrong. What is known as the 'third use of the law' is to view the Commandments as a guide for Christians in their striving after holiness. All three are valuable, but whilst the first two are contemptuously dismissed by our modern society, it is this third use that is chiefly under attack today from within the church.

Too many Christians use the Old Testament just as a book of spiritual illustrations and completely neglect the fact that we learn there what God's standards are for every area of human relationships. It is sad that some Christians think that much of the Old Testament is irrelevant to their life today and so regard it as uninteresting and even boring. To find that all of it is relevant, and to begin to apply it—with the aid of the New Testament as a commentary—to every area of life, may require some hard work but it is very exciting.

Reading the Highway Code must be quite tedious for someone who only ever sails yachts, but it takes on a new meaning when you are on the M25 in the rush hour. The Bible, all of it, was written for real life—and the Ten Commandments are no exception. It is with that frame of mind that we can turn to the Commandments themselves.

No other gods

'And God spoke all these words: "I am the LORD your
God, who brought you out of Egypt, out of the land of
slavery. You shall have no other gods before me."'
Exodus 20:1–3

E very profession and trade has its regulations to ensure safety. There
are right and wrong ways of doing things, and the more potentially
dangerous the outcome, the more precise are the rules. An architect
may design a beautiful building that is aesthetically pleasing in all respects,
but unless it conforms to the fourteen-part *Building Regulations* he will
never get permission to build. This is not because the Secretary of State for
the Environment wants to monopolise the design of all buildings, but
because to ignore the regulations would be to jeopardize the safety of
others.

This principle of guarding public safety by precise and protective rules
holds true for every serious profession whether it is architecture,
engineering, aeronautics or medicine. But in the most serious of all—
religion—it would appear that anything goes.

One God—One way ?
We live in a 'pluralistic' society. This means that in the same community we
have a mix of religions and cultures, races and languages. But the word
'pluralism' goes further. It is used to describe the view that all these
differences, and particularly the religious differences, contribute to the sum
of spiritual truth. No matter what a person believes, that belief must be
accepted as a valid contribution to our full understanding of the ultimate
Principle behind the universe—call it whatever you like. Pluralism, we are
told, helps to maintain harmony in a pluralistic society. No one should
claim an exclusive monopoly of the truth (exclusivism), and we must sift
out what is best from all religions. Christianity must just take its place
alongside all the others. This is certainly the 'politically correct' view

expressed in the media, and many church leaders follow obediently. Phrases like 'their aspect of the truth', 'the valuable insight into the reality of God', 'an important contribution to our understanding of spirituality', are liberally sprinkled into the thoughts and prayers for the day.

God demands, 'You shall have no other gods before me'; Christ claimed, 'I am the way and the truth and the life, no man comes to the Father except by me' (John 14:6); and the disciples insisted, 'Salvation is found in no one else, for there is no other name under heaven given to men by which we must be saved' (Acts 4:12). The inevitable response to this exclusiveness is, 'That's all right for those who want to accept him; for them he *is* the only way. But for other men and women there are other ways.' The media will not allow the Christian faith to assert that there are no other gods, and our children are taught that they must be tolerant of those who follow other religions (a healthy truth) because all religions are right (an unhealthy lie).

When the Ten Commandments begin with the assertion, 'I am the LORD your God… You shall have no other gods before me' the immediate response is that this is perfectly correct—for the Jews. They have only one God and no other; he is the God revealed here in the Old Testament and understood in a Jewish way. But for others whether Moslem, Hindu, Buddhist or whatever else, there are other equally valid gods. This is not just a modern idea either. A Christian leader and politician wrote in his diary: 'The larger proportion of those who profess to believe are eagerly eliminating from their creed all dogma and doctrine. They accept the Scripture just as far as it suits their philosophy. Such will be the religion of the future, in which Vishnu, Mahomet, Jupiter and Jesus Christ, will be upon a level; with some, all equally good, with others, all equally bad.' That was written on 18 March 1868 by the evangelical earl, Lord Shaftesbury.

Pluralism asserts that all religions are really heading for the same destination but that we all give the destination, and the route to it, different names. It may be Heaven, Nirvana or Paradise via Krishna or Buddha or Allah, or we may just call him the Great Architect, or Gaia the great mother goddess of earth. Call God what you like: Mother, Father, it doesn't matter. The Greeks and Romans had Zeus and Hermes, just like God and Christ. The Assyrians had their own god Asshur, and the Egyptians worshipped Osiris and Isis and their hawk-headed son Horus, together with the apis bull and many local gods. The Persians prayed to Ahura-mazda, and so the list continues. Whether we consult New Age 'channels', Spiritist mediums, Hare Krishna, chant Hindu mantras in our local yoga classes, or merely go to church on Sunday, it is all one and the same thing.

In 1993 the General Assembly of the Church of Scotland was faced with a resolution calling on the churches to reaffirm that Christ is the only way of salvation; it was defeated by four hundred votes to three hundred. Presumably the majority of church representatives knew better than Paul who wrote, 'There is one God and one mediator between God and men, the man Christ Jesus' (1 Timothy 2:5), and Isaiah who, on behalf of God declared, 'I, even I, am the LORD, and apart from me there is no saviour' (Isaiah 43:11). Pluralism becomes 'syncretism' when our mutual recognition of one another's gods expresses itself in the ultimate unity of a multi-faith act of worship. This is meant to be good for community relations in a cosmopolitan and heterodox society. Christian certainty, and an exclusivism that maintains there is only one true God for everyone in this world, is to be avoided, and opposed, at all costs. Multi-faith services are popular in our society.

Replying to pluralism
FIRST, IF EVERYTHING IS TRUE THEN NOTHING IS FALSE
If every generation and culture can write their own 'building regulations' for eternity then everything is right and nothing is wrong. That is far more dangerous than allowing every cowboy building contractor to compile his own regulations.

Pluralism assumes that the totally opposite beliefs of world religions must all be stirred into the pot of spiritual enquiry. The moment we suggest that any aspect of a world religion is either false, or at best incomplete, we have assumed a standard by which we make that judgement. But where did that standard come from? Someone, somewhere, must have a measuring line by which to judge how close to truth and reality a particular religion has arrived. For those who have attempted even an elementary study of world religions it is evident that there are great gulfs between them. The character of the supreme Being, how many there are, what the purpose of life is, how we are to find peace and forgiveness (assuming that either is necessary or possible), what lies beyond the grave (if anything) and how we can be prepared for it, what a 'good' life is and how we can achieve it, these and a hundred other issues find totally different answers in a thousand different religions. According to pluralism the only view that is certainly false is the one that claims to have the only answer. But to say that the answers do not matter because it is the search that is all important leads to an even greater problem.

SECONDLY, IF NOTHING IS FALSE THEN EVERYTHING MUST BE TRUE

'Alternative medicine' is a mixture of serious science and quack practitioners. For this reason, in the United Kingdom no one can pose as a doctor and then give medical advice, clinically examine, treat a patient or prescribe drugs unless he is registered with the General Medical Council. The Council has exacting regulations governing both qualifications and practices. The reason is straightforward: not everyone is able to give good advice in such an important field as the health of the nation. Bad advice, however well-meaning, can be fatal.

The high-ground of pluralism is that whatever the religion and whatever its beliefs and practices we must acknowledge that it is a legitimate search for the Ultimate Being or Beings. On what grounds did we outlaw suttee, the practice of burning widows, in colonial India? Presumably because we ignorantly assumed that Christianity knew best. On what grounds can we oppose self-mutilation by devout Hindu worshippers? Or religious and ethnic cleansing? Or the hideous practices of ancient religions?

The ultimate failure of pluralism lies in the fact that logically it must destroy itself. No-one actually believes that everything is acceptable providing it is in the name of religion, but equally no-one can enlighten us how to tell the difference. Pluralism, and its sister syncretism, cannot deny the right of anyone to believe and practise anything providing they are sincerely searching for the truth. Back in the time of the great Babylonian Empire, the terrifying Baal god and the sensual Asherah goddess dominated the lives of many. Presumably these, and even Moloch to whom the people offered children in sacrifice, were all pointing towards the truth and adding a little more to the great pool of spirituality. And if not, why not, if there is no ultimate reality to be known certainly?

THIRDLY, WE HAVE QUESTIONS WITHOUT THE POSSIBILITY OF ANSWERS

If there is no ultimate religious truth of which we can be certain, then we are presumably prepared to acknowledge the existence, or non-existence, of a God, or gods, who has either chosen not to reveal himself, herself or themselves clearly, or is/are incapable of doing so! Thus there is total confusion in the most vital issue we can ever face: reality in life and certainty in death.

How can a belief in reincarnation possibly be squared with the plain teaching of Scripture that there is one death and one judgement, and that that is the end (Hebrews 9:27)? How can salvation by personal effort and merit possibly be valid alongside a belief in salvation as a free gift which is both unearned and undeserved (Ephesians 2:8–9)? Pluralism deliberately begs the most vital questions both philosophy and religion ever ask, 'Who am I? What am I here for? Where am I going? And how do I get there?' For pluralism the answers are far less important than the questions.

FOURTHLY, EVANGELISM IS IRRELEVANT

Pluralism may be a first step to a world agreement that no one will evangelise anyone. All religions will be left free from the evangelical predators of other religions. Perhaps this is why church leaders decline to support evangelism among the Jews for example. Why should we consider 'converting' people from other religions, or from no religion for that matter. It is surely unnecessary in a pluralistic age to want to convert the Moslem, Hindu, Buddhist, or even the animist or pagan.

Some writers are even suggesting that all religions should combine their strength to attack, not each other, but the perceived enemy of religion: humanism. On the contrary, the Christian maintains that humanism is not the greatest enemy to the truth—Christless religion is. Evangelism assumes a possession of the truth which is not shared by those we are evangelizing.

FIFTHLY, A SMALL VIEW OF GOD

The God who revealed himself to Moses and the people of Israel also revealed himself throughout the unfolding revelation of the Bible as a God for all people in every age and culture. As we have already seen, the laws given to Moses were a witness to the nations (Deuteronomy 4:7–8) and were to be taught to the nations (31:12–13). Centuries after Moses, the prophet Jonah was sent to preach repentance to Nineveh, the capital city of the great Assyrian empire, not because the people were lacking in gods and religion but because they were without the true God and true religion. Fifteen hundred years beyond Moses, the apostle Paul stood in the market square of the Greek city of Athens and invaded their centuries-old paganism by introducing them to: 'The God who made the world and everything in it'. He made no pact with Greek mythology, or with their philosophy or priestcraft, when he claimed, 'The Lord of heaven and earth does not live in temples made with hands, as if he needed anything, because he himself gives all men life and breath and everything else' (Acts 17:22–32). Paul went on to assert one true God, to denounce the worship of idols, to insist upon a final judgement to come, and to call for a change of mind, heart and religion.

It is this kind of evangelistic confidence that we meet continually throughout the New Testament, and it is the context for the apostolic insistence that 'Salvation is found in no-one else, for there is no other name under heaven given to men by which we must be saved' (Acts 4:12). Apparently the Christian apostle was ignorant of the tolerance demanded by pluralism!

The influence of pluralism

Pluralistic thinking has permeated the minds of evangelical Christians to an alarming degree. We are ready to assert, 'You shall have no other gods' but are reluctant to accept that the biblical consequence of this is that there can be no salvation apart from personal faith in Christ. A significant debate amongst evangelicals today concerns the possibility of salvation through Christ but without a knowledge of him. On both sides of the Atlantic books, articles and lectures defend the suggestion that those who have never heard of Christ may be saved by Christ. This is a form of inclusivism.

A paper published by an evangelical study group in the *Evangelical Review of Theology* (Vol. 15 No 1 January 1991) explores the salvation of Gentiles in Old Testament biblical history and draws three conclusions: First, whilst acknowledging on the one hand God's implacable hatred of pagan idolatry and its practices, we are reminded that many Gentiles are recorded as living 'in contact with God': like Melchizedek, Abimelech, Jethro, Balaam, Rahab and Ruth. In responding to this we must insist that contact with God and finding salvation outside the covenant of Israel are two very different things. Melchizedek is claimed by the New Testament to be an enigmatic character who was nevertheless a perfect picture of Christ himself (Hebrews 7:17); it is therefore inconceivable that he was a pagan prophet or priest. As for Balaam, it is one thing for God to use the mouth of a reluctant prophet (just as he used the mouth of the donkey) but quite another to assume that the prophet had any salvation relationship with God; in fact the Scriptures strongly suggest the contrary—2 Peter 2:15 and Revelation 2:14. As for Rahab and Ruth we are specifically told that they came under the protection of the covenant with Israel; these girls were converted to Judaism.

Secondly the paper suggests that 'Gentile nations are declared to have their place in the gracious purpose of God' and Isaiah 19:24–25 and Malachi 1:11 are offered as evidence. Insofar as God uses the nations for his purpose and allows them his general providence of sun and rain, this is true. But Isaiah 19 speaks of a day when Egypt and Assyria will 'swear allegiance to the LORD Almighty', that surely is a conversion. Whether this chapter is a picture of Gentile conversion in the age of the gospel will depend upon one's view of Bible prophecy, but the only hope offered here is for an Egypt converted to 'the LORD Almighty'. Nothing could be clearer. To believe anything else comes close to suggesting that Islam could be the salvation of Egypt. Malachi 1:11 reads, 'My name will be great among the nations'— how can that be if the nations remain within their pagan ignorance?

Thirdly the paper concludes that much of the biblical Wisdom literature (e.g. Proverbs and Ecclesiastes) speaks of divine wisdom 'without reference to God's revelation to Israel'. But is this really so? The Wisdom literature is part of Israel's religious literature and as such was never seen as anything other than his revelation to his people. To suggest that 'it has close links in spirit, content, form and method with similar literature in Egypt' is like an evangelical suggesting that Moses may have borrowed some of his laws from Hammurabi's Code. The paper suggests that Job was 'a Syrian Chief outside the context of Israel'; but what were the sacrifices that God clearly accepted (Job 1:5)? They could hardly have been pagan offerings, especially as God introduces him as: 'My servant Job. There is no one on earth like him; he is blameless and upright, a man who fears God and shuns evil' (1:8). There is much we do not know about Job, but that description, together with his decisive faith revealed in the book, introduces us to a man who is very much more than a pagan idolater stumbling out of his ignorance into the twilight of truth. This man knew the true God and worshipped him in the right way. No one denies that a pagan may 'discover' some aspects of true wisdom—in that sense there is doubtless some truth in all religions and philosophies—but knowing God and experiencing salvation is altogether different.

The arguments of this study group are no stronger from the New Testament. Whilst admitting that the apostles had a clear message of the uniqueness and exclusiveness of the Christian gospel, John 1:9 and Acts 17:30 are taken to imply that there is some truth in all world religions. Cornelius (Acts 10:4) is chosen as an example of God accepting the prayers of a Gentile, even though salvation came only through Christ. But this ignores the significant fact that Cornelius was a proselyte who had placed himself under the covenant of Israel—it was in this context that his prayers and acts of charity had been acceptable.

The influence of our pluralistic society on this particular study group is seen most strikingly when Lesslie Newbigin is quoted approvingly, 'The Christian confession of Jesus as Lord does not involve any attempt to deny the reality of the work of God in the lives and thoughts and prayers of men and women outside the Christian church. On the contrary, it ought to involve an eager expectation of, a looking for, and a rejoicing in the evidence of that work ... If we love the light and walk in the light, we shall also rejoice in the light wherever we find it' (from *The Open Secret* S.P.C.K p. 198). If Newbigin meant by 'the evidence of that work' a pagan heart opening to the gospel of Christ, then we must all agree heartily—but that is not what he meant.

Similar loose thinking is revealed when we are told that whilst receiving Christ brings salvation, and that whilst 'those who reject him are lost', those who have never heard the gospel will be judged 'in proportion to light received'. But what does that mean? Sir Norman Anderson is allowed to clarify it for us. After referring to the salvation of the Old Testament saints through the merits of Jesus Christ, Professor Anderson continues, 'May we not believe that the same would be true of the follower of some other religion in whose heart the God of all mercy has been working by his Spirit, who had come in some measure to realise his sin and need of forgiveness, and who had been enabled, in the twilight as it were, to throw himself on the mercy of God?' *(Christianity and Comparative Religion* pp 100–107). But to equate the faith of the men and women under the covenant of Israel with the faith of an 'enlightened' pagan is an incredible misunderstanding of Old Testament religion and its unique relationship to Christianity.

The same arguments are expanded by Peter Cotterell in *Mission and Meaninglessness* (SPCK, 1990) and Clark Pinnock in *A Wideness in God's Mercy* (Zondervan, 1992), and have been ably answered by Hywel R. Jones in *Only One Way* (Day One Publications, 1996). There is no suggestion by any of these writers that salvation can be received from any source other than the atonement of Christ, but one writer does go so far as to suggest that there may be salvation in other religions 'though through the mediation of Christ' (G. Tomlin, *Evangelical Anglicans* SPCK, 1993, p. 89)!

However, the issue is not just a battle for the giants; it goes far beyond the theologians and study groups. The first Commandment is first because its implications are incredibly far-reaching. The statements 'You shall have no other gods before me' and 'I, even I, am the LORD and apart from me there is no saviour' (Isaiah 43:11) are in effect one and the same. God teaches his people that there is no other god and no other salvation and that all else is a lie.

Exclusivism and intolerance

The command 'you shall have no other gods' is not simply a negative comment that all other religions are worthless, it is a positive statement on the exclusiveness of the one true God. The first Commandment says not only 'you must not worship other gods', but that there are no other gods to be worshipped—just as Paul acknowledged in 1 Corinthians 8:4, 'there is no God but one'. The universal exclusiveness of Israel's God is revealed also in Isaiah 44:6, 'This is what the LORD says—Israel's King and Redeemer, the

LORD Almighty: "I am the first and I am the last; apart from me there is no God."' Society may believe that all gods are authentic, but that cannot be true for the Christian unless we are prepared to reduce our Sovereign Creator to the level of the world's gods.

The God revealed in the Old Testament never accepted the gods of the surrounding nations; on the contrary he ordered his people to destroy them. His disgust at the behaviour of the nations is revealed in Deuteronomy 18:9–13. There is no tolerance here. This God, who is everywhere claimed in the Bible to be the Sovereign Creator, never once hinted that there might be another way for other people. When he told the Israelites that they must not worship like the other nations, or live like them, or enquire into their religions (Deuteronomy 12:4,8,30–31) he did not do so as a local deity whose territory extended approximately from the River Jordan in the east to the Mediterranean in the west, and north to south from the Syrian border to Egypt, he did so as the God of the whole universe who is in control of all the inhabitants of the earth and beside whom all other gods are a lie.

However, exclusivism and certainty on our part do not imply aggression and intolerance. Although God was aggressively intolerant of the world religions in the Old Testament, even he allowed them to continue world-wide, and only destroyed them where they threatened the purity of his chosen nation. The New Testament recognises the existence of world religions and advocates a peaceful demolition of their falsehood by the power of the gospel. Christians today, as in the first century, can live peacefully with their religious or non-religious neighbours whilst maintaining a unique and exclusive gospel. It was Rome with all its pluralism that could not tolerate the Christians, not vice versa. And that is exactly what we find today. Nothing is more intolerant of people with convictions than pluralism.

The uniqueness of Christ

When God declared to the Israelites: 'You shall have no other gods before me' he was not saying 'You must not, but others may'. God put forward his chosen people as a model to the world and effectively said, 'You must show the world the meaning of true religion and true worship; what you are to me will be a pattern for all time and for all people because beside me there is no other.'

This is the same God of whom Christ spoke when he declared that the greatest Commandment is that we should love God with all our heart, soul and mind (Matthew 22:37). To believe either that Christ was referring only to the Jews and Christians or that he was prepared to tolerate a definition of 'God' that included the Moslem, Hindu or New Age understanding is frankly either dishonest or stupidly ridiculous. Did the One who claimed, 'Anyone who has seen me has seen the Father' (John 14:9) really believe that Mohammed, Krishna or Gautama could be visible or viable alternatives? If he was mistaken in his teaching concerning his own uniqueness then his egocentric error is no example for us at all; but if he was correct, then why do so many who profess Christianity concede that he is at best the 'highest' or 'nearest' or 'clearest' expression of the truth of God? Have they not read the lives of the other contenders sufficiently to convince them that there is nothing more dangerous than a religious lie?

The value of religions

But is there no value in this smorgasbord of religion? Yes there is. In a strange way there is immense value in them all. First they reveal the deep longing of mankind for God. They tell us that our understanding of the Bible is absolutely right when we claim that God has put eternity into man's mind (Ecclesiastes 3:11). Religions are mankind grasping for eternity.

A second value in the religions of the world is that they reveal humanity's awareness of an accountability to God. This is why most religions have some form of sacrifice through which they will bring their god or gods into a pleasant frame of mind; in much the same way that children put out food for Father Christmas in order to obtain their wishes!

But the religions of the world reveal something more. In the light of accountability we must make ourselves fit for God. In various ways that means self-effort. This may involve acts of charity to the poor and disadvantaged—which is all very good. But equally it may be far more sinister. The suicide bomber is promised all the delights of Paradise on condition that he dies in the act of killing as many of his fellow human beings as he can. That is a salvation by works; a salvation conditional upon shedding as much blood as possible. Acts of mercy and massacre are therefore equally legitimate in the effort to please our god.

On the other hand, Christianity begins with God's solution. Human religion would never conceive of the idea of God coming to earth in order to make the only possible provision for salvation by his death and not by his teaching—and that is why no human religion invented the story of the incarnation and crucifixion. Similarly no human religion would ever conceive the idea of God doing all that was necessary for human salvation and then offering it as a free gift, with the 'risk' that mankind would take advantage of this and pocket the salvation without a change of behaviour. For this reason no human religion ever invented such an offer. Human religion would never by-pass human effort as a major contribution to the solution of individual salvation—and that is why the Buddhist Noble Eightfold Way and the Islamic Seven Pillars of Wisdom are keys to unlock a present change and a future hope. In other words, world religion always focuses upon mankind as the solution to the problems faced by mankind. Christianity focuses upon God as the only ultimate solution.

World religions all suppress the truth about Christ. The Birmingham shopkeeper who put a notice in his window declaring, 'Jesus Christ is not the Son of God, he is only a prophet' was doing what all religions do—he was inventing alternatives to the revelation of God. And that is precisely why God began his Commandments where he did. The religions of the world reveal a deep longing for God by the human race, an awareness of accountability to God and the utter impossibility of finding peace with God apart from Jesus Christ. They do have value if only we would see them as sign-posts to the Cross. They say, 'This is the wrong route. Go to Christ'. Sadly, however, too many conclude that they are pointing the right way.

What's in a Name?

God began with this Commandment in order to clear the rubbish out of the way. All other gods will spell disaster. But in Exodus 20:2 God reveals the kind of God that he is, and only on this basis can we move to verse 3 and the first command. Through the Israelites, God will say to the whole world from here on: 'There is no other God. You must have no other God.' But why not? Who is this exclusive God?

The purpose behind almost all advertisements is to project a name that, during the course of our shopping, we will constantly recall. Companies aim to highlight their name so that we will always associate it with the appropriate product. Getting a name, or making a name, is vital for commercial success. In Exodus 3:14 God met with Moses at the burning bush in the desert. Moses was told to go back and command Pharaoh to let the Israelites go; but first he was to inform the people that God was on their side. Among all the excuses Moses offered was the fact that the people might well ask, 'Who is your God? What is his name?' Moses wanted to know what his answer should be. The word 'Elohim' is the Hebrew word for 'god' but it has no reference to any particular god. Even the gods of the nations are called 'Elohim'. Egypt had their gods as well, so what was different about this God of the Israelites?

God replied by reminding Moses of the special name by which the Patriarchs—Abraham, Isaac and Jacob, had known him. He told Moses to go to the people and say to them: 'The I AM has sent you.' Tell them that the I AM has come and the I AM has spoken to you. The God who is self-sufficient, self-existing, without beginning and without end. The Creator God who does not need anything from you. You do not need to feed him, because he feeds you. You do not need to carry him because he leads you. He has life and power in himself. In fact, he does not need you, but you need him.

Moses and the people could contrast this 'I AM' God with the gods of Egypt. At sunrise the Egyptian priests would knock on the doors of the temples to wake up their gods. Then they would wash them and give them breakfast, stand them out in the sun for the day and, at evening, put them to bed for the night. Moses, told the people that the I AM, the self-sufficient, self-existing, utterly different God had come to set the people free. When the Jews offered their sacrifices to God they were never to think of their gifts as food and drink to sustain their God. Their God needed nothing from them. He was the I AM, he was the LORD.

We will look again at this word LORD in chapter five, but it was never used by any nation other than the Israelites; it was unique to them. It carried with it the guarantee of a God who was entirely trustworthy and who made promises and always kept them. It was the 'covenant' name of the God of Israel. Yahweh (LORD) was the God who had chosen Israel from among all the nations on earth, and through them he would bless all the nations on earth (Genesis 12:2–3). This is why it was important for God to use this title as he introduced his Ten Commandments. He is saying to the people: 'I want you to understand the kind of God I AM. I AM the God who made everything and I AM the God who is self-sufficient. I need nothing from you but I will make promises to you and I will keep them. This is a special relationship.'

Even at their lowest point of backsliding in later years, the Israelites never forgot this special name or its significance; and they never thought of their God as a localized god. For the nations there were the gods of the hills so, if you went up to the hills, you prayed to them. When you went into the valley it was no use praying to the gods of the hills, you had to pray to the gods of the valley. And so on. But the Israelites had their God of the whole world. Abraham had once prayed, 'Will not the judge of all the earth do right?' (Genesis 18:25) and Israel never forgot this. Abraham did not say 'Shall not the judge of the plain around the Dead Sea do right?' That was staggeringly advanced for his time. Few nations considered that their gods have a monopoly on space or time. Read 1 Kings 20:23–28 and you will understand this point.

The God who acts
'I am the LORD your God, who brought you out of Egypt, out of the land of slavery.' Here was a reminder of the powerful activity of God in Egypt. The people had only to recall the terrible plagues, the angel of death who passed over their own homes, the miracle of darkness to halt the Egyptian army, the parting of the Red Sea and the flood that crashed into the elite royal charioteers, to realise how foolish it is to choose any idol in preference to the God who had revealed himself in power. This is why Paul dismissed the gods of the world as no gods at all (Acts 19:26).

God has never left himself without a witness; the whole world and universe demonstrates that God is active and powerful (Romans 1:20), and no one has any excuse for not acknowledging him. From the squalid slums of Calcutta to the rubbish tips of the Philippines, still there is evidence of God at work. There are few who cannot look into a night sky or listen to the song of the birds, or marvel at the incredible form of a young baby. All this is God in action. But for those who have his special revelation in the

Scriptures and can therefore read of his mighty acts throughout history and especially in the coming of his Son Jesus Christ, there is even less excuse when they turn to the idols of western society.

The God who is present

We often entertain overseas visitors in our home, and one of our first enquiries is to ask about their family. More often than not our guest offers, 'Would you like to see my wife and children?' Of course we would, but we never expect them to walk into the room at that point in the conversation. A well-worn photograph comes out of a wallet and we can see the face of the family; they may be six thousand miles away, but we can see them. In the time of Moses to 'see' the face of someone would certainly mean that you were in their presence; no other way of seeing them was possible.

In Exodus 20:2 God drew the attention of his people to something very significant. The phrase 'before me' (v 3) is a translation of two Hebrew words (*al pani*) that mean 'before my face'. Among the items in the Tabernacle, and later in the Temple, was a table on which bread was daily placed in the presence of God. The *Authorised Version* referred to it unhelpfully as 'the shewbread' (for example in Exodus 25:30). A literal and more accurate translation would be 'the bread of the face' or 'the bread of the presence' (NIV); it was bread placed before the face of God. In Exodus 33 God promised Moses that 'My presence (*pani*—my face) will go with you' (v 14) and Moses picked up on this as the basis for his strong appeal: 'If your presence does not go with us, do not send us up from here' (v 15). In each case the root word is the same in the words 'my face' and 'your face'. The NIV 'mystifies' the word by the use of a capital 'P' for 'Presence', but that is not warranted in the original Hebrew.

This phrase 'the face of the Lord' occurs often in the Old Testament and always refers to God being present; as such it is a 'gospel' word because just as the voice of God is grace in that he does not need to speak to us at all, so the presence of God is grace. Sin always results in the withdrawal of the presence of God. The first tragic consequence of the Fall is described in Genesis 3:8 where this same word is used. It is lost in the NIV but is literally 'they hid from the face of the LORD God'. Similarly after the first murder 'Cain went out from the face of the LORD' (Genesis 4:16). There can be nothing worse than this in the whole experience of the human race. It is the experience of total desolation and hopelessness. Sin separates us from the presence of God, and salvation is the restoration of his presence to the sinner; for this reason Christ died in order to 'bring us to God'—to restore us to his presence (1 Peter 3:18).

The presence of God is a distinguishing mark of the Christian, and therefore of the Christian church. A Christian is someone evidently related to God and walking in friendship with him. That is the Fall reversed. Moses was described as a man 'whom the LORD knew face to face' (Deuteronomy 34:10) and the psalmist longed for the same experience: 'My heart says of you, "Seek his face!" Your face, LORD, I will seek' (Psalm 27:8). The Hebrew word *pani* is used on each occasion. It is this very presence of God, and not simply his all-seeingness—what is referred to as his 'omniscience'—that should cause us to fear our God (Jeremiah 5:22). What Moses wanted in his plea recorded in Exodus 33:15 was not only that God would keep an eye on his people, but that he would keep his presence with them.

This phrase 'before me' clearly does not imply that we may have other gods providing he is the first. Neither does it mean that God would be among his people in an 'aura' or ghostly 'Presence'—though the fire and cloud were symbols of his attendance among his people. The word is also more than an affirmation that God is the God who sees; after all, a seeing God could view from a distance, just as we might observe an eclipse of the moon. The vital significance of the command, 'You shall have no other gods before me' is that at once the people are reminded that in the presence of this holy God there is no room for any other god. The nation of Israel, and through them the whole human race, have a straight choice: They can either have God or not. What they can never have is the privilege of his presence *and* at the same time dabble in the false religions of the world around them. According to 2 Kings 17:33 the sin of the foreign tribes who were settled in Samaria after its conquest by the Babylonians, was that, 'They worshipped the LORD, but they also served their own gods.' That would not do. Syncretism, the unholy mix of deities, was never tolerated by the God of Israel. And it still is not. The form of this first command shows not that there are no other gods besides the one true and Sovereign Creator, but that anyone who thinks there are can never experience the presence and reality of God.

The God who creates

When Solomon built the magnificent temple in Jerusalem he might have copied the nations and said, 'Well now, all we have to do is to go in there and God will be sitting inside.' But this is how Solomon prayed at the dedication of the temple: 'O LORD, God of Israel, there is no God like you in heaven or on earth—you who keep your covenant of love with your servants who continue wholeheartedly in your way... You have kept your promise to your servant David my father; with your mouth you have promised and with your hand you have fulfilled it—as it is today... But will God really dwell on earth with men? The heavens, even the highest heavens, cannot contain you. How much less this temple I have built!... Then from heaven, your dwelling place, hear their prayer and their pleas, and uphold their cause. And forgive your people, who have sinned against you' (2 Chronicles 6:14,15,18,39).

Jonah, the disobedient prophet whose submarine experience is well known, stood on the heaving deck of a storm-tossed ship and declared his belief in, 'The God of heaven who made the sea and the land' (Jonah 1:9). No local storm-god for him!

Job spoke of God in the same way: 'He spreads out the northern skies over empty space; he suspends the earth over nothing. He wraps up the waters in his clouds, yet the clouds do not burst under their weight. He covers the face of the full moon, spreading his clouds over it. He marks out the horizon on the face of the waters for a boundary between light and darkness' (Job 26:7–10). Those are not the words of a primitive Syrian pagan who worshipped a local deity. They are the words of a man who knew nothing of the spaceship or of people walking on the moon, who had never looked through a telescope and may have had no knowledge about the roundness of the earth, but who knew the only true God—the God of Israel.

Spy satellites have the ability to identify things on earth just thirty centimetres across. But the Israelites knew of God's perpetual care for their land: 'It is a land the LORD your God cares for; the eyes of the LORD your God are continually on it from the beginning of the year to its end' (Deuteronomy 11:12). Yet their God was far bigger than the land of Israel for he 'marks out the horizon on the face of the waters for a boundary between light and darkness' (Job 26:10), and 'the eyes of the LORD are everywhere, keeping watch on the wicked and the good' (Proverbs 15:3). Similarly Malachi looked forward to the day when the name of his God would be, 'great among the nations, from the rising to the setting of the sun' (1:11). Paul, preaching in Athens perhaps two thousand years after Job, declared to the Greeks with their vast pantheon of gods and goddesses that 'The God who made the world and everything in it is the Lord of heaven and earth and does not live in temples built by hands' (Acts 17:24).

The God who is known

God introduced himself to the people with the words, 'I am the LORD your God'. He never expected anyone to worship him as someone unknown or unknowable. The Hebrew word for God is 'Elohim'. It is the word used of God at the beginning of the Bible when we are introduced to his creating activity. In the Bible, and therefore for the Israelite, there was never any doubt about the fact that God is the Creator. That is not open for intellectual discussion, scientific analysis, or theological debate. The Bible states it as a matter of plain truth.

But in creating man and woman, God created them to be different from any other part of the creation. He created us with eternity in our minds (Ecclesiastes 3:11). That is something that no other part of the creation has: 'Man *became* a living being (soul)' (Genesis 2:7). And when God created man he created him to worship. That is one thing about God's relationship to men and women that does not apply to his relationship with the rest of the creation: God and Adam and Eve had a spiritual relationship of fellowship and friendship together. This is described in Genesis 3:8 as 'the LORD God walking in the garden in the cool of the day.' There was a unity of friendship between man and God that was qualitatively and uniquely different from the rest of creation.

Wherever we find people they are always found worshipping. Never, on the face of the earth and throughout the history of the human race, has there ever been discovered a tribe or nation that does not worship. Atheistic governments have been forced to spend great sums of money to educate men and women not to worship. Worship is the natural inclination of the human race. There is a longing within all of us to worship God—and that has never been entirely lost. However, in this modern age we are squeezing eternity out of our minds, but eternity is still there and it won't go away. It is always there nagging at us. This is what is meant when Christ is referred to as: 'the true light that gives light to every man' (John 1:9). The light that everyone possesses when they are born into this world, and of which the animal kingdom knows nothing, is an awareness of the reality of God.

Many Christian parents, in the course of teaching their children the Christian faith, have used the book *Leading Little Ones To God* (Marian Schoolland, Banner of Truth). Perhaps it is a quaint title, but the book is full of good theology, and it has a sentence that well expresses the God-awareness within the soul of us all. The book explains that 'Some people say there is no God and they don't even pray at all.' Then the writer continues, 'But deep down in their hearts there is that little voice that says "Yes, there is a God."' That is magnificent theology! There are many people who carelessly conclude, 'There isn't a God. I don't believe in God.' But deep in their hearts there is a voice that says 'Yes, there is a God. You know there is.' There are very few true atheists in the world, because God created man and woman with an insatiable thirst to find spiritual reality. Although Satan has written his graffiti all over God's creation, deep down human nature knows there is a God. This explains the growth of interest today in New Age, reincarnation, and the world religions. Our modern age is desperate to find spiritual reality even though we refuse to acknowledge that this is what the thirst is all about.

But do we know that there is *only one* true God? In Romans 1:19–20 Paul makes the position very clear: 'What may be known about God is plain to them, because God has made it plain to them. For since the creation of the world God's invisible qualities—his eternal power and divine nature—have been clearly seen, being understood from what has been made, so that men are without excuse.' It could not have been written more plainly. All are without excuse when they turn to the pantheon of the world's religions. When we look at the heavens around us, we ought to say, as the Psalmist concluded in Psalm 19, 'The heavens declare the glory of God'. This marvellous universe speaks of God. And what is even more important, it speaks only of the Lord God who revealed himself to the Jews.

Whether a religion is intellectual so that the clever can understand it, philosophical so that the wise can enjoy it, moral so that the upright can embrace it, superstitious so that the simple can fall for it, or whether it is paganism, polytheism, animism, occultism or materialism, it is a deceit from God's arch-enemy—Satan. Whatever the religion or no religion, it is a violation of that first Commandment because it refuses to acknowledge the Sovereign Lord God as the only God. Paul wrote of religion and atheism in this way: 'For although they knew God, they neither glorified him as God nor gave thanks to him, but their thinking became futile and their foolish hearts were darkened. Although they claimed to be wise, they became fools, and exchanged the glory of the immortal God for images made to look like mortal man and birds and animals and reptiles' (Romans 1:21–23).

Breaking the first rule

Eight out of the ten Commandments are negative because God knows that sin inevitably brings us into conflict with the will of God, so he needs to start by telling us what we must not do. If we tell people only what they must do they will always be able to say, 'Well, I do that'—and somewhere in their lives we can be sure that they do. Tell a man to love his wife and most men will say they do, or at least they have done. Tell him not to commit adultery and it is a command that stands for the length of life. If we tell a man to love God, he may well protest that he does, but when we remind him of the negative: 'no other gods', he must concede that at that point he has failed. Nothing ever in the place of God? The Christian who loves God is not guiltless on this point; not one of us can say that we never have ambitions, interests, loves, lusts, pride, or selfishness that do not jockey for first place in our lives.

This is the first Commandment because it is the most significant of them all. But although it is the most significant of all the Commandments, it is the one that we most consistently break.

Every form of western superstition is a breach of the first Commandment. Those who touch wood, sprinkle salt or cross fingers, as well as those who read their horoscope, visit the palmist or consult the medium, are all in the same category as the sportsman who 'religiously' puts on his left boot before his right, wears the correct tie to bring him luck, or piously crosses himself before the race.

The cult of personality worship, whether sport or pop star, is a modern form of breaking this Commandment. Pope Pius XII may have hesitated before declaring Mary to be the 'Queen of Heaven' if someone had drawn his attention to Jeremiah 7:18, 'The children gather wood, the fathers light the fire, and the women knead the dough and make cakes for the Queen of Heaven. They pour out drink offerings to other gods to provoke me to anger.'

There are few who will not claim to believe in God in some form, only a fool denies the reality of the obvious (Psalm 14:1), but anything we put as number one in our life takes the place of God, however legitimate it may be in itself.

Shirley MacLaine popularised New Age religion in her best-selling books. In one she expresses her own philosophy in these words: 'I know that I exist, therefore I AM. I know that the God-source exists. Therefore IT IS. Since I am part of that force, then I AM that I AM.' There is no mistaking the intended reference here! New Age philosophy is one of the most blatant modern violations of the first Commandment. When gurus preach that all is one (monism), or that Mother Earth (Gaia) is watching our progress, or that past spirits (channels) can guide us through life, God's greatest law has been broken.

When Jesus was asked which is the greatest Commandment in the law, he replied, 'Love the Lord your God with all your heart and with all your soul and with all your mind. This is the first and greatest commandment' (Matthew 22:37–38). Interestingly that phrase is not here in Exodus 20, however you will find it in Deuteronomy just after Moses has rehearsed the Ten Commandments a second time for the people of Israel (Deuteronomy 5)—it was from Deuteronomy 6:5 that Jesus quoted. He was in effect saying, 'I will tell you what the very first Commandment means. It means that you must love God first and above all; anything less is a breach of this greatest law.' These two verses in Matthew 22 are our Lord's commentary on the first Commandment. It is clearly not enough just to believe in one God; that gives us no great advantage over the demons themselves (James 2:19); we must love God with our heart, soul and mind. A mere theist no more keeps this Commandment than an atheist, and a deist no more keeps it than a pantheist or a polytheist. To 'love' God is to trust and obey. God is never satisfied with a mere intellectual assent; he calls for a belief that is seen in commitment and worship. The philosopher Teilhard de Chardin suggested there are only two options for mankind: adoration or annihilation. He was nearly right. In reality the options are adoration or eternal separation.

Some people say it is so hard to love God because we can't see him. But we can. That is why Christ came, and that is why he said, 'He who has seen me has seen the Father' (John 14:9). That is why the Bible tells us that he is the 'exact representation' of God (Hebrews 1:3), and that in Christ we have seen, 'the glory of the one and only (Son) who came from the Father' (John 1:14). Our obedience to this Commandment is very simply to put Jesus Christ first in our lives. In this way we honour and love the Father. He who loves the Son loves the Father and he who loves the one who was sent loves the one who sent him.

The fulfilment of Exodus 20:2 is to love Christ with all our heart. Every other religion disobeys the first Commandment, because if we do not love Christ first then we do not love the Father first. If we do not love the Father first, then we do not obey this Commandment, and if we do not obey this Commandment we have committed the greatest sin. We must test our obedience to the first Commandment by our love for Christ. How much are we devoted to him? This is why the law is such a good thing for us; it is part of the gospel because it forces us to Calvary. I need his forgiveness for breaking this first Commandment, because I know that it stands supremely above all the other Commandments. There is only one God and I must worship him alone through Christ.

Do not worship idols

You shall not make for yourself an idol. Exodus 20:4–6

In 1878 China suffered one of its worst ever famines. The London *Times* reported that 70 million people were dying of starvation; that was more than the combined population of Great Britain and America at that time. A Confucian scholar Hsi Shengmo had been terrified as a boy by the grizzly faces of the idols in his village, and he suffered nightmares as their twisted features leered at him in his sleep. Now with a terrible drought in the land, with the sun burning down relentlessly from an unclouded sky, and with the ground scorched like a desert and people dying by their hundreds of thousands, the men of Hsi's village turned to these idols for help. At first they feted and feasted them in a desperate attempt to put them in a better mood. The villagers arranged theatre shows so that the idols would enjoy themselves. But still the rain did not come. Finally the people took their idols out of the temple and sat them in the blistering sun until their paint peeled— so that they might know what it felt like for the villagers! The vain hope was that in self-defence the idols might make rain. How futile, how tragic. It was sadly reminiscent of Elijah's contest with the prophets of Baal on Mount Carmel: 'There was no response, no one answered, no one paid attention' (1 Kings 18:29). The only value of that miserable episode in China was to convince Hsi Shengmo that there must be a greater power than these foolish idols. It prepared his heart for the coming of the gospel of Christ.

The history of the human race is the history of idolatry; every race and each generation manufactures its own idols in one form or another. Modern Western civilization is no exception.

We may wonder why God distinguished between making an idol and having 'no other gods'. It would seem that if we make the one we must break the other. But God is wiser than to repeat himself unnecessarily. The first Commandment establishes the kind of God we worship: He is one and alone; there never has been nor can there be any other God. The character of the God revealed in Scripture does not place him apart from all other gods but it declares that all other claimants thought up by human imagination are in fact no gods at all. This God is not above the others, as Zeus ranked highest in the Greek pantheon: there simply are no others. To worship anything else is not to worship at all.

The second Commandment focuses upon how we so easily break the first: 'You shall not make for yourself an idol in the form of anything in heaven above or on the earth beneath or in the waters below. You shall not bow down to them or worship them; for I, the LORD your God, am a jealous God.' As we saw in the previous chapter, men and women do not find it difficult to believe in God—the evidence is all around us. The whole world is without excuse for unbelief because it is the most natural and most obvious thing to believe in God (Romans 1:19–20). Atheism is a very hard religion to swallow because it flies in the face of the evidence. We must worship because we have an eternity-mindset. We think about eternity, we are aware that there is an eternity, and we are afraid of eternity because we have a sense of accountability to God.

Those who extol the virtues of, for example, Hindu and Moslem holy writers, and claim that they are all equally acceptable to the true deity, have overlooked the fact that to be consistent they must allow the same for the pantheist (God is everything), the animist (everything is God), and the New Ager. The door of pluralism cannot logically be closed on anyone, whatever their belief. To do so is to claim standards for judging true and false religion—and where do those standards come from?

In the time of Moses the surrounding nations did not lack their idols. They backed a fair number of deities and chief among these were El, Baal (or Hadad the storm god), and Dagon; there were the goddesses as well: Asherah, Astarte, and Anoth (the goddesses of sex and violence). Baal was in the form of a bull and Asherah in the form of a carved pole. Every god was represented by its physical form, and this was the idol. The ancient world could not believe in a god it could not see, and that was part of the uniqueness of the faith of Israel—their God was invisible! The nations looked in vain for Israel's God. Every pagan city had its gods, temples, sacrifices, priests, priestesses and cult-prostitutes. Possibly some employed adult sacrifice and certainly many practised the grotesque child sacrifice associated with the god Moloch. It is not difficult to imagine the kind of life-style of people who worshipped gods like this.

It is true that the ancient civilizations had laws, like the code of Hammurabi, but these laws were chiefly centred upon property, not people. What is certain, however, is that there was no relationship between the idols and the moral laws of the tribal cities. These carved rocks and trees did not give moral laws, they did not inspire moral laws and they did not approve moral laws. They were at best amoral in their expectation and immoral in the example set by the stories surrounding them. Their inspiration is seen clearly in the description of Ahab, King of Israel: 'Ahab behaved in the vilest manner by going after idols, like the Amorites the LORD drove out before Israel' (1 Kings 21:26); and the final indictment against Manasseh was that he did 'more evil than the Amorites' (2 Kings 21:11).

Idols for all

A century ago John Paton went as a missionary to the New Hebridean islands in the Pacific Ocean. After years of fruitful work, during which he saw many cannibals converted to Christ, Paton visited Australia. Whilst there he discovered that the white men had concluded that the aborigines were no better than animals because it appeared that there was no evidence that they worshipped. No one had seen them worship so they must be like the brute beasts. From his experience Paton was convinced that they must worship something and he set out to find what that something was. Paton eventually discovered that the aborigines carried little bags around with them filled with tiny pebbles. He persuaded one aborigine to concede that those pebbles were nothing less than their gods. The reason they had hidden them was that many years earlier white men had laughed at their pebble-gods and the aborigines decided that never again would a white man see their idols. Paton was right when he claimed that the aborigines were 'not brutes, incapable of knowing God, but human beings yearning after a god of some kind.' He continued, 'Nor do I believe that any tribe of men will ever be found, who, when their language and customs are rightly interpreted, will not display their consciousness of the need of a God, and that divine capacity of holding fellowship with the unseen powers, of which the brutes (animals) are without one faintest trace.'

God began his Commandments by ordering, 'You shall have no other gods before me' because he knew that humanity would believe in God or gods and therefore it is important that we should know who the only true God is. Then God added the second Commandment because he knew that our next step would be to say, 'We can't understand this God. He is too big, too vast. We will reduce him to a size we can understand.' And so with pebbles, rocks or trees, man would make God 'man-size'. In other words, God gave the second Commandment to guard the first.

The story of the golden calf in Exodus 32 illustrates this. The people wanted God. They had been talking with Moses, the representative of God. They had heard the voice of God, had seen the thunder and lightning, and they felt the awesome sense of the presence of God. But it was all too much for them. They wanted a god they could see and feel and touch—a god they could control. It was no coincidence that when Aaron melted the people's gold in the fire 'out came this calf' (Exodus 32:24). The Apis bull had been worshipped in Egypt from the earliest times as a symbol of fertility and strength. Apis represented the chief god of Memphis as well as the god of the River Nile and the regular and essential Nile flood. The bull was also one of the three representations of Pharaoh, along with the falcon and the lion. In Egypt the Apis bull was a live animal that received great honour and worship throughout its life—on average eighteen years—making its 'window appearance' to adoring crowds. When the Apis bull died it was buried with honour in the great vaults of the dead, and the priests scoured Egypt to find the new bull calf to bring in triumph to his special 'Apis house'. It is clear just how infected with Egyptian idolatry the people of Israel had become during four hundred years of slavery.

This desire to visualise our God is practically irresistible; it lies behind almost all the pictures of Mary and of the Saints and the images associated with 'Christian' worship. Even Moses longed to see his God (Exodus 33:18) and was told to be content with somewhat less than that (v 20).

Idolatry makes a mockery of mankind. It is the devil's graffiti written all over the soul of the idol worshipper. That is why the Old Testament prophets scoffed at the idols of the nations. The mockery of Isaiah is so vivid that it is worth quoting at length:

'All who make idols are nothing, and the things they treasure are worthless. Those who would speak up for them are blind; they are ignorant, to their own shame. Who shapes a god and casts an idol, which can profit him nothing? He and his kind will be put to shame; craftsmen are nothing but men. Let them all come together and take their stand; they will be brought down to terror and infamy. The blacksmith takes a tool and works with it in the coals; he shapes an idol with hammers, he forges it with the might of his arm. He gets hungry and loses his strength; he drinks no water and grows faint. The carpenter measures with a line and makes an outline with a marker; he roughs it out with chisels and marks it with compasses. He shapes it in the form of man, of man in all his glory, that it may dwell in a shrine. He cut down cedars, or perhaps took a cypress or oak. He let it grow among the trees of the forest, or planted a pine, and the rain made it grow. It is man's fuel for burning; some of it he takes and warms himself, he kindles a fire and bakes bread. But he also fashions a god and worships it; he makes an idol and bows down to it. Half of the wood he burns in the fire; over it he prepares his meal, he roasts his meat and eats his fill. He also warms himself and says, "Ah! I am warm; I see the fire." From the rest he makes a god, his idol; he bows down to it and worships. He prays to it and says, "Save me; you are my god." They know nothing, they understand nothing; their eyes are plastered over so they cannot see, and their minds closed so they cannot understand. No one stops to think, no one has the knowledge or understanding to say, "Half of it I used for fuel; I even baked bread over its coals, I roasted meat and I ate. Shall I make a detestable thing from what is left? Shall I bow down to a block of wood?" He feeds on ashes, a deluded heart misleads him; he cannot save himself, or say, "Is not this thing in my right hand a lie?"' (Isaiah 44:9–20).

The mocking is almost cruel. Isaiah says, 'Did you notice the blacksmith working away on his anvil? What was he doing? He was sweating so hard that at the end of the day the poor man was worn out; he was tired, hungry and thirsty. He was making a god—how clever of him! And do you see the carpenter? Now his was an even more ridiculous case. He went out into the woods and he found a suitable tree and he chopped it down and brought it home; he laid it in front of himself, he eyed it up and down, and said "Ah yes, that half will make a good fire to cook my dinner and the other half will make me a very attractive idol." You foolish people. Your idols have eyes, because you made them carefully—but they can't see a thing! You carved them ears, but they cannot hear. You actually gave them mouths and you put food in front of them every day, but do they eat? If you can afford to, you cover them with silver; but whether or not you cover them with silver eventually they rot. You even cover some of them with gold, and in case someone runs away with them you chain down your gods of gold!'

Jeremiah presents a similar picture and vividly refers to the idol as 'a scarecrow in a melon patch', and then jeers, 'Do not fear them; they can do no harm nor can they do any good' (Jeremiah 10:5).

Contrast all this with Isaiah's description of God:

'Who has measured the waters in the hollow of his hand, or with the breadth of his hand marked off the heavens? Who has held the dust of the earth in a basket, or weighed the mountains on the scales and the hills in a balance? Who has understood the mind of the LORD, or instructed him as his counsellor? Whom did the LORD consult to enlighten him, and who taught him the right way? Who was it that taught him knowledge or showed him the path of understanding? Surely the nations are like a drop in a bucket; they are regarded as dust on the scales; he weighs the islands as though they were fine dust… Do you not know? Have you not heard? Has it not been told you from the beginning? Have you not understood since the earth was founded? He sits enthroned above the circle of the earth, and its people are like grasshoppers. He stretches out the heavens like a canopy, and spreads them out like a tent to live in. He brings princes to naught and reduces the rulers of this world to nothing… "To whom will you compare me? Or who is my equal?" says the Holy One. Lift your eyes and look to the heavens: Who created all these? He who brings out the starry host one by one, and calls them each by name. Because of his great power and mighty strength, not one of them is missing… Do you not know? Have you not heard? The LORD is the everlasting God, the Creator of the ends of the earth. He will not grow tired or weary, and his understanding no one can fathom' (Isaiah 40:12–28).

One of the most pathetic stories of idolatry in the Bible is found in Judges 18. At that time the land was in total lawlessness; everybody did what was right in their own eyes. The tribe of the Danites planned to move out from where they were and to settle in Laish. In Laish there was a man called Micah who had a Levite, one of God's priestly tribe, to look after his religion for him, and his religion was in the form of a collection of household idols. They were lined up in the private chapel. When the Danites came to the land, they broke into the house, stole the best of the idols, and left, taking the Levite with them. Micah woke up and ran after the six hundred Danite raiders. He was very upset. But the Danites turned on Micah and in effect warned him, 'What's the matter with you? You'd better be careful or we'll set some of these ruffians onto you.' And Micah responded, 'You took the gods I made, and my priest, and went away. What else do I have? How can you ask, 'What's the matter with you?' (Judges 18:24). How pathetic!

When Adam and Eve fell into sin, every part of their life was tarnished and corrupted. As a result, in the totality of our nature, we too are spoiled by sin. Not least in our soul—the very part that was created to worship and enjoy God and to have fellowship with him. Instead of worshipping and glorying in the invisible yet holy and all powerful Creator, people worship idols of their own making. This is both ridiculous and tragic. 'All the gods of the nations are idols', said David in his prayer as he brought up the ark into Jerusalem, 'but the LORD made the heavens' (1 Chronicles 16:26).

New Idols for old

At root an idol is that which represents God; it is an object of religious veneration or affection, fear or devotion standing in the place of God— either ignorantly or knowingly. This Commandment is not against the innocent painting or sculpture that is not intended for religious veneration. However, the word came to refer to all the gods of the nations (1 Chronicles 16:26), and by the time Paul was writing his letter to the church at Colossae he had extended the meaning of the word to everything that becomes the centre and goal of our life (Colossians 3:5).

However, this second Commandment is not only against the *worship* of idols. God is careful to warn the people not even to *make* idols—and it is possible to do this unintentionally. That which is not made for worship soon becomes an object of worship because of our fallen nature. There is an example of this in Numbers 21. Israel had grumbled against God so much that he sent a swarm of snakes among them and thousands of the people died. They cried for God to take the snakes away and God told Moses that he was to make a bronze snake and put it on a pole; when the people looked at the bronze serpent they would be healed of their snake bite. However, it was not long before the nation had turned that bronze serpent into an object of worship (2 Kings 18:4). Whilst it is true that human nature is sufficiently perverse as to turn almost anything into an

object of magical trust or worship—holy animals, water, jewellery etc.—
God warns his people to be alert to anything that may become an idol. The
Nehushtan of 2 Kings 18:4 is left as an example of this very danger.

One of the great failures of the church at the time of the collapse of the
Roman Empire in the fifth century AD. was that it took over the images of
the deserted pagan temples. As Roman paganism collapsed, the Christians
occupied the temples as places of worship and retained the images of the
gods. The statues of Zeus and Isis were renamed Christ and Mary and this
was justified as an aid to worship. No one intended to worship these idols
but simply to use them as aids. Soon the inevitable happened and they
became objects of worship. The people began kissing the images of Mary
and of Christ and the images of the saints; they lit candles in front of them
and burned incense to them, just like the pagan worshippers had done
before Isis and Zeus. The Eastern Orthodox churches do not worship
images but instead they use 'icons' to aid their worship—pictures of Mary
and Christ and the apostles and the martyrs who are 'saints' in the history
of the church. When these icons become objects of worship in themselves
they are idols. In the same way when the bread of communion is declared to
be 'the body of God' it is inevitably followed by the superstition of idolatry.
It is not sufficient to claim, 'But we do not worship the icon or the image',
God is not here warning only of *worshipping* an idol—that surely must be
prohibited by the first Commandment—he is forbidding the *making* of
anything that is likely to be worshipped.

The Puritan preacher Thomas Watson is wise to remind us that if the
first Commandment is against worshipping a false god, the second
Commandment is against worshipping the true God in a false way. When
the people of Israel worshipped Baal *and* the Lord, they were worse than
the nations from which they had been redeemed.

The word 'idol' immediately brings to mind the image of the Indian
totem pole or the stone-carved god; it refers to the household gods of the
Hindu or the temple effigies of the Buddhist. For most of us that is another
world of religion. But there are religious and secular idols worshipped
amongst even those who profess Christianity.

The first century Christians used symbols to identify themselves. They
were living in dangerous times, like many Christians in both atheistic and

religious countries today. They devised ways by which they could recognise one another. Most commonly they used the symbol of a fish. The Greek word for a fish is *ichthus* and each letter of that word forms the initial letters of the words 'Jesus Christ God's Son Saviour'. For this reason a fish was a useful symbol for identification—and it still is. That fish symbol would become an image the moment it received honour, veneration or worship.

In the New Testament God gave us only two visual aids to help us in our worship: Baptism and the Lord's Supper. The form of each was deliberate. Assuming that baptism takes place in a river or lake, it is a moving body of water and it is not easy to worship a moving body of water—though some religions, both ancient and modern, manage it! The elements in the Lord's Supper were eaten and drunk, and similarly it should be hard to worship something you eat! The pagans were not so foolish as to eat their gods—no one ever made beefburgers out of the Apis bull in Egypt! Sadly, however, the fallenness of man knows no bounds. Even these two Christian visual aids have been abused. Men take 'holy' water from the Jordan and attribute to it some kind of supernatural power. The bread and wine of Christian communion are thought by some to turn into the physical body and blood of Christ, and inevitably the elements are treated first with care and then with the veneration and worship that we would expect if we are handling the 'body of God'. It is hard to imagine how such things could happen in Christianity, but they have. The water of baptism and the bread and wine of the Lord's Supper were intended as symbols only, but they have become like *Nehushtan*—the snake on a pole.

Some symbols are more likely to become images and for this reason should be avoided altogether. A crucifix can so easily become an idol, so can a cross. But idolatry for others can be something far more subtle. It may be a ring, a necklace, a pendant or even a tie. Anything that becomes a lucky charm or mascot is idolatry. Anything that we always carry with us because somehow we feel safe and secure with it. That is an idol. If in doubt we would be well advised to take it out and destroy it. Our willingness to do that is a sure test of whether or not it has become an idol.

Today some Christians have begun to ape the religions of the world by their icons. It has become customary in some circles for Christians to place an object on the table and, as a supposed aid to worship, to allow their minds to empty and concentrate on the object. Apparently this will bring us closer to God. Whether we focus on flowers, a cross, a Bible, a piece of bread or a candle, that is precisely how the idolatry of icons began. It is exactly the reasoning behind the images that sit in every corner of the ornate church building and the justification for the great street processions of 'the Mother of God' or 'Corpus Christi' in Spain and South America. They are not idols, we are told, just aids to worship. But why all the kissing and kneeling? The test is to suggest that the image be smashed and the ornate decorations be sold to help the poor and we will quickly see how important the idol is.

Writing on tradition, a Christian journalist describes how his diocesan course in theology was so far from biblical truth that he felt obliged to object. In responding, the church authorities told him that truth is subjective and that he had no need to believe what he did not agree with. Yet when it came to worship in the cathedral, the stole was considered an essential article of the priests' vestments; without it they could not officiate. Tradition becomes idolatry when it is elevated above the revelation of God.

The faith-healing aids of some evangelists are idolatry. To send for pieces of cloth 'blessed' by the prayer of the evangelist is idolatry. The 'holy' water from the Jordan or that which had been blessed by a 'priest' is no better than idolatry. What God thinks about the horoscopes avidly sought by the readers of our local rags and national tabloids is clearly revealed in Deuteronomy 18:10–12. But sadly this does not hinder millions from betraying their post-modern idolatry. My local paper followed the headline 'What's in the stars this week?' with the question: 'Is it love, money or luck?' That probably sums-up the religion of millions. It is idolatry.

There are secular idols too. Os Guinness, commenting on the way the Israelites left Egypt (Exodus 12:35–36), remarks that 'Christians are free to plunder the Egyptians, but forbidden to set up a golden calf'. All that belongs to the world is not wrong. But it becomes sin with misuse. Anything from religious austerity to secular gluttony can become idolatry. The difference between an ascetic and a profligate may be the same as between a Pharisee and an idolater—it is just that they have a different idol.

To make an idol of self-denial is no better than making an idol of self-indulgence. The religious Pharisee and the secular hedonist are one and the same—idolaters. Anything that takes the place of God and his laws is idolatry.

Writing to both the Ephesians and the Colossians, Paul lists a number of sins that belong to what he calls our 'earthly nature'—'sexual immorality, impurity, lust, evil desires and greed'–and he calls them all 'idolatry' (Ephesians 5:5, Colossians 3:5). The gods of our society are sex, violence and greed. If these three ingredients were cut out of the films and advertisements in just one evening's television there would be little else left on some of our channels. These gods have taken centre stage, so much so that many are seriously concerned that our children are rapidly becoming desensitised to the idols of lust and violence; they no longer react with either disgust or fear as a child should. When Paul wrote of greed as idolatry he made an important point. It is not just what we have that we turn into idols, but what we don't have; greed is not simply holding on to possessions, but grasping for more. The green eye of envy is discontent not simply because I do not have sufficient but because others have more than me. That is idolatry.

The National Lottery has become probably the number one idol of the United Kingdom at the present time, with thirteen million people 'playing' each week. The mocking of Isaiah against the idols of his day would be no less scornful of those who need to invest ten pounds each week for twenty-thousand years to be reasonably certain of winning the Jackpot! This 'Saturday night idol' has duped even sections of the evangelical church into considering it right to share in the Lottery grants. When our principles are adapted by the lure of greed we are worshipping Mammon—whatever its current name may be.

To allow sport, a hobby or leisure to take the place of the worship of God is idolatry. But so is the gratification of sexual pleasure by treating others as playthings to this end—however secretly it is done. Idolatry can be identified by the magazines we collect at the newsagent and by the films we hire from the video store.

The company director or financial speculator whose 'securities' are his religion and whose motivation is the greed of wanting more and more is an idolater. The nation that specialises in rating individual achievement higher than personal morality, and overlooks the most indecent lifestyle providing the man is a succeeder, is in the grip of idolatry. The nation that ignores the laws of God when it drafts its laws for men is unquestionably idolatrous.

Anything we honour in the place of God is idolatry; anything that commands our attention more than the call of God to holiness or service. Our idol may be a person as easily as a sport or hobby. The words of William Cowper, our national poet, have lost nothing over the past two hundred years, and at the time of writing the idol in his life was Mary Unwin:

> The dearest idol I have known,
> whate'er that idol be,
> help me to tear it from thy throne,
> and worship only thee.

Idolatry is not merely the habit of primitive cultures, it is the rebellion of modern man—and for both it is sin. Ours is, without a rival, the age of idolatry.

What's wrong with idolatry?

Does it matter whether or not men and women create their own idols? In view of the terrible warning in Exodus 20:5 it clearly does matter: 'I am a jealous God, punishing the children for the sin of the fathers to the third and fourth generation of those who hate me.' But why is idolatry so wrong?

IDOLATRY ROBS GOD OF HIS RIGHTFUL HONOUR

The illustration of John Paton and the Australian aborigines teaches us that idolatry trivialises the greatest thing we possess, namely a knowledge of God. When sin came, it spoilt everything, including our longing for God. Idolatry reduces God to the size that will fit our own capacity to understand, our own ability to grasp. Paul tells us what the human race does: 'For although they knew God, they neither glorified him as God nor gave thanks to him, but their thinking became futile and their foolish hearts were darkened. Although they claimed to be wise, they became fools and exchanged the glory of the immortal God for images made to look like mortal man and birds and animals and reptiles' (Romans 1:21–23).

God is a 'jealous' God. That word found in the Hebrew of Exodus 20:5 does not carry our idea of furious rage and selfish possessiveness, still less that of vindictive envy or a fearful pride of being displaced. It means that God is protective of his own honour and intolerant of disobedience (Isaiah 42:8 and 48:11). But God is protective and intolerant for our benefit also. He is a God who wants us to worship him alone, for only in this way will we find our spiritual fulfilment, satisfaction and peace. We were made by God and for God; our soul is hungry to know God, and every substitute is a cheap mockery of the real thing. For a marriage partner to expect and jealously guard faithfulness to the marriage vows is not to be dismissed as 'selfish possessiveness'; on the contrary, it is for the benefit of both partners. The husband or wife who is angry at any violation of the 'covenant' is to be commended not condemned.

The colour of God's jealousy is certainly not green, but red. It is protective anger rather than possessive envy that is expressed in this Commandment. We are robbing God of the honour that should be his when we 'exchange the truth of God for a lie, and worship and serve created things rather than the Creator' (Romans 1:25). God's honour is fulfilled by obedience to the second Commandment.

IDOLATRY ROBS HUMAN LIFE OF ITS DIGNITY

Recently I was idly turning the pages of a magazine whilst waiting for an appointment when I came to a picture of a religious procession. As I looked at the serious faces of the men carrying their lavishly adorned idol I thought to myself, 'That man may be a banker, and that one a university professor, and that man may be a shop keeper or a doctor.' Perhaps they were all intelligent men, yet there they were trundling through the streets a hideous image of one of their gods. It made them look foolish in the extreme. They were unwittingly rubbishing themselves as plainly as do the ridiculous antics of the drunkard. Idolatry is the graffiti of Satan written right across humanity. When men and women place their confidence in something they have made, it reduces them to the level of blind and ignorant fools. The image and likeness of God has been tragically defaced. Nothing so dignifies human nature than when it worships, honours and obeys the glorious God who created it. Idolatry not only robs God of his honour, but the human race of its dignity. To watch a man or woman devote their entire life to making money or a name for themselves whether in politics, education, finance, sport, the arts or even religion or unbelief is to watch an idolater at work. This is no less a tragedy than to study the bewildered fear of the tribesman at his totem pole.

To what idol can anyone look and say, 'I want to live like that'? Idols have no life-style because they have no life, and therefore they have no example to offer us. The idols of the ancient world took no interest in city life and expressed no personal care; they never moved and never gave moral instructions. Modern idols never offer a 'clean' way of life that dignifies their devotees.

We too often forget what happened in the Garden of Eden: there the temptation was to plant a new religion in the place of the worship of God: 'You will be like God' (Genesis 3:5). When we believe we are gods we behave in a self-commending way. No one is going to tell us what to do; our lifestyle is for us to decide. In Romans 1 Paul traces the tragic decline in morality when a society takes to the religion of idolatry. The Roman Christians would understand well enough the inevitable downward spiral since they had been rescued from it by the gospel. Paganism began by suppressing the evidence of God in creation (vs 19–21) and it was natural to substitute man-made idols for the 'glory of the immortal God' (vs 21–23). What followed was the inevitable result of rejecting the truth: sexual impurity, lesbian and homosexual relationships, greed, deceit, malice, murder, gossip and pride are some of the 'every kind of wickedness' that Paul lists (vs 24–32). Idolatry degrades humanity.

In the summer of 1993 the British government coined the expression 'back to basics'. It was an attempt to resolve the immorality of a degenerating society. Significantly the only morality offered amounted to neighbourliness, government policy and some reference to family values! Westminster had no idea what moral advice to offer the nation and this was hardly surprising. The contemporary idols we have identified already can never offer morality to a nation.

On the contrary, we can look at Jesus Christ the Son of God and say, 'I want to live as he lived.' He lived on this earth and set a pattern for us; for thirty years he lived and ate, walked and talked and was tempted exactly as we are. Yet there was one remarkable difference: He was utterly without sin. No idol can set us any standard, let alone such a high and holy standard.

IDOLATRY SPOILS FUTURE GENERATIONS

The phrase in Exodus 20:5, 'I am a jealous God, *punishing the children for the sin of the fathers to the third and fourth generation* of those who hate me' (compare Exodus 34:7) causes confusion for some, but it need not. Elsewhere God promised that men and women would be punished for their own sin and not for the sins of their fathers; Ezekiel 18 is clear on this (see verses 14 to 20 especially) and also 2 Chronicles 25:4. However, there is no doubt that children suffer greatly for the sins of their parents, not by some arbitrary decree of a vengeful God but by the law of cause and effect. Sadly and unavoidably the punishment that falls on the parents often afflicts the children too. The son smarts for his father's sin—that is true of millions of divorce-orphans across the world. Sadly also the sins of the fathers are too frequently aped by the children and grandchildren.

It is a fundamental law of humanity that we never sin to ourselves alone. Every generation sets the agenda for tomorrow's world. We show our children how to live and by passing on our idols we demonstrate our priorities. All our sin affects others, and it affects our children particularly. Our idolatry in whatever sphere, from money-making to drug-taking, is passed to our children with a vice-like grip. Christ can break that grip, and this warning in Exodus 20:5 is only a general statement; but it is a terrible warning that the superstition, idolatry, false religion or no religion, of the parents will be indelibly marked on their children so that only the power of God can erase it.

The most serious warning Christ ever gave was in connection with the next generation. Addressing those responsible for their welfare, and with the visual aid of a little child standing beside him, Christ warned that anyone who caused a child to stumble into the sins of its guardians— presumably whether parents or society—would be better to be weighted down and drowned in the sea (Matthew 18:1–5). His radical and offensive challenge to cut out everything and anything that hinders the true spiritual and moral development of a child is in this same passage (v 6–9). This is what is meant in Exodus 20:5 by the punishment continuing to future generations. We are reaping in our children today the fruit of our idolatry of yesterday.

Seneca, the Roman philosopher who was tutor to the children of the Emperor Nero in the first century, once complained bitterly at the cruel violence of the contests in the stadium: 'Come now', he protested, 'can't you people see even this much, that bad examples rebound on those who set them.' If our nation will not listen to the law of God they might show passing interest in the words of a Roman philosopher. But then, *he* was forced to commit suicide on the orders of the emperor because of the too high standards of his life!

The reference to the 'third and fourth generation' does not put a limit on the effect of punishment there; it will continue even beyond that unless there is repentance; that is what is meant by the phrase: 'of those who hate me.' However, for any and every generation, God shows love to those who 'love me and keep my commandments.' The evidence of this is the fact that King Hezekiah of Judah witnessed remarkable spiritual blessing and revival (2 Chronicles 29–31) even though his father Ahaz had been an apostate and idolater (2 Kings 16:3–4). Similarly Josiah enjoyed a true reformation in the spiritual life of the nation (2 Chronicles 34–35) whilst both his father Amon and his grandfather Manasseh were idolaters (2 Chronicles 33:1–7; 21–23).

IDOLATRY HOLDS PEOPLE IN FEAR

There can never be peace, security and certainty in idolatry. The idol can never be a great comforter, helper or deliverer. Peace, in the Christian sense of the word, was unknown to the nations around Israel. They could babble to their gods as long as they liked, but they never got so much as one syllable in response (1 Kings 18:29).

The idolatry of greed that the New Testament speaks of (Ephesians 5:5 and Colossians 3:5) holds its devotees in an iron grip of fear: the fear of letting go and losing the prize. We cannot rest when the stock markets roller-coast; every national event, every significant death, every cabinet minister's statement can affect the fortunes of thousands. And there is always someone waiting to scoop the spoils of another's hard work. The idolatry of sex and violence bring their own fear of incurable disease and inevitable revenge. Little wonder that Paul expressed confidence in the fact that 'godliness with contentment is great gain' (1 Timothy 6:6).

IDOLATRY IS INCAPABLE OF GIVING SPIRITUAL LIFE

Not infrequently I find myself in an unfamiliar town or city asking for directions. Knowing that the normal routine is to ask a visitor who has 'only been here five minutes, mate' or a foreigner who 'not speak English', I try to assess who is most likely to be able to help me. I often still get it wrong. Recently I asked three people for directions to the parish church which proved to be just two hundred metres away—but none of them could help me! I am learning also to suss out the person who tries to be helpful but clearly has no idea how to get me to my destination. Sometimes there is no one to ask. At a country cross-roads, where the locals assume that everyone knows where each road leads so no sign-post is necessary, I have never yet walked across the field to consult the distant scarecrow! I am at least sufficiently wise to know that a scarecrow cannot help me. Yet the prophet Jeremiah ridicules idolatry in all its forms as: 'Like a scarecrow in a melon patch' (Jeremiah 10:5). Admittedly scarecrows can do no harm but, the prophet concludes, 'nor can they do any good'. Unlike a scarecrow, the idols of the world *are* harmful because they do pretend to possess answers—but they cannot deliver.

To believe in an idol may give some kind of psychological boost, but it is incapable of giving anyone new life or spiritual strength. Our modern idols have sapped the moral energy of the nation. Many people are working harder and for longer hours than at any time through the past century. The United Kingdom tops the European poll for the number of hours our work-force devotes to employment. But we have little of satisfying significance to show for this. Violence in the home and the street increases: currently forty percent of all marriages will end in divorce; the abuse of alcohol is responsible for forty thousand premature deaths each year, takes up one in five of our hospital beds and accounts for nearly eighty percent of all assaults; and AIDS, the 'silent holocaust', irresistibly extends its grip across the nation. All this is the result of what God calls idolatry—a life-style that has no place for God and his laws.

Jesus said that the only way into the kingdom of heaven was by the new birth: 'Unless a man is born again he cannot see the kingdom of God' (John 3:3). He went on to explain what he meant by this. To be born again is to have God the Holy Spirit come and live in one's life. What idol can do that? If there is any spirit associated with the idol, it does not come from God. On the contrary, the Holy Spirit gives life, power and peace. Millions consult their horoscopes before setting out on a new day, settling a piece of business or confirming a relationship, but they would be better off talking with a scarecrow in the cornfield.

IDOLATRY CANNOT SHOW US THE WAY TO ETERNAL LIFE

In the rooms of Egyptian antiquities at the British Museum in London a number of ancient Egyptian coffins are on display. They are large, elaborately painted wooden caskets that contained the mummified remains of important people in Egypt. Inside many of the coffins are carefully drawn maps intended to lead the dead safely through the underworld. Nobody today seriously imagines that these are reliable guides, if only because they are all different!

None of today's idols even attempt to offer hope for the future. Sex, violence and greed are idols for today but not for tomorrow. Their devotees dare not think of the grave, for when it comes they have nothing to say to it and nothing to offer beyond it. Besides, to plan for tomorrow will spoil the pleasure of today. Idols have nothing to say about the future; they have no sure word for the life to come. It is said of the comedian Tommy Cooper that before his last performance he commented in the dressing room: 'I'm alright tonight; my show is alright. The only problem is, I don't know how to finish it off.' He never did finish off that show because Tommy Cooper died on stage that night. In the same way, idolatry may think it knows how to live, but it has no idea how to die. None of us will be on stage for ever.

Sitting inside the great fish somewhere off the coast of Phoenicia in the ancient world, the prophet Jonah rebuked himself for his callous indifference to the eternal welfare of the inhabitants of the capital of the

Assyrian empire by his refusal to go and preach to Nineveh. Nineveh was an idolatrous and violent city whose wickedness had come before God. Their only hope was Jonah's message calling them to repentance. Recognising that salvation 'comes from the LORD' Jonah reflected on the possibility of hope for the otherwise lost nation: 'Those who cling to worthless idols forfeit the grace that could be theirs' (Jonah 2:8). Nothing has changed. Idolatry, whether ancient or modern, denies men and women the privilege of enjoying their Creator as he intended. To cling to their idols will forfeit the grace that could be theirs.

An invitation to worship

There is a positive side to this Commandment: whilst idolatry is degrading and humiliating, the very fact that the Commandment is there is evidence that God has a better plan for us. This is always the case. Not one of the Commandments is intended for our hurt or to spoil our enjoyment of the best life. In prohibiting idols, God is not only forbidding but inviting. He does not leave us without our idols in an empty vacuum of hopelessness. The invitation is to come and worship the Creator as he always intended; and in our worship of him we will always find our highest value. Our *felt* needs may be for meaning, purpose, authentic relationships, self-worth and so on—all those objects the present day encourages us to strive for. But our *real* need is for reconciliation with our Creator and then all other things of value will be found as well.

God dignifies humanity by commanding us to lay aside our idols and worship only him. He honoured us even more by making that possible. The incredible step of the incarnation, when God in Christ became human, is God's invitation for us to find our real worth by finding the true God. It is like a father taking poison berries out of his child's hand, and replacing them with delicious and nutritious fruit. The first action may cause tears but it was only for the purpose of something better; the second action brings life and joy. We may reject God's warning by neglecting this Commandment but, as Jonah knew from experience: 'Those who cling to worthless idols forfeit the grace that could be theirs' (Jonah 2:8).

Do not blaspheme

You shall not misuse the name of the LORD. Exodus 20:7

When Salman Rushdie published the *Satanic Verses* in 1989 he unintentionally exposed his life to the death sentence of an Islamic *fatwa* imposed by the Ayatollah Khomeini, and opened the whole debate about the meaning of blasphemy. The courts have ruled that in the United Kingdom blasphemy can only refer to the Christian God, but it is doubtful for how long that judgement will stand. The *Times* suggested that we ought to abolish the blasphemy laws because nobody really understands them and added, 'The concept of an offence to God is beyond the philosophical concept of most Englishmen.' The *Times* could well be right that the idea that you can offend God no longer registers with modern man, but that is what he is doing all the time.

This third Commandment deals with the way we talk about God. Many avoid offending against the second Commandment but crash into the third. This is fast becoming a significant sin of our modern society.

The meaning of this command depends partly on the word 'misuse', which in the older translations reads, 'take in vain'. It comes from a root meaning 'to be waste' and it carries the idea of something that is empty of meaning and therefore wasteful. The word is found in Psalm 24:4, 'He... who does not lift up his soul to an idol or swear by what is false', where 'idol' translates the same word (empty, wasteful) and the word 'false' translates the word for deceit or fraud.

But the meaning of the third Commandment more significantly depends upon the word 'name'. The use of that word would remind Moses of his encounter with God at the burning bush in the Midian desert (Exodus 3). Moses expressed a dilemma that he needed to have resolved before he could go any further in speaking on behalf of God. The problem was not in a burning bush; Moses had doubtless seen that kind of thing many times before. In a dry, hot wilderness, shrubbery can ignite spontaneously under the burning desert sun. However, as Moses watched this bush, he noticed that it did not burn up nor did the fire go out. When he turned aside to look at this strange phenomenon I doubt whether he went with any sense of spiritual awe; he was just interested and inquisitive. But as he came near to the bush that seemed to burn brighter and brighter he heard the voice of God—and the whole inquiry changed direction.

God began to speak to Moses, telling him that he must go back to Egypt and set the people free from their slavery to the Egyptians. God promised to bring them out to this very mountain and to set the people in a marvellous land that was now currently occupied by wild and idolatrous tribes. Moses liked the sound of that, but his problem was that if he went to the people of Israel and said to them 'God says', they would understandably respond, 'Which god are you talking about?' After all, the Egyptians had any number of gods. Moses needed to know what name he could put to the God for whom he was spokesman (Exodus 3:13).

God replied in the words recorded in Exodus 3:14, 'I AM who I AM.' In the Hebrew of our Old Testament 'I AM' is just one word and it is the word that is translated sometimes in our English versions 'Jehovah' or 'Yahweh', though more often it is simply printed as LORD in capital letters. It was the special name used only by the Jews to describe God. No other tribe or nation or people in the world ever used that name to describe a god of any kind; it was unique to the Israelites. There is another Hebrew word which is used more generally for 'God', it is the word *Elohim*. This word describes all the false gods of the nations and the true Creator God. But the other word, LORD or Yahweh, referred to the self-existing eternal God who revealed himself to Moses here in the wilderness of Midian.

The exact meaning of the word is an open question, but it probably means, 'I AM WHAT I AM' and refers to the eternal God who is unchangingly the same and who has existence within himself, needing nobody to add anything to him. The reason we need to understand this is that whenever there is a reference to his 'name' in the Old Testament, and particularly here in this Commandment, it was not merely a handle by which to refer to God. It was a summary of his holy character.

The name Yahweh (LORD) was the description of the God who entered into a covenant with his people. It was the word that reminded them of the fact that they were a chosen people with whom God had entered into a special relationship and had promised that he would never abandon them.

To show their reverence for this name, and so that their enemies could not learn of it and either ridicule it or add it as another in the list of their own pantheon, the Israelites later refused to speak the name aloud when they were reading the Law of God; instead, they would substitute the vowels of the common word for 'master'—the word that a servant would use of his 'lord'. The Hebrew for that is *adonay*. The vowels of *adonay* put to the consonants of 'Yahweh' formed an unpronounceable word so that to this day no one can be sure how the word should be pronounced. Whether or not they were right never to utter the sacred word aloud is a matter for debate, but at least it demonstrated their deep reverence for 'the name'.

This special word LORD referred to the character of God as a promise-giving and promise-keeping God. Whenever the Israelites went up to the temple to offer their sacrifices it was this character of the LORD that they remembered. Although they did not all realise the fact, it was the name that pointed forward to the coming of Christ who, as the self-existing one who has life and immortality in himself (John 5:26; 1 Timothy 6:16), gave his life to establish the covenant of forgiveness with those who, from all nations, would form the new Israel of faith.

The first promise of the good news is found in Genesis 3:15. In that verse, so close in time to the tragic rebellion of Adam against his Creator, God guaranteed that at some point in the future he would intervene by sending an offspring from the woman to challenge the power of Satan. This offspring, though bruised by Satan, would infallibly crush the arch deceiver. The whole of the Old Testament is actually the unfolding story of God preparing the way for the fulfilment of that promise. It was a promise repeated to the Patriarchs: Abraham, Isaac and Jacob. The priesthood and sacrifices all pointed to the coming of Christ. This revelation of the 'name' to Moses at the burning bush (Exodus 3:15) was just one more step in God's revelation of his great plan, a plan that became clearer as the time of the incarnation drew near.

The name was not new. The Patriarchs clearly knew of this special name and had heard it used by God himself. Abraham 'called on the name of the LORD' when he built an altar east of Bethel (Genesis 12:8) and again at Mamre (13:18); he even used the name in his pleading with God (for example 15:2). But it is doubtful whether the Patriarchs understood the full significance of the word, and the Israelites had perhaps lost it altogether during their four hundred years in Egypt. Certainly God could say to Moses at the bush: 'I am the LORD. I appeared to Abraham, to Isaac, and to Jacob as God Almighty (Hebrew: El-Shaddai, see Genesis 17:1) but by my name the LORD (Hebrew: Yahweh) I did not make myself known to them' (Exodus 6:3). The uniqueness of the revelation to Moses was not the word Yahweh, but the deep and rich significance of that name.

So, this third commandment is not merely about the misuse of a word consisting of four Hebrew consonants, but an abuse of all that the name means. To misuse his name is to tread carelessly upon God's covenant offer of salvation and to treat his holy character with contempt. We may therefore break this commandment even though we never allow the words 'God' or 'Christ' to pass our lips as a swear-word. The Israelites blasphemed the name of their God when they lived and behaved in a manner that brought ridicule to him or when they attributed his work to the work of Satan, as Christ made clear in the context of Matthew 12:24–36 when he referred to the blasphemy against the Holy Spirit.

So, how is it possible for us to misuse the name of God?

Blasphemy—a common swear word

The ninth edition of the *Oxford Concise English Dictionary*, published in 1995, has a significant entry at the word 'Jesus': 'An exclamation of surprise, dismay, etc.', and then in square brackets this explanation is added: 'Name of the founder of the Christian religion d. c. AD 30'. The first part of the definition is preceded by the words *int. colloq.* which means that the expression is a colloquial interjection. In other words, 'Jesus' is to be understood first and foremost as a common expletive and only secondarily as the name of the founder of Christianity!

That is a tragic concession to our modern society. But the use of the names of the triune Godhead as swear words is so common today that people hardly know they are doing it; yet it is one of the most serious of all sins since it arrogantly involves God himself.

There is a form of social swearing today where some uses seem to be reserved by convention for certain sections of society. One group swears by using the words 'Christ' and 'Jesus', but with a little more education and 'class' the word 'God' or the phrase 'my God' is the vogue. You can often judge the education and earning capacity of people by the form of their swearing. However, whichever category we are in, the third Commandment is very clear: to use the name of God as a casual expletive is never innocent, because it brings the whole character of a sovereign and holy God to the level of a curse. Blasphemy is slandering the name of God.

But professing Christians should be careful also. We can as easily use the name of God in a careless and a frivolous manner. We can say 'God knows' as a casual claim that I don't, so somebody must. That is hardly better than using his name as a swear word. We can even say to somebody 'God bless you' when all we really mean to say is 'good-bye'—and even this expression originally meant 'God be with you'. We have taken no care for the use of the word at all; it simply tumbles off our lips without a thought. Whenever we use God's name we should use it thoughtfully or else we misuse the name of the Lord our God.

Perhaps there are more expressions than we care to believe that treat holy things lightly. In addition to 'good Lord' and 'my God', 'good gracious' and 'goodness knows' are both references to God; a careful assessment of our modest expletives is not only in order, it is essential if we are to avoid transgressing this Commandment.

Leviticus 24:11 relates the story of the son of an Israelite woman who blasphemed the name of the Lord with a curse and for that he was put to death. This may not be the punishment that is dealt by our judiciary today, but God is no less severe in his ultimate judgement of those who take his name cheaply and use it as a common swear word. And the God who put that young man to death in Leviticus 24 was only doing summarily and immediately on earth what he will do in the final judgement to those who use his name as a swear-word.

That is perhaps the easiest understanding of the phrase and many never think beyond it. But it is not the only way we can misuse God's name and neither is it the most serious breach of the third Commandment.

Blasphemy—misusing his name in false worship

The translation: 'You shall not misuse' is in some ways unfortunate. The emphasis of the original word in Hebrew is to 'lift or raise up'. Psalm 24:4

captures the meaning perfectly in the words 'who does not *lift up* his soul to what is empty (an idol)'; and there it is used in the context of worship. Perhaps the most significant use of this Commandment has to do with worship.

There were times in the Old Testament when the people had the arrogance to worship the Baal gods *and* the Lord. In the evil days of the Judges recorded in the book that relates the tragic cycle of Israel's disobedience, punishment and repentance, there is a short story told of a young man from Ephraim whose name was Micah. His mother discovered that some of her money had been stolen and she put a curse on the unknown thief. Eventually her son came to her and confessed to being that thief. In Judges 17:2–3 we read these incredibly blasphemous words from the mother: 'The LORD bless you, my son! I solemnly consecrate my silver to the LORD for my son to make a carved image and a cast idol.' The mother seemed to imagine that by using the word LORD the sin of idolatry could be made acceptable.

Our pluralistic society boasts many religions that will happily use the name of Christ. Islam acknowledges Christ as a prophet and Hinduism is content to add his name to the endless list of deities; even New Age will allow Christ as one of many 'channels'. But to use the name of Jesus Christ or God does not make worship right. On the contrary, to use his name in an approach to God that is not according to his revelation through his prophets and apostles is to misuse his name altogether. The Israelites were warned more than once that they must not try to worship God in the way of the nations or just as they themselves pleased (Deuteronomy 12:4,8,13). They must not worship anyhow and anywhere.

This third Commandment is directly opposed to the idea that all religions are a legitimate way of worship and to the suggestion that each contains some valid truth. God never allowed his people to dip into the storehouse of the collected wisdom and morality of the world faiths and to add the best to what he had on offer through Judaism. Neither did he ever allow the thought that, in the absence of a knowledge of Israel's God, the religions of the nations would do. The whole Old Testament presents a powerful case for the exclusivism of Judaism as the only way to God for the entire human race. The New Testament makes it even more clear that the fulfilment of Judaism in Jesus Christ is the only way of salvation (John 14:6 and Acts 4:12).

Multi-faith services are in vogue today. They are hailed as a triumph for racial harmony and religious tolerance. People are excited at the act of worship that levels the name of Christ with Gautama, Krishna and Mohammed, and reduces the importance of the Bible to a shared place alongside the Three Pitakas of Buddhism, the Dharma-Shastras of Hinduism and the Koran of Islam. But to introduce the name of Christ into a multi-faith service, however sincere and well-meaning the worshippers may be, is to commit the sin described in Judges 17:2–3 by 'lifting up his name worthlessly'.

Many in our modern society will recoil from this conclusion, but it is precisely why God has given us this third Commandment in addition to the second. It is not enough to pity the worshipper of the idol. To allow the name of Christ and God to be placed alongside any other religion is to misuse his name. False worship is blasphemous worship, however many times and with whatever high motive the name of God or Christ may be invoked. We are never to worship as everyone sees fit (Deuteronomy 12:8).

This is precisely the reason why Christ taught his disciples to pray, 'Our Father in heaven, hallowed be your name' (Matthew 6:9). The word 'hallowed' means 'separate' or 'different'. God allows no rivals and certainly has no equals, and his name is not set apart or treated with respect when it is stirred into the potpourri of world religion.

Blasphemy—the name of the Lord in careless worship

The preacher in Ecclesiastes warns, 'Guard your steps when you go to the house of God. Go near to listen rather than to offer the sacrifice of fools, who do not know that they do wrong. Do not be quick with your mouth, do not be hasty in your heart to utter anything before God. God is in heaven and you are on earth, so let your words be few.' (Ecclesiastes 5:1–2).

Nadab and Abihu died when they made an offering before the Lord with 'unauthorised fire' (Numbers 26:61). They came to God their way. They may have been sincere but they were careless. Perhaps one of the most serious failures amongst Christians today is precisely the sin of offering unauthorised or unholy worship to God. It was part of God's law for his people that they were to worship in the way he had prescribed and not to please themselves (Deuteronomy 12:4,8). In our search for happiness we become careless in our worship. But the test of true worship is not whether it makes us happy but whether it makes us holy; not whether it pleases us, but whether it pleases God. Worship is not always a pleasure, sometimes it is very painful.

Shakespeare put some wise words into the mouth of Prince Hamlet: 'My words fly up, my thoughts remain below. Words without thoughts never to heaven go.' We sing of God's character and use magnificent words extolling his worth, but our mind is a thousand miles away from our hymn book. We sing of deep and serious commitment, pledging our life, our soul and our all to the service of Christ our King, but we have no intention of leaving the building any differently from the way we came in. We sing of Calvary and the broken body of Christ on the cross, and we can sing it a hundred times with our mind everywhere except at the cross. We make serious promises to God that we do not keep—and often have no intention of keeping. We can pledge to do all manner of things in the name of our God but fail to keep our word. It has been well said that Christians do not tell lies, they just sing them in their hymns! All this is a violation of the third Commandment.

The idle repetition of the word 'Jesus' in worship is also a clear violation of the third Commandment, especially when we do it to impress others with our spirituality, or without a serious thought for the full character of the one whose name we are using. The same is true of the magical tag at the end of a prayer for which we had only half a mind: 'In the name of Jesus Christ. Amen.' Can it be any better when we engage in 'worship' whilst our mind is full of criticism for the one leading or bitterness for another worshipper or anger against God himself?

There is a flippancy in some modern worship which violates this Commandment. In our determination to be modern and to demonstrate our personal relationship with the Creator, a trivial and over-familiar use of words like 'dad' and 'daddy' are used. We appear to have forgotten the awesome privilege of being adopted into the family of the Sovereign of the universe. It has been wisely commented that the Almighty has too often become the 'all-matey' in some of our contemporary worship.

Similarly coarse language and cheap joking is hardly the way to 'lift up' the name of our God with honour and respect. And the arrogant use of John 14:14, 'You may ask me for anything in my name, and I will do it', without respect for God's will or holy character is no less a misuse of the meaning of his name.

It is surely on this understanding of the third Commandment that all the King's men and women fall down!

Blasphemy—using the name of the Lord to support a lie

With all of these Commandments there are expansions later in the history of Israel. In Leviticus 19:12 God adds, 'Do not swear falsely by my name and so profane the name of the LORD your God. I am the LORD.' It is all too easy for us to confine our understanding of that to the lies of those who perjure themselves in court.

A young prophet was sent to Jerusalem with a prophetic warning to King Jeroboam. The prophet was told that he was to deliver the message and immediately to return home; he was not to talk to anybody on the way nor to accept an invitation to anyone's home. On his way back the young man passed through Bethel where an old prophet lived who had been starved of fellowship for some time; the old man offered hospitality to the Lord's messenger but was met by the correct response: 'I'm sorry but I can't. I am under strict instructions to return straight back home.' The old prophet then supported his invitation with these words: 'I too am a prophet, as you are. And an angel said to me by the word of the LORD: "Bring him back with you to your house so that we may eat bread and drink water"' (1 Kings 13:18). That was a blatant lie, as the rest of the sorrowful story makes so clear.

A lie or deceit wrapped up in spiritual language does not become a truth. Jacob similarly broke this Commandment when he assured his father, Isaac, that the speed with which he had been able to hunt and prepare a meal was because 'The LORD your God gave me success' (Genesis 27:20), when in fact a young goat had been taken from the flock and prepared by his mother. Ananias and Sapphira committed a sin against the third Commandment when they wrapped up deceit in spiritual language (Acts 5).

This all comes uncomfortably close. Few who read this have a significant problem with swearing and so we consider we are keeping well within the third Commandment, but the net is far wider than that. The Christian serves a holy God whose standard is nothing less than his own purity.

We live in days when 'prophecy' is very fashionable. Many meetings in Christian churches have become more 'prophetic' than biblical. Leaders, members and even little children are encouraged to wait upon God for a word of knowledge or a prophecy. This is not the place to discuss how far such things can be expected in the church today, it is sufficient for us to recognise that for anyone to offer a word of prophecy as a direct revelation from the Lord when the Lord has not spoken, is committing blasphemy by a breach of the third Commandment. The old false prophet said, 'An angel said to me by the word of the LORD', but the Lord had not spoken—that was a blasphemy. But worse still is the fact that his false prophecy caused the young prophet to 'defy the word of the LORD' (1 Kings 13:21). Some churches claim that they have regular prophetic communications from God. That may or may not be so, but to claim, 'This is what the Lord says', when he has not spoken, is to violate the third Commandment and 'The LORD will not hold anyone guiltless who misuses his name.' Alarmingly many groups appear unperturbed by that possibility and exercise little or no discipline. Of the six things that the Lord hates, one is 'a lying tongue' (Proverbs 6:17).

Miracles and fulfilled prophecy are no final test of a true prophet, as Deuteronomy 13:1–3 makes adequately clear. So much of the contemporary prophetic scene is described in Jeremiah 14:14 as 'delusions of their own minds.' In fact the prophet goes on to deal with this issue in stronger terms in chapter 23 and concludes, 'You claim, "This is the oracle of the LORD"… even though I told you that you must not claim, "This is the oracle of the LORD"'(v 38). To bring the name of the Lord into a false prophecy, however sincere and well-meaning it may be, is a serious violation of the third Commandment.

Ezekiel warned of the same danger: 'Their visions are false and their divinations a lie. They say, "The LORD declares", when the LORD has not sent them; yet they expect their words to be fulfilled' (Ezekiel 13:6). He does not say they were insincere, in fact they expected their words to be fulfilled, but in reality they were prophesying lies. One of the most terrifying activities among Christians is when somebody claims to have a special word from the Lord; if they are mistaken then they are breaking the third Commandment—and God warns, 'My hand will be against them' (Ezekiel 13:9).

Sadly there are Christians who will agree with all that has been earlier written about the blasphemy of swearing and of multi-faith worship but who will now move away from the clear application of the third Commandment in their own direction! In all the current debate about modern-day prophecy we read and hear little about testing what is true, and almost nothing about disciplining that which is manifestly false—especially when national and international leaders are involved!

In the Old Testament a prophet who prophesied falsely could face only one judgement—death. His ministry was finished. Jeremiah warned, 'The prophets are prophesying lies in my name. I have not sent them or appointed them or spoken to them. They are prophesying to you false visions, divinations, idolatries and the delusions of their own minds. Therefore …I will pour out on them the calamity they deserve.' (Jeremiah 14:14–16). To encourage children in this places us under the awful judgement of Matthew 18:6, 'If anyone causes one of these little ones who believes in me to sin, it would be better for him to have a large millstone hung around his neck and to be drowned in the depths of the sea.'

Blasphemy— mocking God

When my headmaster warned us schoolboys of our behaviour whilst we were travelling to and from school he would invariably close the lecture by reminding us that the honour of the 'name' of our school was dependent upon us. How much we really cared about that is open to question; but for the Jews it was very different.

The word blasphemy in Old Testament Hebrew is the word *na'ats* and it means to despise or insult. Cheap jokes that poke fun at God and Christ are scheduled for some of the biggest audiences today. Second only to sex, religion—exclusively the Christian religion of course—is the hunting ground for some of the most pathetic and vicious humour. No sensible person considers for one moment that the rash of banal books and films in recent years about the life of Jesus has anything to do with art, literature or the interests of historical research.

Almost three thousand years ago God complained through his prophet Isaiah, 'All day long my name is constantly blasphemed' (Isaiah 52:5). It could have been written today. *The Times* is right when it suggests that, 'The concept of an offence to God is beyond the philosophical concept of most Englishmen.' Modern man has drifted so far away from truth that he does not even realise that he is blaspheming the name of God when he turns his back upon God and dismisses as irrelevant the laws of this holy Creator.

However, much of the guilt for this blasphemy by a mocking world lies at the door of the 'Christian' church. Too often professing Christians give other people good cause to insult God. When we live and behave in the office, the factory, the classroom, the workshop, or in our home, in such a way that we give the unbelieving world cause to sneer and mock God then we have lifted up his name worthlessly. That must surely be blasphemy.

The man who wrote so many of the exquisite psalms in our Bible was King David. In composing those psalms he revealed something of his deep love for God, but David also sinned seriously. In 2 Samuel 11 the tragic story of his double sin of adultery and murder is recorded. In the following chapter the prophet Nathan came to convict the king of his sin. Nathan reminded David of an unexpected additional sin: 'By doing this you have made the enemies of the LORD show utter contempt.' (2 Samuel 12:14). The word that is translated 'utter contempt' is the word for blasphemy, *na'ats*. By his sin David had made the enemies of the Lord blaspheme. How had he done that?

The nations around David's kingdom had been watching this king and they concluded that he was an incredibly powerful warrior and that he must have a strong God on his side. The message drifted back to the nations that David was not a king to be trifled with and that he had some special relationship with his God, a relationship that was totally unknown to them in their relationship with their own idols. They stood in awe of him and they concluded, if we may borrow a phrase from earlier in the history of Israel, 'Surely this great nation is a wise and understanding people. What other nation is so great as to have their gods near them the way the LORD their God is near them whenever they pray to him? And what other nation is so great as to have such righteous decrees and laws...?' (Deuteronomy 4:6–8). But then one day gossip began to circulate: 'Have you heard what the king of Israel has done? Well his God is clearly not very different from our gods after all.' And they held the name of David's God in utter contempt.

When Moses came down from the mountain with the law of God in his hands, he first heard the noise of the people partying in the valley and then he 'saw that the people were running wild and that Aaron had let them get out of control and so become a laughing-stock to their enemies' (Exodus 32:25). Perhaps it was this that made Moses so angry. It was bad enough that they had already broken faith with the God who had delivered them from Egypt, but their actions had led to the nations around jeering at them and thus at their God. They were hardly an example of the holiness and distinctiveness of a people belonging to the Lord. The nations blasphemed because of Israel—but who bore the greatest guilt?

The behaviour of too many Christians today, and especially Christian leaders, is unquestionably causing the world to be contemptuous of our God. The world may blaspheme, but the Christian shares in that guilt. Does God treat lightly those who give cause for his name and that of his Son to be trampled under foot? Christian leaders are forced out of office by their scandalous affairs or their money-grabbing greed and the world sneers at their hypocrisy and at their God. Others encourage bizarre and unscriptural behaviour that leads a watching world to laugh at such crass stupidity and provides it with an excuse for rejecting the Christian faith. Church members behave towards their leaders or towards one another in such vicious and unloving ways that even the world is disgusted. Christian business men conduct their trade in a way that appals those who deal with them. These are all responsible for the blasphemy of a scornful world.

Paul presents the issue plainly: 'You who brag about the law, do you dishonour God by breaking the law? As it is written: "God's name is blasphemed among the Gentiles because of you"' (Romans 2:23-24). There are many professing Christians today like those of whom Paul wrote to Titus nearly two thousand years ago: 'They claim to know God but by their actions they deny him' (Titus 1:16). According to Paul, such people must be 'silenced' (v 11), presumably by rebuke and sound teaching (v 13 and 2:1), and not encouraged and applauded. It is precisely for this reason that Paul urged Timothy to ensure that church leaders 'have a good reputation with outsiders' (1 Timothy 3:7). When the world scorns the Christian faith because of the disgraceful or deceitful life-style of Christians, those Christians are 'misusing the name of the LORD' and it is the Christian who is blaspheming as well as the world.

Blasphemy—the name of the Lord in idle oaths

When Christ preached on the making of oaths (Matthew 5:33–37) he did not specifically tie in his subject with the third Commandment, though his Jewish hearers would almost certainly make the connection. Significantly he warned against swearing by heaven, earth, Jerusalem and ourselves, but made no reference to the name of the Lord. According to Alfred Edersheim (*The Life and Times of Jesus the Messiah*) the various modes of swearing referred to by Christ were adopted by the Pharisees to avoid pronouncing the divine name: 'Accordingly, they swore by the Covenant, by the Service of the Temple, or by the Temple. But perhaps the usual mode of swearing... is "By thy Life"'.

It is a tragic comment upon human nature that we feel the need to take oaths at all. The only reason why for centuries it was the custom of our English courts to expect witnesses to swear on the Bible that they would tell 'The truth, the whole truth and nothing but the truth' was in order to put 'the fear of God' into those whose word could not otherwise be trusted. The taking of oaths by reference to an independent third party reveals only that men and women are by nature liars!

It was unthinkable for a Jew to swear an oath involving the name of his covenant God—a name that he would not even pronounce in the course of worship—yet he was quite willing to offer up an oath based upon some comparatively trivial object. The tragedy of this was that he felt less obligated to a promise if the guarantee of his commitment was considered less significant. In other words, according to Christ in Matthew 23:16,18 there were grades of loyalty to an oath: 'You say, "If anyone swears by the temple, it means nothing; but if anyone swears by the gold of the temple, he is bound by his oath"... You also say, "If anyone swears by the altar, it means nothing; but if anyone swears by the gift on it, he is bound by his oath."' And with barely disguised anger the Lord concludes, 'You blind fools! You blind men!' To grade lies by the importance of the oath is nonsense.

On the other hand God does allow the making of oaths or pledges: 'When a man vows to the LORD or takes an oath to bind himself by a pledge, he must not break his word but must do everything he said' (Numbers 30:2, NKJV, and compare Deuteronomy 23:21–23). But notice that the significant words here are 'bind himself' and 'he must not break his word'; there is no reference to a third party (whether object or person) brought in to support the promise, the man's word must be his bond. That is precisely the conclusion of our Lord in Matthew 5:37, 'Simply let your "Yes" be "Yes" and your "No", "No"; anything beyond this comes from the evil one.' According to Paul in 2 Corinthians 1:18–20 and James 5:12, that is the example God himself sets us.

There is something peculiarly offensive to God in the oath that is taken 'by the name of God', or 'in the name of Christ' when the party is insincere. Such a person can be sure of the solemn warning that 'the LORD will not hold him guiltless.' The prophet Jeremiah refers to such empty promises: 'Although they say, "As surely as the LORD lives", still they are swearing falsely' (Jeremiah 5:2). On the other hand the same prophet looks forward to the day when God's people can 'in a truthful, just and righteous way… swear "as surely as the LORD lives"' (4:2). For this reason it cannot be blasphemous to call God as witness to the truth of our statement, even though Christ said it should be wholly unnecessary since our word should be our bond. But to invoke the name of God to a lie is a fearful sin and it will not go unpunished.

Blasphemy—the name of the Lord in complaint and unbelief

In a series of statements that demand a response, the prophet Malachi forced the nation to admit their own disobedience and sin: '"You have said harsh things against me," says the LORD, "Yet you ask, 'What have we said against you?' You have said, 'It is futile to serve God. What did we gain by carrying out his requirements and going about like mourners before the LORD Almighty?'"' (Malachi 3:13–14). A spirit of grumbling and discontent was also the sin of the Israelites in the wilderness (Numbers 14:27; 1 Corinthians 10:10) and for this the people suffered severely.

It is a violation of this third Commandment when we profess the name of Christ and God and yet complain that he has acted unfairly towards us or that he has not cared for us. We lift up the name of the Lord worthlessly when our conversation or grumbling spirit implies that he is a God who is not to be trusted. Others are hearing what we say about our God, and especially when circumstances are running against us. To imply that 'it is futile to serve God' or to keep his Commandments dishonours his name.

It is not unusual for Christians to explain the behaviour of someone who is going through some tragic or trying period of their life by concluding that they have 'not learned to accept it.' That may be true, but very often the problem is at another stage. They may well have learned to accept that the circumstances that have so changed their life are from the hand of God and they do not blame him or accuse him of unfairness; in this regard they are blameless. However, what they have not learned yet is *how* to accept it'. They can handle the fact of the circumstances, but their complaining and moody spirit, and the grumbling way they resign themselves to 'the will of God', destroys the value of their supposed trust in God. In other words their theology is denied by their reaction.

This surely was Jonah's sin when he stood on the deck of a storm-tossed ship and declared his belief in 'The LORD, the God of heaven, who made the sea and the land' and then added that he was running away from this God (Jonah 1:9–10). His theology was impeccable, his reaction was despicable. It is a blasphemy when our response is a denial of the God we profess to serve.

Blasphemy—in mishandling his word

Two or three decades ago the doctrine of biblical inerrancy (the belief that the whole of the Bible is God's word without error) was a significant issue. It was surely a blasphemy to say that God had not said when in fact he had, or to say that he had when in fact he had not. Today the greatest challenge to the evangelical is that of 'hermeneutics'—the correct interpretation and understanding of the Bible.

A charge levelled against the evangelical by critics is that we claim to believe in the Bible as the revelation of God and then proceed to interpret it according to our preconceived notions, our cultural context, or our desire to remain 'politically correct'. To a greater or lesser extent we can all be guilty of this. This is not the place to deal with the matter in detail, but the range of issues is widespread. What is alarming is the way some Christians select a few passages to 'prove' what is contrary to the whole tenor of Scripture, reject what they do not like as either culturally conditioned or not a genuine part of Scripture, and make unwarranted assumptions of specific texts.

Some interpret the gospel primarily in terms of health, wealth and happiness and believe that we have only to imagine or 'conceptualise' what we want and it is simply ours for the asking—name it and claim it; they have selected a few out-of-context verses from the Bible to give a grotesquely false picture of God's revelation.

Others have recently attempted to justify homosexual behaviour by forcing novel interpretations upon the clear teaching of Leviticus 18:22 and 1 Corinthians 6:9, and by such unwarranted assumptions as that David and Jonathan enjoyed a 'homo-erotic' relationship and that the servant of the centurion (Matthew 8:5–13) was a homosexual slave. Similarly, on the role of women in leadership and ministry in the church some have suggested that 1 Corinthians 14:34 is not really part of Paul's original letter; but their evidence for this conclusion is so slim that they would not treat any other text in the Bible in the same way. The current debate about whether or not hell is for ever has produced a cluster of unusual reinterpretations of words and phrases, the meaning of which had rarely been questioned before in the long history of evangelical scholarship.

More could be said, but hermeneutics is not our subject here. The point at issue is this: We may all be mistaken in our understanding of particular passages and verses in the Bible, but if we violate accepted principles of interpretation in order to force our preference upon a passage, we are misusing his word and therefore his name. We are claiming, 'This is what the Lord says' when it is patently obvious that he did not say this.

It is not that scholarship can ever claim to have reached finality, but when previously accepted sound conclusions are stood on their head we must at least question whether integrity has passed into peddling God's word (2 Corinthians 2:17). It is blasphemy to misuse the Bible, whether wilfully or ignorantly, in such a way that we make it say what it clearly does not say. Not all that Paul wrote is 'hard to understand' (2 Peter 3:16) though much of it is hard to accept. However, to pretend the first in order to avoid the second must come perilously close to blasphemy.

Does it matter?

This Commandment does matter, because to use the name of the Lord carelessly is to downgrade his character or to bring ridicule upon his Son Jesus Christ. To misuse his name is really to say that our God and our Christ are of no particular value. It may have been going too far for Jews to refuse to speak the name of Yahweh, but at least their reverence for the name implied a reverence for his character and person. Our worship also reveals what we think of our God and since worship of the true God is the highest point of human activity, so worship that is blasphemous is the lowest point to which a man or woman can sink.

It matters also because to downgrade God is to downgrade ourselves. To speak cheaply of the God who created us inevitably reveals that we have a low view of the value of the human race.

It matters because God places a serious warning at the end of this Commandment. He will not 'hold anyone guiltless who misuses his name.' This means that he will not hold such a person innocent or acquit him. The one sin that Christ spoke about as unforgivable was, 'the blasphemy against the Holy Spirit' (Matthew 12:31). The Pharisees were attributing the work of Christ to the work of the devil (v 24), but more than this, they were claiming that the character of Christ himself was little more than devilish. The unforgivable nature of this sin is an unwillingness or inability to give the honour that is due to the name of Christ. We may withhold this honour deliberately, through carelessness or through ignorance, but to withhold the worth of his name, in whatever way, and to use his name therefore in a worthless manner, is a sin for which God will not acquit us.

If anyone thinks the standard is becoming impossible, that is precisely the purpose of the Ten Commandments. They reveal the nature of the God we worship, and this should cause us to tremble before him and drive us to the Cross of Christ for forgiveness.

Using his name

Because, as we have seen, the 'name of the LORD' refers not merely to a collection of Hebrew letters but to the whole character represented by it, the phrase stands for the various names used to describe the triune God—

the Father, Son and Holy Spirit—and it is intended to guard the honour of each member of the Godhead.

Like all the Commandments there is a positive aspect to this warning against treating the name of God carelessly. If we are warned not to misuse the name of the Lord, it is because we are also invited to use it. The name of our God and Saviour is a powerful name. It is the name of Christ that opens access for us into the presence of God through prayer (Romans 5:2); and that is surely our greatest privilege on earth. It is the same name that gives us confidence to ask in prayer and to believe that we shall receive (John 15:16). The powerful name of Christ was used by Peter in the healing of the lame man at the Gate Beautiful: 'Silver and gold I do not have, but what I have I give you. In the name of Jesus Christ of Nazareth, walk' (Acts 3:6).

But this name is no magical formula to be used without a personal knowledge of the Saviour and a careful regard to his holiness. Seven sons of a Jewish chief priest named Sceva tried to gain authority over evil spirits just by using the name of Christ, and all they received in response was a severe beating from a madman (Acts 19:13–16). That is a significant warning to anyone who believes that there is some kind of automatic authority in the 'name' of Christ.

This was also the one name that the early church used in its evangelism. Peter boldly asserted, 'There is no other name under heaven given to men by which we must be saved' (Acts 4:12). The name of Jesus Christ, like the name 'LORD' in the Old Testament, is a summary of the whole work and character of the Saviour. It was not merely a handle by which the apostles referred to him but a description of the one who expressed the wholeness of God (Hebrews 1:3), and who came to fulfil the promise first given in Genesis 3:15. Jesus Christ is all that the name LORD implied under the old covenant.

It is our privilege to use the 'name' of our triune God—the Father, Son and Holy Spirit—both in worship and in witness. But we must use it carefully. There are few things more wonderful than to use the name of our God and Saviour—and nothing more dangerous than to abuse it.

Keeping the Sabbath day

Remember the Sabbath day by keeping it holy.

Exodus 20:8–11

One thing about the Ten Commandments upon which all Christians will agree is that the fourth is the most controversial. Yet this Commandment happens to be the one that offers the greatest blessing and is cast in the most positive way; it is one of only two Commandments that begin with a positive encouragement rather than a negative prohibition.

The first three Commandments are concerned with our relationship with God himself and that, as we saw, is an essential way to begin. What matters more than anything else is our relationship with the Creator. There is no value talking about loving our neighbour who is next door whilst all the time we are out of line with our Creator who is in heaven. The fourth Commandment is something of a bridge between the two parts of this 'Decalogue' (the 'ten words'); it stands between the first three and the final six in dealing with our relationships both with God and with those who live around us. In fact this Commandment always proved to be an effective barometer of Israel's spiritual relationship. When Israel was in touch with God they kept the Sabbath day holy, and when they gave up on that it was evident that they were wandering away from him.

A Sabbath no longer?

Today, the Christian principle of Sunday as a special day is significantly under attack, not only by secular governments, which we would expect, but by a new generation of Christians who affirm that the fourth Commandment is no longer valid as a binding law for everyone in general and for Christians in particular.

The stand Christians take on many issues often reveals their commitment to tradition or their capitulation to contemporary culture rather than a clear-headed conviction concerning the teaching of God's word. This debate is no exception. Across the world, Christians express such a variety of viewpoints on the Sunday issue that it must be bewildering to anyone who observes their fair degree of unanimity on the meaning and application of the other nine Commandments.

A rush of books and articles in recent years has made a strong challenge to the two thousand year history of Sunday observance. It is a sad comment that far more has been published on the fourth Commandment over the past ten years than on all the other nine put together. We have inevitably lost sight of the forest by focusing exclusively on one tree. This is not the place to deal exhaustively with the various arguments, but they differ widely.

The consistent view of the church during its history is represented by those who believe that the Sabbath is a creation ordinance and is therefore universally and eternally valid. Christ freed us from the rigid application of the Pharisees, and the first century church of the apostles moved its observance from the Jewish Saturday to the Christian Sunday—that is, from the last to the first day of the week. (Beckwith and Stott, *This is the Day*, Marshall, Morgan and Scott 1978). This view regards Sunday as the Christian Sabbath.

Others maintain that the Sabbath is an order of creation with eternal and universal relevance, but that the apostolic church followed the Jewish Sabbath and that the day was only changed to Sunday during the second century in the time of the Emperor Trajan in order to distinguish Christian worship from Judaism. (Bacchiocchi, *From Sabbath to Sunday*, Pontifical Gregorian University 1977). This view regards Saturday as the Christian Sabbath.

More recently the case is presented that the Sabbath was not a creation ordinance and therefore has no lasting or universal application; on the contrary it was a sign of the covenant with Israel, and the ministry of Christ and the first century apostolic church is evidence of a 'shaking free' not only of Pharisaic legalism but of the burden of the Sabbath altogether. Nevertheless there is biblical approval for first-day worship and the force of the Sabbath Commandment lies in the fact that it points towards the end-time rest in heaven, in our ceasing to work for salvation, and in our sanctification as we set apart every day for God. However, neither Saturday nor Sunday are regarded as the Christian Sabbath (Carson, *From Sabbath to Lord's Day*, Zondervan 1982).

Those representing each view use the same biblical and historical data and yet arrive at significantly opposite conclusions. How confusing!

The third position is increasingly popular today across a broad spectrum of evangelicalism, and it is the view that, whilst not intended by its proponents, enabled many Christians to support the 'Keep Sunday Special' campaign during the early 1990s in an attempt to keep Sunday Observance laws in England intact, but then to abandon all restrictions once the legislation had been abolished. In other words they were defending not theological but pragmatic convictions: a day of rest is good for the nation and convenient for the church, but it has little more significance than that.

Back to the beginning

Since the Christian must not be bound either by historical or contemporary tradition, the wisest course of action is to go back to the beginning. So much of the debate on this Commandment has traditionally revolved around what we should or should not do on Sunday. That is wholly irrelevant as a starting point. The Christian is always to be known as a 'first cause' thinker. We go back to beginnings. On this subject the beginning is in Genesis chapter one—and there is very little beginning before there.

Have you ever wondered why God created the world in six days? He could have created all things instantaneously or in six seconds, six hours, six months, six years or in six millennia. It would have been no more difficult for God to create in a microsecond than in an hour or a day. One word, one thought from the sovereign, triune Creator and everything would have come into being. After all, when it was required, Christ created bread immediately, and wine in the same way on another occasion. During his lifetime he healed the limbs and cured the diseases of so many people instantly. At the resurrection our bodies will be raised and changed in a moment—in the blink of an eye (1 Corinthians 15:52).

So why did God not create the universe in an instant? Or, if there is some particular value in the number six, why did he not create it in six seconds? The answer to that question is found in Genesis 2:2–3. The whole debate must start there: 'By the seventh day God had finished the work he had been doing; so on that day he rested from all his work. And God blessed the seventh day and made it holy, because on it he rested from all the work of creating that he had done.' There is a deliberate purpose here. God was setting a pattern. Six days of work were followed by one day of rest. According to Genesis 2:1 after six creating days everything was completed; the whole of creation, the universe and its vast array was finished. And God rested. What did that mean? We are not to imagine that God was worn out with the labour of creating. In Hebrew the word *Shabath* can mean simply 'to cease' (compare Genesis 8:22). God stopped creating, not because he was tired or could think of nothing else to make, but because in his divine plan he had scheduled quite deliberately that in six days he would accomplish everything. By the dawning of the seventh day there would be nothing left to be done.

God set a pattern for the human race. Six days of work were to be followed by one day of ceasing from work. The respected nineteenth century Hebrew scholars, Keil and Delitzsch, point out that Genesis 1 and 2 are connected by a conjunction that implies that the completion of the work of creation has two parts to it: 'Negatively in the cessation of the work of creating, and positively in the blessing and sanctifying of the seventh day.' In a carefully worded argument Keil and Delitzsch continue by explaining their conviction of what this 'finishing' and 'resting' means. It was because of God's great satisfaction and pleasure in what he had done that he invested his creation with 'blessing and holiness' (Genesis 2:3) which, for Keil and Delitzsch meant placing creation in a living relationship to God himself and raising it to a participation in the clear light of the holiness of God. In other words, when God declared the universe to be 'very good' (Genesis 1:31) this meant far more than that it looked pretty. It was morally and in every way perfect. The seventh day was a celebration of that fact.

The word 'sabbath' does not occur in Genesis 1 or 2 but the root of the word is found in 2:2 which says God 'rested' from all his work. And God did something else. We are told in Genesis 2:3 that he blessed the day and made it holy. That is exactly what he reminded the people of in the fourth Commandment: 'Remember the Sabbath day by keeping it holy' (Exodus 20:8). Those two words 'blessed' and 'holy' in Genesis 2:3 mean that God set the day apart as a day of special privilege and treatment; it was to be different from all his other working days. It was the day on which men and women could enjoy what they had been doing during the past six days. This lies behind the words: 'God saw all that he had made, and it was very good' (Genesis 1:31). On the evening of his final creating day he took pleasure in all his work.

It is true that in Genesis 2 there is no instruction that we are to follow that pattern; it is a simple statement of fact. When God created woman as a compatible companion for Adam, the on-going lesson is applied, 'For this reason a man will leave his father and mother and be united to his wife, and they will become one' (Genesis 2:24). But here there is no interpretation, no application, and no reference to a chosen people; just a statement that this is what God did.

However, the seventh day was a very special day simply because God made it so. He did not have to say anything about the day beyond what is written in Genesis 2:2–3. God made it holy by his own decree and his own example, and it was self-evident that if God treated it as a special day, it would be treated so by his creation. In what other way was the day holy and blessed unless some form of perpetual recognition was intended?

The argument against this special day being part of God's creation plan is faced with the insuperable problem of Exodus 20:11 where, in a direct reference to the six days of creating and the following rest day, God reminded his people: 'Therefore the LORD blessed the Sabbath day and made it holy.' If the 'Sabbath day' here refers to a newly innovated pattern for the Israelites this is a remarkably strange way of saying so! Every natural reading implies that the 'Sabbath' God blessed and made holy was that seventh day after creation. In other words that first seventh day was the first 'Sabbath' day and the Israelites were to remember that as the pattern for all Sabbath days. Genesis 2:2 *is* therefore referred to as a 'Sabbath' day; Moses effectively says in Exodus 20:11, 'This is that'.

Why seven days?

This period of seven days is actually very interesting because it doesn't fit naturally. If we were compiling the story of creation and we had to gather all the ingredients of Genesis 1 into so many days, we would most likely come out with a ten-day week: On day one we would create light; on day two we would create sky and on day three the dry ground; day four, the vegetation; day five, the planets (sun, moon and stars); day six, the water creatures; day seven, the flying creatures; day eight, the animals; day nine, the human race, and day ten would then become the day of rest. This would give us a thirty-six and a half week year, which isn't any more odd than our present fifty-two week year with a little over!

In discussing the origin of the seven-day week, some maintain that the Hebrews discovered it from the Canaanites who in turn had received it from the Babylonians. The earliest practice of civilizations was to divide time into years and days, later into months and finally the weeks were added for convenience. In the ancient world there was no general agreement. In parts of West Africa a four day week was used, in Asia five days constituted a week, the Assyrians adopted a six day week, the Babylonians seven or ten, ancient Rome chose eight or nine days and in Egypt it was ten. There is little evidence of anyone regularly using a seven-day week until it was introduced by the Israelites. God's original pattern was clearly lost as the human race drifted further and further away from the Creator.

But the seven days is still not what we would expect, because it does not quite fit into the lunar year. The lunar year of 354 days would give us fifty-nine weeks of six days exactly, and the solar year of 365 provides seventy-three weeks of five days. People have at times tried juggling with the length of the weeks. During the French Revolution the Republic changed the calendar and introduced a ten day week in 1792, but thirteen years later it was abandoned. In 1929 a Revolutionary calendar was proposed in the Soviet Union but it was never adopted. The proposed International Fixed Calendar would retain the seven day week but reduce each month to a neat twenty-eight days. One thing is certain, the seven-day cycle appears to fit human requirements perfectly. Verna Wright, as Professor of Rheumatology at Leeds University and a Consultant Adviser to the Department of Health and Social Security, commented on the wisdom of this seven-day cycle of work and rest. He noted that just as the body requires its twenty-four hour cycle, so the one in seven rest day fits perfectly the needs of the body and mind in modern man.

The final act of God after six days of creation was to create one more day and to set it aside as special from all the others. And so God created the Sabbath day. After that the days and the weeks, the months and the years continued in a cycle. Civilizations have been forced to change the calendar to conform to a more accurate understanding of lunar and solar time, first during the rule of Julius Caesar (the Julian calendar) and then in the time of pope Gregory (the Gregorian calendar of 1582). Even though the seventh day of rest is never again referred to in the Genesis record, the seven-day cycle is clearly foundational to the life of the early inhabitants of the earth (for example Genesis 7:4,10; 8:10,12; 29:27)—a fact that is often ignored by chronologists today.

For how long, if at all, the descendants of Adam and Eve followed the one day rest pattern of their Creator is unknown. It is hardly unreasonable to assume that in the perfectly holy relationship between God and his creation, Adam and Eve marked as special this one day set aside so clearly by their Creator. Like everything else it was doubtless neglected after the Fall until the concept was virtually lost to the human race. However, as we have already seen, from the way Exodus 20:11 refers to the day following the six days of creation as 'the Sabbath day' it is evident that something of God's plan was known among the first inhabitants of the earth. On the other hand, nothing else is said of this day until we come to Exodus 16. When God covered the desert with manna the people were told that on the sixth day they were to gather twice as much. Moses explained that the following day was to be a 'day of rest, a holy Sabbath to the LORD' (Exodus 16:23). It was made clear that this would be repeated every sixth day, and those who went out on the seventh day looking for manna, found nothing. Moses reminded the people to 'Bear in mind that the LORD has given you the Sabbath' (v 29). This was before the law-code of the fourth Commandment.

Apparently then, during the long years since that creation day and the fall of Adam into disobedience, the day had been neglected. We cannot know whether Noah and the Patriarchs observed this day; certainly it would have been hard for the Israelites during four hundred years of slavery in Egypt to keep a seven-day Sabbath, since they were tied to the Egyptian ten-day week. But still the principle was known. For this reason when God gave the fourth Commandment to the people he could simply remind them of what they already knew. The reminder was not just because of the recent instructions in Exodus 16; God took his people right back to the beginning: 'For in six days the LORD made the heavens and the earth, the sea, and all that is in them, but he rested on the seventh day. Therefore the LORD blessed the Sabbath day and made it holy'(Exodus 20:11).

It would not be hard for the Israelites to understand the value of this day because the principle was well established in their story of creation. The pattern set by God in Genesis 2:3 would, at the very least, have been an intriguing record for any Israelite; none could have overlooked such a significant phrase. Through the remainder of the Old Testament their observance of this law became a hallmark of whether the people were with God or away from God. In Isaiah 58 the people had been regular in their sacrificial offerings to God and in their activity at the Temple, but God said in effect: 'I am not interested in your outward form, I want to know where your heart is. And I can tell where your heart is because I see how you view the Sabbath.' If the people viewed the Sabbath as a delight, a holy day, an honourable day, then they would show what they were really like and would find their joy in the Lord himself (Isaiah 58:13–14).

When Christ came

Some claim that of all the Commandments this one is endorsed neither by Christ nor by his apostles. If anything, it is argued, Christ down-graded the fourth Commandment by deliberately healing on the Sabbath, which the Jews saw as working, and by refusing specifically to support it. The same is thought to be true of the apostles. These arguments are more apparent than real.

When Christ came, the Sabbath was firmly fixed in the life of Israel— sadly to a fault. They had invented many petty and ridiculous laws to make sure that nobody broke the fourth Commandment. Alfred Edersheim, in his monumental study of *The Life and Times of Jesus the Messiah*, says of the Pharisees in the time of Christ: 'They provided for every possible and impossible case. They entered into every detail of private, family and public life, and with iron logic, unbending rigor and the most minute analysis they pursued and dominated man, laying on him a yoke which was truly unbearable.' Nowhere was this more true than in the laws invented by those Jewish lawyers to protect the Sabbath. Here are just a few examples:

A limit was set on how far you could travel on the Sabbath day—2000 cubits from home. But it was always possible to overcome this restriction.

The night before the Sabbath you could take some food and set it out 2000 cubits away from home, when you arrived at that spot you could say, 'This is my new home because there is the meal all ready for me.' From there you could travel a further 2000 cubits. But it was possible to be even more subtle than this. If in some way you linked the buildings together with a piece of rope or a beam then you could claim your neighbour's home to be linked with your own, thus making the two, one. In this way it was possible to travel all the way down the street before you actually started your 2000 cubits!

The household fire was to be extinguished prior to the Sabbath because there was to be no cooking on that day; you were not even allowed to let an egg bake itself in the sun. You could ride your donkey on the Sabbath day providing you saddled him the day before. The way you dressed on the Sabbath was carefully controlled as well, particularly if you were a woman. Women were not allowed to wear any pin or jewellery on the Sabbath because if they took it off to show to a friend they would be carrying a burden on the Sabbath day. If you cut your finger you could always put a little piece of cloth round it to stem the bleeding, but if you suspected that by doing this you would help the healing process this would be breaking the Commandment—a significant Pharisaic law in the light of their criticism of Christ.

The rules became ever more ridiculous. You were allowed to dip a radish in salt but you could not leave it too long or you might be pickling it. If you found some dirt on your dress you could brush it off but you must not rub it. You could throw something in the air and catch it with the same hand, if you caught it with the other hand that was considered work. If you were moving hay for the animals you must use a different hand than the one you used during the week. Even the animals were not exempt from these rules. Perhaps the most pathetically amusing of the Pharisaic rules was that concerning the chickens. If a hen that was being fattened for the table laid an egg, the egg could be eaten since egg-laying was not the hen's daily work; however if an egg-laying hen laid an egg on the Sabbath she was working and that egg could not be eaten!

Tragically, in spite of hundreds of sermons and pages of the Talmudic literature devoted to this subject, little is said about the spiritual purpose of the Sabbath day. The Pharisees were not concerned to tell the people why the Sabbath was given in the first place. This is all sheer legalism.

That is the background against which Christ came. So, how should we respond to the suggestion that both Christ and the Apostles played down the importance of this fourth Commandment and deliberately broke it? Mark 2:27–28 are significant verses and are frequently used in this debate. Our Lord is talking about the Sabbath and has been accused of not keeping it simply because his disciples walked through the corn fields, pulled a few ears of grain and rubbed them between their hands to eat. There was nothing illegal about their action; it was not considered to be stealing, so that was not the issue. The issue was that they did it on the Sabbath, and whilst the law of Moses was silent on this, the Pharisees were vocal.

In response to the criticism of the Pharisees, Jesus said, 'Have you forgotten that the Sabbath was made for man, not man for the Sabbath?' (v 27). There are three things of importance in that sentence.

First, 'the Sabbath was *made*'. The Greek verb used (*ginomai*) means 'to become' or 'come into existence' and in John 1:3,10 the same word certainly carries the meaning of being created. Immediately this leads us back to the plan in creation. The Sabbath was one of God's great acts of creation; its origin was not in Exodus 20. After his work in creation, the Sabbath came into being. God had no other creative act after he had made the Sabbath.

Secondly, the Sabbath was made for *man;* 'mankind' is the word and it refers to the human race rather than to male gender. Our Lord did not say 'for Israel' and although it is argued that since he is talking to Jews the word is to be understood in that context, he at least implies that it was for all mankind.

Thirdly, we are told the Sabbath was made *for* man. That means it was made for the benefit and well-being of mankind.

Significantly, Christ did not take his hearers back to Exodus but to Genesis. The day was made so that through it God could bless the whole of the human race and Christ endorsed that creation plan of God. Neither the action of the disciples nor the instruction of Christ in Mark 2 can be taken as a down-grading of the Sabbath. Certainly both they and he violated the petty rules of the Pharisees, but that was in order to confirm the purpose of the Sabbath at the beginning. This passage highlights that the Sabbath was intended as an enduring benefit for mankind. Professor Verna Wright gives a simple illustration for this affirmation that 'the Sabbath was made for man, not man for the Sabbath': 'I am driving along a clear road early one morning. As I approach a set of "keep left" bollards a child darts out from the pavement. The only way I can avoid the child is to drive to the right of the bollards. I do so unhesitatingly because the bollards were made for man, not man for the bollards. Yet as a general rule I still keep to the left of the bollards.'

God always intended the Sabbath to be for the good and the enjoyment of mankind; this much is clear in the promise that it was a day 'blessed' by God, and by his invitation in Isaiah 58:13–14 for the people to take delight and joy in it. The rules he gave about it were, like the bollards for us, intended for the benefit of his people, but if ever the observing of the rules would hinder the greater blessing of the day then the rules could be broken. That is a vital principle to remember and it is what our Lord meant by his reference to David eating the consecrated bread in the days of Abiathar (Mark 2:25–26). It was certainly not the Sabbath law that Christ was seeking to correct here, but the Pharisaic abuse of it. If he had been intending to take out the fourth Commandment from its place in the Decalogue this was a strange way of achieving it, since he did nothing more than re-affirm his Father's plan for the Sabbath day.

The parallel passage to Mark 2 is found in Matthew 12, and the context of that chapter is important. The weariness and burden that our Lord refers to in 11:28 is a reference, not primarily to the hard circumstances of life, but to the legalism of the Pharisees; by contrast his yoke is easy and his burden is light (v 30). As if to illustrate that point we move straight into the story of the disciples picking and eating the grains of corn. It was never the law that Jesus criticised, but the abuse of it.

It is sometimes claimed that the Commandments are all quoted in the New Testament with the exception of the fourth. It is true that it is not quoted, but that does not mean that Christ and the Apostles therefore side-lined the fourth Commandment. Besides, it is not the only Commandment that is not specifically *quoted* in the New Testament, neither are the first three! We do not abandon those. Presumably we believe that the first three

Commandments are implicitly taught throughout the New Testament and are fundamental to the Christian faith. But, as we have seen, our Lord endorsed the fourth Commandment in his teaching in Mark 2, so on what grounds can we assume that this one is not foundational to the Christian faith also? Christ could hardly have been more clear in his affirmation of the continuing value of the fourth commandment. On the other hand his principle was clear: if ever the rules hindered the fulfilling of the purpose of the day then the rules could be broken.

Paul and the Sabbath

Did Paul break free from the fourth Commandment in Romans 14:5 when he declared, 'One man considers one day more sacred than another; another man considers every day alike. Each one should be fully convinced in his own mind'? Nowhere does Paul refer to the Sabbath in this chapter and he is hardly likely to fly in the face of the example of creation and the command of the Decalogue without at least some explanation. It is surely more satisfactory to conclude that in Romans 14 Paul is referring to the observance of both Jewish and Christian festival days which we are at perfect liberty to invent and observe if we wish—providing we do not make them mandatory for others. The celebration of a Harvest Sunday, Good Friday, Easter day, Pentecost and Christmas day, and any other Christian 'holy-day' is a matter of personal preference—and nothing more. We are neither wrong nor right to celebrate them, but we are certainly wrong to make them a rule for others, or to think less of those who choose to ignore such days altogether. Significantly the Puritans in the seventeenth century abolished the celebration of Christmas, but were strong observers of the Sabbath day.

The same point is reiterated by Paul in Colossians 2:16. He refers to 'a religious festival, a new moon celebration or a Sabbath day'. Unfortunately the *New International Version* offers us a poor and misleading translation here. The *New King James Version* has 'or sabbaths', and that is a more accurate translation of the Greek. Paul was not thinking of the Sabbath day that he knew to be rooted in both creation and the law, but of the many other religious rest-days that the Jews observed. The Jewish festival days, such as the Feast of Unleavened Bread, the Feast of Harvest, and the Feast of

Ingathering (Exodus 23:14–19), were all known as 'sabbaths' among the Jews. New moons and sabbaths are referred to in Isaiah 1:13 and Hosea 2:11 for example; the seventh year was known as a sabbath year (Leviticus 25:2–5), and the fiftieth year, or jubilee, was a special sabbath (Leviticus 25:8). All these were Old Testament signs or pictures of the coming of Christ ('a shadow of the things that were to come' Colossians 2:17), and as such were fulfilled when the Saviour came.

Nowhere did Paul or any of the Apostles specifically instruct the early church against the application of the fourth Commandment. The fact that they had relatively little to say about it probably tells us no more than that the subject was not debated in their time. The churches had no intention of losing the blessing of such a special day, and the only change concerned the day of the week on which they celebrated the Sabbath.

Ever since the first century it has been the practice among Christians to observe the first day of the week, Sunday, as a day of special rest and worship. The pattern of one special day in seven was copied, as we have seen, from the practice of the Jews throughout the Old Testament. During the early years of the infant Christian church the Christians changed their Sabbath day, which had followed the Jewish pattern of Friday evening to Saturday evening, to one whole day on Sunday. It became what the Christians called the 'Lord's day', a phrase that meant, 'a day belonging to the Lord'; the expression is found only once in the New Testament in Revelation 1:10.

The apostles used the synagogue meetings on the Sabbath day as an evangelistic opportunity but also because that was their custom. There is no evidence that at this time they had any other intention than to keep to that biblical pattern (Acts 13:14,44; 16:13; 17:2 and 18:4).

Probably the change came in order to distance themselves from the Jews; Christians needed to do this so that they were not seen simply as a Jewish sect. But more particularly the first day of the week (what later the Christians referred to as 'the eighth day') was their day to celebrate the resurrection of Christ. What better day to meet than on the day when they recalled the fact that Jesus had risen from the dead. Had he not first appeared alive from the grave on that day (John 20:19)? And a week later on the same day of the week he re-appeared to his disciples (John 20:26). Was not this the true fulfilment of Psalm 118:24 'This is the day the LORD has made; let us rejoice and be glad in it'?

But this was also the day when the Spirit was poured out on the church. The 'day of Pentecost' (Acts 2:1) was the Old Testament 'Feast of weeks' and, according to Leviticus 23:15–16, that was the day following the Jewish Sabbath; the significance of that could not have been lost on the disciples. However, the early Christians retained a link with the older covenant by referring to Sunday as the 'Lord's day' because in Isaiah 58:13 the Sabbath day is referred to as the 'LORD's holy day'. So the Christians picked up this expression and called it the 'Lord's day'. They simply changed the day of the week.

In AD 54 when Paul was writing to the Corinthians he gave them special instructions for what they were to do when they gathered together on the 'first day of the week' (1 Corinthians 16:2). That was their Sunday worship. A year later at Troas Paul met with the church 'on the first day of the week' to share in the communion service (Acts 20:7). There must surely be some significance in this reference to the 'first day' because nowhere in the New Testament do we read of the second day, or the third day and so on.

Almost half a century later in Revelation 1:10 the day is called for the first time, 'the Lord's day'. That is how Christians very often refer to the day even now. The phrase 'the Lord's day' (*kuriake hemera*), translates as 'a day belonging to the Lord'. The word *kuriake* is used elsewhere only in 1 Corinthians 11:20 where it refers to the 'Lord's supper'. The Grimm-Thayer Greek lexicon suggests that 1 Corinthians refers to a supper instituted by the Lord, and Revelation 1 refers to a day dedicated to the Lord.

A short history of Sunday

Many of the early church leaders write about the first day of the week as their worship day. Justin Martyr, writing in his *Apology* to the Emperor, around AD 155, describes a service which included prayers, the Lord's Supper and baptism at which: 'the memoirs of the apostles or the writings of the prophets are read, as long as time permits'; then followed, 'a discourse by the president, instructing us and exhorting us to the imitation of these noble words.' More prayers followed and an offering for the poor.

Almost certainly such a service was before daybreak. In the same century Tertullian comments, 'In Sunday worship, Christians avoid every trace of gloom and put aside business which might interfere with prayer.' When they were able, the Christians stayed together and in the late afternoon shared the *agape* (love) meal after which, according to Justin, they each sang a hymn—some from Scripture or 'one of his own composing'. They continued as long as they could and in this way absent members were easily noted and could be followed up.

Clement of Alexandria provides a delightful picture of a husband and wife going to church: 'decently attired, with natural step, embracing silence, possessing unfeigned love, pure in body, pure in heart, fit to pray to God...' In evidence that nothing ever changes, he lamented that some leave what they have heard from the 'discourse' inside the church and spend the rest of the day foolishly. Clearly he expected the whole day to be kept differently.

In the third century, Origen wrote of the 'Christian Sabbath', referring to Sunday. Eusebius, who was born in AD 260, is the clearest of all in insisting that the Jewish Sabbath had been transferred to the Christian Sunday. However, Athanasius and Chrysostom (bishop of Constantinople in 398), distinguished the Lord's Day from the Sabbath and did not consider that they were under an obligation to the fourth Commandment. Chrysostom wrote, 'If you keep the Sabbath, why not be circumcised?' He placed the Lord's Day above the Sabbath. In fact Sunday became known as the 'Eighth Day'. Just as circumcision and the sacrifices and the Temple were replaced by a circumcision of the heart, spiritual sacrifices and the temple of the people of God, so the Sabbath was replaced by the Christian Sunday. However, it was a very significant day for these early Christians. Chrysostom is clear on this: 'Let us write it down as an unalterable law for ourselves, for our wives and for our children to give up this one day of the week entire to hearing and to recollection of the things which we have heard.' These early church leaders all believed that they were under an obligation of one day of rest—for worship and not idleness—because of the pattern of creation.

By AD 321 the Roman Emperor Constantine, having made a profession of Christian faith, and influenced by Eusebius, codified the seventh day rest, because its use was widespread: 'On the venerable day of the sun let the magistrates and people residing in the cities rest, and let all workshops be closed. In the country, however, persons engaged in the work of cultivation may freely and lawfully continue their pursuits; because it often happens that another day is not so suitable for grain-sowing or vine-planting; lest by neglecting the proper moment for such operations the bounty of heaven should be lost.'

There is no evidence of a legalistic observance of Sunday in the church for the first five hundred years. There were no detailed rules and, providing the believers spent all the time they could in fellowship and worship with the Christian community, there was little that was denied them that was lawful at any other time. Generally it was considered that the Sabbath was specifically Jewish, and Sunday was a pre-Mosaic and Christian day for rest and worship.

But times were changing. The *Apostolic Constitutions* in the late fourth and early fifth centuries reveals that the Lord's Day was being held in increasingly legalistic regard. The liberty of the first three centuries is passing, and the web of legal requirement is tightening. In England from the seventh to twelfth centuries laws became more and more restrictive, and by the eighth century Alcuin observed that the laws and customs of the Jewish Sabbath had been transferred to the Lord's Day: 'by the custom and consent of Christian people.' In 829 ploughing, markets and law business was forbidden, and by 958 Edgar the Peaceable ordered that the Lord's Day should begin at 3.0 pm on Saturday and continue until dawn on Monday. The first reference in English law where the words Sunday and Lord's Day are used is in 1384 and the lord of the manor was forbidden from making his serfs work on Sunday. By 1009 markets, fairs, hunting and ordinary labour were forbidden, and by 1031 travelling was not allowed, except for necessity and acts of mercy. By 1221 everyone was obliged to hear the whole mass and the sermon—generally twice.

From the fourteenth century regulations became often minute and legalistic. Tostatus, Bishop of Avila in central Spain, set out detailed regulations which included the following: Meat may be prepared on the Lord's Day but the dishes must not be washed up. A cook, if hired by the month or year, may work on Sunday, but not if hired by the day. A man may pilgrimage to a shrine on Sunday but not return home on that day.

Labourers may not work on Sunday unless their work is 'a small thing'. This was the very Pharisaism that our Lord condemned

Understandably the Reformers from the sixteenth century reacted against this legalism. Calvin declared that as the fathers had substituted the Lord's Day in place of the Sabbath we were not under the obligation of the original Sabbath. He wrote, 'There is no use in changing the day and yet mentally attributing to it the same sanctity.' Calvin was against what he called, 'The gross and carnal superstition of Sabbatism.' Commenting on Deuteronomy he made it clear that he saw the Christian Sunday as a day for rest and worship; the creation pattern was significant for him. Cranmer in his *Catechism* (1548) did not feel obligated to the Sabbath Day either. He wrote, 'We have liberty and freedom to use other days for our Sabbath days, therein to hear the word of God and keep an holy rest.' Melanchthon, Hooker, Luther and Tyndale were all against legalism and Sabbatariansim, but they still considered that there was an obligation to use one day as a day of rest and worship. Tyndale in reply to Thomas More declared, 'We be lords over the Sabbath, and may change it into Monday or any other day as we need.' Luther similarly wrote, 'The fourth commandment was abrogated by the New Testament, and ideally there should be no distinction between days. But human nature requires a day of rest from labour; the soul demands leisure for joint worship; therefore a day of rest be fixed for all. We cannot do better than follow the tradition which sets apart the first day of the week.' The Reformers and Puritans laid great stress on the service and the sermon—which was anything up to three hours long. The day was expected to be spent in spiritual duties and not frivolous sports, but it was not a community activity; the Christians went to church and immediately returned home.

The Reformers did not abandon the value of the fourth Commandment but what they did was to claim that the detail was part of the ceremonial law, though the principle was everlastingly relevant. By loosening the tie between the commandment and the observance, the day was less rigidly observed. In most Protestant countries (Holland, Belgium, Switzerland, Germany, France) Sunday was much like any other day with regard to business and sport.

In the sixteenth century England of Elizabeth I and Shakespeare, the use of Sunday became slack and almost all recreations were enjoyed. People attended church both morning and evening but spent the rest of the day: 'riding abroad and walking forth to take the ayre, or otherwise to refresh themselves, and following their honest pleasures at such times as are not designate to the public meetings.' They went to the theatre after morning church, and archery was practised by law.

In reaction to this, Hooper's *Exposition of the Ten Commandment*s (1550) took a more strict line, as did Nicholas Bound in *The True Doctrine of the Sabbath* (1595). Bound advocated a return to Sunday as the Jewish Sabbath which should be enforced by the state. George Herbert's *The Country Parson* and William Perkins' *A Golden Chain* both advocated the same position. King Charles I responded with *The Book of Sports* by Bishop Morton (1618) in which almost all recreation on Sunday, apart from bear and bull baiting, was allowed.

In the seventeenth and eighteenth centuries English Protestants reacted, partly because of their strong affinity with the Old Testament. The Puritans burned *The Book of Sports* in 1643, and restrictions were even stronger in Scotland where the *Westminster Confession* of 1647 stated that the Jewish Saturday Sabbath was transferred after the resurrection of Christ to the Christian first day Sabbath; Edinburgh Town Council forbade golf on Sunday (1592) and virtually everything was banned—except drinking! The word Sabbath was now regularly used for Sunday.

The Restoration of the monarchy under Charles II swung the pendulum back so far that by 1676 a compromise was required in the Sunday Observance Act: 'for the better observation of the Lord's Day, called Sunday.' The Protestant Revolution of 1688, when King William came to power, led to stricter observance of Sunday, but there was a further reaction under the Georgian Hanovers in the early eighteenth century.

The Evangelical Awakening in the eighteenth century re-established Sunday, though the sermons had generally reduced to no more than an hour. Two services a day were normal and most simply attended church and returned home immediately. In the Victorian period church clubs and societies met on Sunday. This included 'Pleasant Sunday Afternoons', which were an oasis for hardworking labourers. For many, the church was the only social gathering they had and it provided the origin of Sunday Schools to teach children and adults to read. Ragged Schools were later added to Sunday Schools and Victorian evangelicals placed a strong emphasis on 'charitable' work on Sunday.

The first half of the twentieth century included two world wars that drastically changed English customs in virtually every area of life. This, together with a steady spiritual decline across the nation, led to the use of Sunday becoming one of the many casualties of this social upheaval until, by the opening of the twenty-first century, the remains of Sunday observance was little more than a half severed vestigial organ.

Not under law?

It is suggested that if we follow an Old Testament model on Sabbath keeping we must be brought back under the rules and regulations of the law—and that this is a denial of the freedom that Christ won for us through his cross. Those who believe in a continuing Sabbath, we are told, must either be rigid in the way they apply it, or remain inconsistent.

We have already given our response to this which has been covered in chapter two. Perhaps we need only recall one conclusion stated there: Grace and law are only opposites for those who are on the outside of grace. Once we are on the receiving end of grace the law itself becomes grace. It is no longer a tyrant condemning us but a friendly force to keep us in check. This may be hard for some to understand, but it is vital to grasp. The psalmist loved God's law for it brought him freedom, not slavery. He thought about it often and delighted in it (Psalms 1:2; 119:70,77,97,113,163,174). He wanted nothing better than to have the perfect law of God in his heart (37:31; 40:8).

If all that was said in chapter two is a correct understanding of the relationship between law and grace, then the fourth Commandment stands with the other nine as an expression of God's great love in providing a standard of correction for our lives. Of course the gospel always highlights new aspects of the law. That is exactly what Christ was doing in the Sermon on the Mount (Matthew 5–7); he was not annulling the law of God but explaining its full dimension. We have seen that there was nothing new in the commandment that we should love our neighbour as ourself (Matthew 22:39), that was well-established in Leviticus 19:18. The new covenant dimension that Christ added is that we should love our neighbour *as Christ has loved us* (John 13:34).

In the same way there is a new covenant dimension to the fourth Commandment. The pattern is found in Genesis 2:2, but to Moses, God expanded on the purpose and blessings attached to the observance of a six-day work and one-day rest cycle (Exodus 20:8–11), and seven hundred years after Moses, God expanded the value of the Sabbath day still further through Isaiah (58:13–14). However, the new covenant dimension is added by Christ in Mark 2 and elsewhere. Something of the rigid control found in Exodus is relaxed.

Whilst there is some continuity between the Old Testament law and its application today, there is also a break—a 'discontinuity'. The Sabbath is one example of this and the laws concerning adultery are another. On the principle of discontinuity we no more stone a man to death for working unnecessarily on Sunday (Numbers 15:32–36) than we stone adulterers to death (Leviticus 20:10 compare John 8:1–11). The severity of the punishment demonstrates the seriousness with which God holds any breaking of the law, the fourth no less than the seventh. His mind has not changed just as the law has not changed, though in the present age of the gospel his law is tempered with mercy. This is part of God's unfolding and developing plan found as the story in the Bible progresses. It is part of what we call God's 'progressive revelation'.

We have seen the clear link with the past throughout the New Testament, but Christ's handling of Pharisaic abuses went beyond dealing with the immediate regulations and moved the Christian position in the direction of even greater freedom and enjoyment of the day, whilst never abandoning the principle. All this enhances rather than diminishes the value of the fourth Commandment.

No special day?

Another reason that is put forward for limiting this particular commandment is that the Christian counts every day as the Lord's day, so no special day is required. What we would not do on Sunday we should not do any other day of the week. This argument has nothing to commend it.

Of course we are to live every day for God. Every Jew in the Old Testament knew this much. However, it was God who, at the end of his activity in creating, set one day aside as special and 'made it holy'. That was not man's idea. Similarly it was God who revealed his perfect plan to Moses in the fourth Commandment. A true Israelite, no less than the Christian, was expected to live every day of the week in a manner pleasing to the God he worshipped, but this did not detract from the need for one special day. If we stop to consider the reason for this seventh day it will be evident that only a day protected from the rush and business of the regular week day can serve the purpose fully.

Besides, as we have already seen, there was no doubt that for the apostles and the early church there *was* a special day. It was known as 'the Lord's day' and it commemorated the resurrection of their Lord and the giving of the Holy Spirit to the church, for both of these events took place on the first day of the week. To suggest that we do not need a 'Lord's day' because we should make every day a 'Lord's day' is to be wiser than God who gave his chosen people one special day, Christ who maintained its value as 'made for man', and the apostles who maintained the principle first by regular worship on the Jewish Sabbath and then on the special *kuriake hemera*, 'the day of the Lord' (Revelation 1:10).

Nothing before Sinai?

It is a significant problem to some that after the one reference in Genesis 2:2 there is virtually total silence regarding the Sabbath day until Exodus 16. Why, if it is so significant, is it not mentioned and why is there no evidence of the Patriarchs observing it?

But there are many issues that are later codified by God in his instructions through Moses that are either not mentioned in Genesis or are introduced with the assumption that more was known than we are aware of. For example, where is idolatry expressly forbidden in Genesis? Or adultery or even theft? Yet it is clear from the narratives that there was some understanding of these issues. Where did Joseph find such a high standard of morality that he could resist the temptation to adultery in the seductive culture of Egypt (Genesis 39)? Similarly, where did Abraham and Jacob receive their understanding of the importance of the tithe (Genesis 14:20 and 28:22)? These two accounts allow us to assume that God had given instructions that are simply not recorded in Scripture. Is this the case also of Cain's offering? We must surely assume that Cain was aware of things about which we are not told (Genesis 4:3–7). It is therefore perfectly reasonable to suggest that the introduction of the Sabbath in Exodus 16 and 20 presupposes some understanding reaching back into the history of Israel. Certainly the pattern was clear from Genesis 2:2–3.

A covenant with Israel alone?

One common argument is that the Sabbath command is part of the ceremonial law which marked out the Jews as a distinctive people from the surrounding nations and as such it has been fulfilled in Christ. The argument points to Exodus 31:16–17 where the Sabbath was 'a sign between me and the Israelites for ever'. Surely this is evidence that the Sabbath was a unique covenant requirement for Israel and was never meant to go beyond that.

It is a fact that the whole of the Ten Commandments are set in the form of a special relationship with Israel. Exodus 20:2 introduces them with the reminder: 'I am the LORD your God who brought you out of Egypt, out of the land of slavery'; and this is reinforced in Deuteronomy 5:2 when Moses reminded the people that, 'The LORD our God made a covenant with us at Horeb.' Consequently there are those who argue that this is precisely why the Ten Commandments should not be taken as a moral code for humanity as a whole and that we should view it simply as God's plan for his ancient people; just as the other festivals were fulfilled in Christ and are therefore no longer expected to form part of Christian worship, so the Sabbath has passed away.

But this overlooks the fact that of all the special festivals, this one is uniquely contained *within* the Ten Commandments and the only one that can trace its origin back to creation. Those two facts alone mark it out as special.

You may recall that we argued in the first chapter that it is just because the Ten Commandments *are* the standard for his chosen people that they become so relevant for every society and culture. God does not have one standard for his chosen people and another for the unbelieving world. These laws certainly marked out the Israelites as a special people of wisdom and understanding whose 'righteous decrees and laws' far surpassed those of any other people on earth (Deuteronomy 4:6–8). It is therefore perfectly true that this Commandment, together with the rest, is a special part of his covenant with Israel (Exodus 31:16–17) since no other nation came near to such a high moral code based upon the worship of such a unique and holy God. But that is a pattern for the whole world.

We have already seen that not one of these laws is annulled either by Christ or his apostles and we can rightly claim that the Ten Commandments are still the hallmark of the people belonging to God. From the time of Israel entering Canaan to the present day, via the Apostles and the early church, obedience to the Ten Commandments marks off the true believer as different from the world around. Some of the other Commandments are certainly endorsed by other cultures—but not this fourth; this one is uniquely Jewish and Christian.

This is an important point, so let me express it another way. Israel alone was chosen to correctly interpret and apply the Creator's plans for the human race. Israel would set marriage exclusively in the context of a man and a woman rather than two men or two women, and would stand against all forms of homosexual practice, bestiality and sexual indecency. Israel alone would worship only one God as Architect and Creator of everything that exists. Israel alone received what we refer to as 'the Christian work ethic'—that work is God's plan for mankind and not to be avoided. Significantly one foundation argument for the 'work ethic' is found here in the fourth Commandment: 'six days you shall labour and do all your work'—was that only for Israel? In these and many other ways Israel was expected to be an example to the nations (see Deuteronomy 4:5–8), and all because they alone knew the creation laws of God. So, Israel set apart one day in seven as a day of rest and worship for an example to the nations.

Christ our Sabbath?

It has become commonplace to take as one argument for the cessation of the Sabbath law the presumed fact that Christ has fulfilled the fourth Commandment in himself. The argument claims that this command is part of the ceremonial law which is all fulfilled in Christ. Further, Christ is spoken of as our 'Sabbath rest' and in this sense all that was intended in the fourth Commandment has been realised in Christ.

This is nice thinking, though wholly without Scriptural support, and it betrays a misunderstanding of the purpose of the Sabbath day. Nowhere in the Bible is Christ spoken of as our 'sabbath'. There is a reference in Colossians 2:17 that religious festivals, new moons and sabbaths are 'a shadow of the things that were to come; the reality, however, is found in Christ' but this is beside the point. It is true that the Jewish festivals (referred to as sabbaths) were clearly part of the Jewish ceremonial and were fulfilled in Christ, but we have seen already that those 'sabbaths' are hardly likely to refer to the Sabbath day without some significant explanation from Paul.

On the contrary there is nothing ceremonial about the purpose of the Sabbath day revealed in Exodus 20:8–11 and Deuteronomy 5:12–15. The physical *rest* for man and beast, the opportunity for *remembering* and for *worshipping* can never be said to be fulfilled in Christ. The Christian needs all three—regularly. Consistency demands that if the Sabbath law is seen as part of the ceremonial which was fulfilled in Christ, then the other nine Commandments must follow. There is no justification for dividing the Ten Commandments in this way.

The only other passage that is brought to bear on the claim that Christ is the fulfilment of the Sabbath Commandment is Hebrews 3 and 4. The warning against the sin of unbelief and disobedience in chapter 3 is based upon the generation of Israelites who died in the wilderness and never entered 'God's rest'. This point is made twice, in vs 11 and 18. Hebrews 4 develops a long argument in which the apostle asserts the future expectation of 'a Sabbath-rest for the people of God' (v 9). The question that commentators discuss is simply this: What is this 'Sabbath-rest'?

When the apostle in verse 3, quotes from Psalm 95:11, the 'rest' that was denied to disobedient Israel was clearly the Promised Land of Canaan. The apostle goes on to argue that when David wrote Psalm 95 he clearly was looking forward to another 'rest' that could be obtained by faith and lost by disobedience; Joshua's eventual entry into the Promised Land was not the final rest or else David would not have written as he did (v 8).

Some maintain that the 'rest' is the final homecoming of the people of God into heaven whilst others see it as our entry into the privileges of a gospel in which we 'rest from our own works' (Hebrews 4:10). Keil and Delitzsch, quoted earlier, see the seventh day as: 'The beginning and type of the rest to which the creation, after it had fallen from fellowship with

God through the sin of man, received a promise that it should once more be restored through redemption, at its final consummation.' In other words, the Sabbath day is a picture not to be fulfilled in redemption (Christ) but in the final consummation (heaven). The strong indication is that Keil and Delitzsch are right, especially in the light of the fact that our 'rest' is compared with God resting from his work in creation (v 10). The comparison is therefore not rest from salvation works, but rest from labour.

However, whichever way we understand the 'rest' that the apostle refers to, two things should be noted: First, Christ is nowhere mentioned as the Sabbath rest in this extended passage; in fact he is not mentioned at all in Hebrews 4 until the apostle is well beyond his treatment of the 'Sabbath-rest'. Second, it is significant that the fourth Commandment is not mentioned either. The nearest reference is to Genesis 2:2. Surely this would be the place to expound Christ as the fulfilment of that Commandment.

My conclusion is that 'God's rest' (Hebrews 4:10) refers to heaven, and that the seventh day in Genesis 2:2, and therefore the Sabbath day of the fourth Commandment will find its glorious fulfilment, not in the gospel, but in the eternal rest of heaven.

Delighting in the day

What is particularly sad in this whole debate is that Christians are not looking at the day as a joyful privilege but as a grudging duty. Possibly the fault for this lies too often with those who try to protect the fourth Commandment by allowing no pleasure and no normal relaxation on the Sabbath: those who take delight only in denying delight and find satisfaction only in the absence of joy! The Christian church has been plagued by misguided miseries for centuries, but that is no argument against the kind plan of God.

This fourth Commandment should be a joy to us. We are not bound to keep the Sabbath for our salvation but we are bound to keep it because of our salvation. I will not earn my salvation by obeying any of these Commandments, but having been saved by the death of Christ on the cross, I delight to keep all of them, even those that run against my convenience at times. When I find any of the Commandments irksome it is either because I have misunderstood the gracious law of God, or because I am trying to break free from it. There is no other reason possible.

The tragedy is that there is a spirit of worldly indiscipline amongst us, so that too often we want to have done with the great benefits that God has given us. We should not need to spend our time discussing what we should and should not do on Sunday. If we are right on the principle and we understand what the day is for, then we are bound to enjoy it. We cannot improve on Isaiah: 'If you keep your feet from breaking the Sabbath and from doing as you please on my holy day, if you call the Sabbath a delight and the Lord's holy day honourable, and if you honour it by not going your own way and not doing as you please or speaking idle words, then you will find your joy in the Lord' (Isaiah 58:13–14).

We must turn to the purpose of this wonderful day.

Chapter 7

The purpose of the Sabbath day

In the Victorian classic, *Black Beauty* spent his declining years working as a cabman's horse in London. The name of the cabby was Jerry Barker. At one point in the story Jerry is talking to a colleague, Larry, about Sunday cabmen who claimed that they could not afford to leave off Sunday work and, besides that, they were needed to take the church-goers 'to hear their favourite preachers.' Jerry Barker's high principle is illustrated in his vigorous defence of Sunday: 'If a thing is right it can be done and if it's wrong it can be done without, and a good man will find a way and that is as true for us cabmen as it is for the church-goers.' That is an excellent principle in this context: 'If a thing is right it can be done, and if it is wrong it can be done without.'

One reason why the fourth Commandment is under attack today, especially by those who ought to be its friends and therefore should find the greatest enjoyment from it, is that too much of the debate centres around what we must not do on Sunday. For those who are agreed on the conclusions of the previous chapter there is little more that needs to be said. Most of the discussion on do and don't, how and why, will be resolved by the wisdom of Jerry Barker: 'If a thing is right it can be done, and if it is wrong it can be done without.' Although there are certainly difficulties in applying this Commandment in a modern, fast-moving, leisure-orientated, and profit-controlled society, I want to focus in this chapter on the positive value of the day.

I suspect the traditionally negative attitude that so many have had toward the use of this special day, plus the complexity of applying the Commandment in a modern age, have both contributed to a felt need of finding a way to avoid its clear implications. This is understandable, but neither wise nor right. After all, which of the Commandments has ever been easy to obey? And in our twenty-first century culture they are all becoming ever harder to keep. I am so convinced of the privileges of this special day that we might even have started at this point. If a trusted friend offers you a good gift, you hardly respond by presenting all the reasons why you should *not* accept it! That would be discourteous and foolish—to say the least. So let's now consider the privileges of keeping Sunday special.

It is a rest day

For many at the end of a hard-working week this may be the most encouraging aspect of the Commandment. Exodus 23:12 elaborates God's plan for the nation; it is an interesting and very full verse: 'Six days do your work, but on the seventh day do not work, so that your ox and your donkey may rest and the slave born in your household, and the alien as well, may be refreshed.' One Hebrew word is used for the phrase 'Do not work', but a different word is used for the reference to the 'rest' of the ox and donkey, and a third word is translated by the slave and alien being 'refreshed'. Three different words are therefore used to describe what happens on the Sabbath day.

The master is not to do any work. The verb forms the root of our noun 'Sabbath', and the word Sabbath means 'rest'. The estate owner must rest presumably for three reasons: in doing so he can fulfil the purpose of the Commandment in his own life; he will also set a good example to those who work for him; and thirdly, there will be no need for his servants to work since if he worked, they would have to as well.

The animals are also to 'rest'. This is not the word for Sabbath but a different word which means they are to settle down and be quiet. Animals used for carrying burdens or hauling a plough are to be set free simply to spend one whole day grazing. When God placed mankind in charge of creation he did not expect this to result in abuse and cruelty: 'A righteous man cares for the needs of his animals' (Proverbs 12:10). There is a significant principle involved in this instruction regarding the animals. Their inclusion in this part of the Sabbath day purpose shows how all-embracing God intended the 'rest' to be. Certainly the animals would not benefit from a reminder of the spiritual purposes of the day, but the wise Creator indicates that the principle of rest is vital for every living creature under the control of man. The 'beasts of burden' were not simply to be left tethered and waiting for the next day. The word implies that they are allowed to settle and be quiet; it carries the idea of grazing at leisure.

The servants and the visitor are to be 'refreshed'. The word used here is the strongest of all. It comes from a root meaning breath, life or soul. It is as if God is saying, 'Let your servants take a breath; let them be rejuvenated; let them rest on that day so that new life comes into their body and they are ready for the next six days of hard work.' Once again, it is a demand that is intended for our good.

The cycle of one rest-day in seven has a physical benefit that is of value for its own sake. This is one reason why Christians should insist that governments allow for a national day of rest, so that even those who have no intention of using the day for worship will at least benefit from one part of God's good plan for mankind. This day has social as well as religious benefits.

Sadly, a society which could benefit so much by observing this Commandment has squandered the opportunity by insisting upon its right to work a seven-day week. That is not freedom but slavery, and governments would be well advised not to ignore the wisdom of God by violating his beneficial laws. Four hundred years before Christ was born, Nehemiah took strong action to close down the Sabbath market in Jerusalem. In guarding the Jews against a violation of the fourth Commandment, he also forced a day of rest on the non-Jewish traders and their animals (Nehemiah 13).

It is a memorial day

For the Jew in the Old Testament the Sabbath was a day to call to mind two particular acts of God. The first was creation and the second was redemption. In Exodus 20:11 the people were told to observe this day: 'For in six days the LORD made the heavens and the earth, the sea, and all that is in them.' This was reinforced in Exodus 31:16–17.

A Sunday ought never to pass without the Christian acknowledging God as Creator, both in private and, where possible, in public worship. This is probably more relevant today than ever before, in a society of advanced technology. In our bid to elevate man's achievements and self-sufficiency, we are in danger of forgetting the simplicity of creation and our total dependence upon the Creator. The warning in Deuteronomy 8:11,17 stands for both Jew and Gentile: 'Be careful that you do not forget the LORD your God, failing to observe his commands, his laws and his decrees... You may say to yourself, "My power and the strength of my hands have produced this wealth for me."'

If a reminder of creation was necessary for a people wandering under the desert stars and wholly dependant upon God for their necessities of life, how much more is it necessary today. As we have drifted from bothering with 'the Lord's day', so we have lost a vital weekly reminder of our total dependence and significant insignificance.

Much of modern worship is focused upon personal experience and expressions of affection for Christ. These are good themes and should never be absent in our approach to God, but our concern for God's presence *now*, often overlooks the fact that he is beyond us; our desire for an experience of his immanence has sadly blocked our appreciation of his transcendence. Christian worship should always be grounded in the adoration of an awesome and holy Creator. Our songs and psalms should reflect this as a prelude to any focus upon redemption and the response of love. We are in danger of forgetting that the Christian's privilege is not only to know Christ, however glorious that is, but to know the Father. That, after all, is why Christ came. Our Lord taught his disciples to begin their prayers by addressing, 'Our Father in heaven' (Matthew 6:9), and he himself prayed, 'This is eternal life: that they may know you, the only true God, and Jesus Christ, whom you have sent' (John 17:3).

The Sabbath was also a day in which to remember that God had redeemed his people. When the law was repeated in Deuteronomy, a significant addition was made to this particular Commandment: 'Remember that you were slaves in Egypt and that the LORD your God brought you out of there with a mighty hand and outstretched arm' (Deuteronomy 5:15). On this day we should focus on the God of creation and on the God of redemption—in that order. Redemption is never understood in its full glory unless we appreciate the character of the God who hates sin, yet becomes the friend of the sinner.

Deliverance from Egypt was gained at the blood cost of the first-born throughout the land, and God set aside one special day for the people to remember this. Of course it was possible for them to remember the mercy of God on any day and at any time, but knowing human weakness God set aside a particular day for his people to be in 'recall mode'. In the same way we can remember the cross at any time, but our Lord established a simple supper to put us in mind of his sacrifice of redemption. So, does the Lord's Supper take the place of the Sabbath? Of course not. Both the Day of Atonement and the Passover sacrifice reminded the Israelite of his redemption from Egypt and from sin, but in addition God used the Sabbath as a memory aid. When the master set his animals out to graze and his servants free from work, he was to recall that that is exactly what God had done for him.

We discussed in the previous chapter the reasons for the Christian change from the Jewish Sabbath to the 'Lord's day'. On this day the Christian is reminded that our God is the God of the resurrection. On the Lord's day Christ rose again from the dead; he is therefore the powerful Lord and Sovereign over death and hell and sin. Because God intended that it should be a day of rest and a day of recall we should spend almost no time arguing about what we should and should not do on this day, and most time using the day for its great purpose of remembering the God of creation and of redemption. The first day of the week was also the day on which the Holy Spirit was given to the church. Pentecost, according to Leviticus 23:15–16, fell on 'the day after the Sabbath'—the first day of the week. God had planned a special celebration day for the Christian church back in the early days of Israel's history.

It is a worship day

The purpose of this day is both for rest and worship; but the Jew saw no real distinction between those two activities. Rest enabled the day to be set aside as a special day for worship.

We saw in the previous chapter that this day also points us to the ultimate eternal rest in heaven (Hebrews 4:9)—the glorious rest that awaits those who are trusting in Christ. Therefore, like one aspect of the Lord's Supper, this day is pointing forward. It reminds us that there is going to be an eternal rest in heaven, but not just a sitting at ease; the Sabbath, like eternal heaven, is primarily for the worship of God.

On this day, through our memory we can aid our soul. Numbers 28:9–10 reveals specific requirements for the Sabbath day. The normal daily offering is given in verse 3, 'two lambs a year old and without defect' but in verse 9 we are told of the Sabbath offering: 'On the Sabbath day, make an offering of two lambs a year old without defect, together with its drink offering and a grain offering... *in addition* to the regular burnt offering and its drink offering.' In other words, on the Sabbath the Israelites doubled their worship. This meant, of course, that the Levites and the priests had to work double-time on the Lord's day. Incidentally, there is no command in the Old Testament that the priests should have another day off in lieu! The reason for this is that God considered true worship to be rejuvenating not enervating.

We must not miss the important principle here that worship was to be based upon the response of an active mind. When God called his people to 'remember' and then turned their minds back to creation and redemption his purpose was clear: he intended his people to worship, but not in the mindless ecstasy 'enjoyed' by the religions of the surrounding nations; rather his people were to worship with a mind that was alert and constantly recalling the character of the God they approached. To lay aside our mind in worship is never acceptable to God; true worship should always begin with the mind and flow into the heart. To be encouraged to 'empty our mind' is wholly unbiblical. Our Lord defined worship as 'in spirit and in truth' (John 4:24). True worship in both the Old and New Testaments is the intelligent response of an active mind to the character of a holy God.

Since worship is such a great privilege, it is hard to understand why some Christians struggle to edge their way out of the 'restrictions' of this fourth Commandment. If God has given us a command that is intended to allow us more time to spend in worship, why should we ever want to take less time? The Israelite whose heart was right counted the day as one of great joy, and only those who wanted to do as they pleased considered the whole thing an intolerable burden (Isaiah 58:13–14). Finding our 'joy in the LORD', riding 'on the heights of the land', and feasting 'on the inheritance of your father Jacob' is surely Isaiah's Old Testament language for the privilege of enjoying God in friendship through adoration and worship. However busy we may be during the week, and however diligently we bring our 'daily offerings' to him, on the Lord's day we have more time to worship.

Shortly before he was posted to the Crimea in 1854, Captain Hedley Vicars of the 97th Regiment wrote a letter to a friend expressing his enjoyment of Sunday. The language may be 'quaint' for a modern reader but the sentiment is real: 'I remember, alas! too well, the time when I dreaded the return of Sunday and considered it both dull and tedious, but now surely no day is so cheering and delightful; and there is none that passes away so quickly. I recollect that for several months the only inward sanctifying proof I could, on examination, bring to assure myself that I had indeed been made an "heir of Christ", was this longing desire for the Lord's day.' Vicars, who died in his first battle, wrote the same way from the mud-filled trenches before Sebastapol. Something has happened to our life with God and his people, or to our understanding of the purpose of this day, when we do not feel like this soldier did.

For the Israelite then, the day was a day of rest, a memory aid, and a day of worship. It included his body, mind and soul. But it was never allowed to be just one of these three; it had to be all of them together. Each one is inter-related to the others.

Never say 'ought'?

Some Christians say that we shouldn't do anything simply because we must, but only as the Spirit leads us; in other words, we ought never to say 'ought'. Is that how we get out of bed in the morning? Is it never because it is the right thing to do—or because of what the boss will say if we are three hours late? That is a disciplined habit. It is unquestionably right for Christians to do things because they are right—whether they feel like it or not. For the Christian there is both an obligation and an opportunity in keeping the Lord's day special. The obligation comes from the Commandment. We cannot escape it. It is there in the Scripture from the pattern at Creation to 'the Lord's day' in Revelation. It was reinforced at Sinai.

But the fourth Commandment is also an opportunity. If the obligation comes from law, the opportunity comes from grace. It is a day to refresh ourselves, not in idleness but in worship: worshipping the Creator for the covenant and his salvation, meeting together with God's people and gaining all the benefits that we ought to find in that. Just as the Israelite remembered Egypt and the Passover and their deliverance from slavery, so the Christian remembers the Saviour dying on Calvary, rising again from the dead, giving us new life and salvation through his Holy Spirit. Never should a Sunday pass by without our minds turning to Christ and the cross and our hearts responding with a deep sense of indebtedness to him for all that he achieved on Calvary in order to bring us into fellowship with the Father.

That is our privilege on Sunday. It is a day specially set apart. How many times do we consciously stop from Monday to Saturday and thank God and worship him as the Creator and Saviour? How often do we think of Calvary and worship Christ for what he did on the cross? We have to admit to being often so hassled, busy and distracted that we hardly have a moment to think about God's word, and there is little time to pray.

In this fast-moving world when the demand of our employment daily sucks us into the frustration of our journey into the office, classroom or factory as part of the earth's digestive commuter system, we never seem to be able to accomplish the things we set out to do. We enter each new week with a backlog from the previous week. Any talk about spending time worshipping the Creator, approaching Calvary and pouring out our heart in indebtedness to him seems to be so far away from the realities of Monday to Friday. This is precisely why God has given us this special day. Thank God for Sunday because if nothing else it should make us stop and worship. That is why the day is as necessary now as it ever was.

But for the Christian alone?

We have already seen in chapter two that the law of God was intended for both the law-keepers and the law-breakers; for both Israel and the nations. To imagine that the Sabbath was simply part of the special covenant with Israel intended to mark them out as different from the surrounding nations, fails to appreciate that God has a claim upon the worship of all men and women everywhere, and that in his grace he has included in his moral law a facility to encourage this. The Sabbath was a recognition not only that Israel was to be different—though they were—but that the whole human race needs this special provision designed to call society to remember and worship.

The nations may ignore this Commandment just as they do many of the others. They may even legislate against it, but the fact remains that it is part of God's general grace to the whole of fallen humanity. Are Christians alone in living under an obligation and privilege to remember their Creator, to recall his mercy in the offer of redemption, to worship him in sincerity, and to take time out to do all this? And if they are not, how can we suggest that this great gift of the Sabbath was not intended for the benefit of the nations beyond Israel—just as the other Commandments certainly were.

Using the day wisely

How then are we going to use this day properly? John Wesley, the powerful 18th century evangelist, was once asked by a lady whether or not she should go to the theatre on Sunday. Wesley avoided a direct answer and instead turned her attention to the greater issue: 'Madam, you need only ask, "What is the purpose of the Sabbath?"' So long as we fulfil the whole purpose of the Lord's day we can surely do anything! The reason why some are against observing the fourth Commandment is because they have a false view of the Christian's relationship to the law of God. This day should be a joy to us. None of these commands are made for our misery, but for our freedom and encouragement.

It is only the disobedient Christian who tries to reason a way out of the seventh Commandment—and isn't the same true of the fourth? Remember that God not only set apart the seventh day but he 'made it holy' (Genesis 2:3 and Exodus 20:11); that word 'holy' means separate and different from the commonplace, and that surely cannot be a bad thing. It means that God intended something special for this day and he promised that those who keep it special would benefit from it. If we constantly keep in mind the purpose of this wonderful day then we will know how to celebrate it and how to use it. It is a day for rest, memory and worship, for body, mind and soul.

So, how can we be careful to keep this day special?

First of all, by careful preparation.

Before any important event—a wedding, a social occasion or a job interview—most people spend time getting ready, and they leave sufficient time not to arrive late. If this day is so important should we not prepare for it? It is significant that the Jewish Sabbath actually started at six o'clock on Friday evening and ran through to six o'clock on Saturday evening. For us, Saturday evening ought as far as possible to be a preparation evening; we should do whatever work is reasonable in order to avoid all unnecessary work on the special day. Without running into the Pharisaic danger of a ridiculous slavery to legalism, there are surely many things we can do on Saturday to leave us free from the clutter of the world on Sunday.

We should not keep Sunday free so that we can smugly tick off the rules we have obeyed and list the things we are not doing, but so that, as far as is possible in our modern society, we can spend a day apart from our regular involvement in the world; this will give us time for resting, remembering and worshipping. This is why we may choose to prepare our meals on Saturday, and refrain from the household chores and shopping that have occupied us during the week; and why the student will finish revision and write-up the assignment by Saturday evening.

John Paton was a missionary to the Indians on the island of Aniwa in the Pacific in the middle of the nineteenth century. When some of them were converted to Christ, Paton commented that life on the island was changed as the people's lives and habits were transformed. Among the changes he observed was that Saturday became known by the tribes-people as 'cooking day' because all the cooking was done on Saturday so that when Sunday dawned they could spend more time in the place of worship. There was nothing new in this; God had made provision for the Israelites in the wilderness by providing double the quantity of manna on the day before the Sabbath, and by prohibiting cooking on the Sabbath (Exodus 16:22–23). Cooking for them would have been more of a 'chore' than it is for us with our microwaves and ovens, but we can still prepare in every way possible so that there is less for us to do on Sunday.

We prepare for Sunday by a reasonable night's rest. To be up until the early hours of Sunday morning means that we will never be fit for the worship of God later in the day. We will prepare also by getting up on Sunday morning at a sensible time and by an unhurried and early arrival at church. To rush into a congregation five minutes late is hardly preparation for the benefits of this special day. The day is not intended to be one of idleness but of rest; there is a world of difference between the two. Rest rejuvenates and recreates, whereas lying in bed for half the day achieves nothing positive for the mind, soul or body.

A disciplined mind is needed to use the day as God intended. We may not actually go to work on Sunday, but to spend the day with our mind poring over the problems of the coming week is no more obedient to the command of God than if we had gone to work; our minds are muddled and busy about other things. Surely the best preparation is to pray *before* we arrive at church so that we are ready to hear what God has to say through his word.

Secondly, by disciplined habits

Our Lord went to the synagogue on a Sabbath day 'as was his custom' (Luke 4:16). A good individual and family habit is to be regularly at the house of God when God's people meet together. Only illness should be allowed to interrupt it. Not tiredness or business, or pleasure and leisure. Some Christians have more grit than others, but if we absent ourselves because we are too tired then we should go to bed at a reasonable hour. Otherwise we are robbing both God and his people.

I have met Christians who, strangely, do not go to church when they are on holiday or when relatives or friends call unexpectedly. Far from exercising their Christian 'freedom' they are revealing that Sunday is a great bore and that it is good to have an excuse for a 'day off'. I wonder if these Christians were intending to watch their team playing on Saturday afternoon when friends arrived, whether those friends would either join them at the match or be hurried on their way!

Henry Martyn went out to serve God in India during the middle of the nineteenth century and he died on his way home, alone and somewhere in Persia. Martyn penned these words in his diary: 'We may judge by our regard for the Sabbath whether eternity will be forced upon us or not.' He is right. Christians who long for eternity want to be as near eternity as they can be and as often as they can be; whatever will help them to think about eternity—they want to be part of it. The opposite is also true; those who see nothing of value in eternity will not want to be near to eternity here on earth. Surely anything that can distract the mind from being constantly absorbed with this world and can direct it to the realities of heaven must be very attractive to those whose citizenship is in heaven. For this reason the response of the Israelites in the Old Testament to the fourth Commandment was a barometer of the people's love for God. It still is. The regular meeting together is a good habit (Hebrews 10:25).

Thirdly, by wise use

We must not legislate for each other. God has given us the law, and both our Lord and the apostle Paul warned against adding human regulations to that. Each person must be persuaded before God on the detail. Some will not answer the telephone on Sunday, use electricity, travel in a car, kick a ball, go for a walk or swim in the sea. We should never mock those who have strong personal convictions concerning what they should and should not do on the Lord's day. However, they must not make laws about these things for others. We must all ensure that the day is used for the purpose of resting, remembering and worshipping in such a way that it becomes a day to delight in the Lord. Clearly as far as possible we should put aside all our daily work. To immerse ourselves in reports, newspapers and videos that fill our minds with the business or values of this world will not be using the day as God intended. These things may not be wrong, and many of them will occupy us from Monday through the week, but our purpose must surely be to clear our minds for God on this day. It is the purpose that is all important, not the obedience to regulations.

The Puritan Thomas Watson urged his readers in their preparation for Sunday, 'Having dressed your bodies, you must dress your souls for hearing the word of God'. Some Christians choose to have a 'no television day', not only because studies have demonstrated that television is a poor way to relax, but because to have a mind filled with television ads and media images is hardly the way to approach a holy God and to hear him speaking through his word. To make that kind of personal decision is not 'narrow-minded legalism' but the refreshing liberty of a heart in search of God.

In many evangelical churches family life is disrupted on Sunday and children actually see less of their parents—particularly their father—than they do during the week. This cannot be right and is certainly a violation of the purpose of the law of God. He has kindly planned for a rest that is both refreshing and allows the family to be together. Families should make every effort to ensure that this is a special day.

If Sunday is boring for our children it is generally not the church that is to blame—that may take up less than three hours of the day. But how do we spend the remainder of our time? It is not hard to make Sunday a different day for the family and to do things together for a change. Certainly many evangelical churches would do well to reassess their programme of Sunday activities to make sure that families do have time to be together and not to so overload the day with 'spiritual' activities that the three-fold purpose is lost under the heavyweight of Christian busyness. A little imagination and freedom from traditional, but unbiblical, taboos will both guard the day and treat it as a delight (Isaiah 58:13–14). However, neither sport nor any other recreation should interfere with the primary purpose of a day of seeking and finding God.

We should not make others work unnecessarily either. No Christian has to shop on Sunday. That is wholly unfair to those who have to serve us; whether they recognise that or not doesn't matter. Far from it being an expression of Christian 'freedom', it is a mark of being enslaved by the values and mindset of our post-Christian world. Business can cease for one day. Many have proved this: a modern nation like Germany, and others across Europe, have found little hardship in closing all shops from midday on Saturday. Driving through the Czech Republic a few years ago we stopped at a fair sized country town and were amazed to discover the neat and clean shopping centre almost deserted; then we realised it was Saturday afternoon—it was as if Sunday had already begun. Centuries earlier the prophet Jeremiah and the governor Nehemiah both insisted that the best use of the Sabbath was to stop the daily round of business (Jeremiah 17:19–27 and Nehemiah 13:15–22).

Pastoral dilemmas

We have to come to terms with the fact that the option of refusing to take a job that demands some Sunday working is gradually coming to an end. Already the retail trade has virtually locked out the Christian who refuses ever to work on Sunday. For a long time industries have worked a seven-day rota, in some cases unavoidably because of the nature of the equipment used.

Our Lord sanctioned necessary labour. In our pagan, post-Christian society the edges are often blurred and we are compelled to do things that we would not do from preference. There are times when in our employment we have no option but to work on the Lord's day. We are not living in the 'theocracy' of Moses' day when God's laws were the only ones for society. The first century Christians were not in this privileged position either. The Christian slave was not able to say to his master: 'Excuse me boss, but I am a Christian now, so you will need to roster someone else for Sundays. I will be in the catacombs for worship.' As a matter of fact Christians *are* often still able to make that sort of demand—and where they can, they should—but how long this freedom will last is debatable. We must be prepared for the dilemma that forces us to choose between occasional Sunday work and no work at all. As we have seen, the first century Christians met early in the morning—before work—and continued this way until the Sunday laws of Constantine in AD 321.

The newsletter of an evangelical pastor included this item: 'We still have many of our men who have to travel abroad on business regularly. A few Sundays ago we had five of them away (in four different continents of the world). Not only do they miss out on continuity of the teaching, but their wives cannot attend the evening service or the mid-week meetings when they are away. Our two policemen still only have one whole Sunday off a month; and other people have to work either on Sundays or all night on Saturday.' That is becoming typical. Businessmen are not infrequently expected to travel on Sunday in order to be ready for an early appointment on Monday, and few companies will be prepared to pay for a hotel room for the Saturday as well. Besides, airline and hotel staff work on Sunday for Christians in business or on holiday.

These are pastoral issues that compel us to face, not the principle of the abiding obligation of the fourth Commandment—that is clear as we have seen—but the application of that principle in a modern society.

When we have the choice of working on Sunday or not, then our duty is clear, but many are faced with the choice of accepting employment that demands Sunday working, or of remaining unemployed and therefore expecting the state to support their family. In some countries the option is even more stark since there will be no state aid as an alternative. We cannot be the conscience of another man or woman in these dilemmas. Remember the first century slaves and the fact that our Lord softened the law with grace. But remember too the advice of Jerry Barker: 'If a thing is right it can be done, and if it is wrong it can be done without.' Balancing these two perspectives is often hard. But this is not the only Commandment that presents dilemmas in a modern world. The Christian child ordered to shop on a Sunday by unbelieving parents may consider that it is faced with the straight decision of choosing between Commandments four and five!

'Call the Sabbath a delight'

John Paton tells us that on the island of Aniwa he used to call Sunday 'the day for Jehovah'. This day is still 'The Lord's day' and the fourth Commandment is no less for our good than any one of the other nine. It is not a day on which we can do just as we please, and yet we *can* do as we please providing that all we do fulfils the triple purpose of rest, remembering and worship. It is an 'honourable day' (Isaiah 58:13), a day to be honoured; it is also a 'holy' day, set apart as different and special; and it is a 'delight'—a day to be delightfully enjoyed. Isaiah 58:13 reflects the New Testament approach to this day. With all the stern warnings of God to his people concerning this day, he never intended them to keep it just because of the penalties incurred for failure, but because of the benefit to be harvested by its observance. In that sense God's concern for the day and his plan for the day has not changed. It is the day to follow the Creator's good example. On this day he enjoyed the fruit of his creation—and it was very good. It is not the day to dig the garden, clean the car, paint the house or work for the family—rather it is the day to enjoy all these good things.

Stripped of unnecessary labour and excessive leisure, the Lord's day is ready to be employed for the maximum benefit. The ideal use of this day is to spend time with God's people in worship and ministry so that we have turned our hearts towards our Creator and Redeemer; and our minds towards his word so that we have listened to his voice and have stored up truth and practice for another week ahead. We will also have time to relax and refresh our bodies whether alone or with a family. But we cannot be one another's conscience in the detail of this. Anything is legitimate, providing that it is governed by the purpose of this day, and that we do not expect others to work unnecessarily for our leisure. It must surely also be a day for good works whether in evangelism or visiting the sick and needy.

Like all of God's Commandments, the fourth is intended for our freedom and joy. Freedom is not necessarily freedom to do what we want, but freedom to do what we were created to do and freedom to be what we are meant to be. Those who destroy this day by ignoring it altogether, or who blunt the force of the Commandment by softening its relevance, are no better than those who destroy it by the addition of human regulations. Rebellion and legalism are incompatible twins. To embrace this fourth Commandment equally with all the others and call its observance our joy and delight, *that* is truly Christian.

Honouring parents

Honour your father and your mother. Exodus 20:12

Something has gone wrong in our homes. In 1994 ten thousand schoolgirls became pregnant, thirty thousand children were added to the child protection register in England alone, and one hundred thousand ran away from home or from care. Perhaps none of this is surprising when we consider that one hundred and fifty thousand children and young people were affected by their parents' divorce in that year.

The United Nations' Universal Declaration of Human Rights, drawn up in 1948, stated clearly that 'the family is the natural and fundamental group unit of society.' How far we have travelled since then was illustrated by the agenda at the United Nations Fourth World Conference on Women held in Beijing in September 1995. Motherhood was virtually overlooked in favour of the role of women in politics and business; the aim was for women to achieve fifty percent representation on political and economic bodies, with no thought of the consequences of the radical shift in motherhood and homemaking that this would demand. The international right of women to abort their children was also high on the agenda. No one tabled the right of women to be women, or babies to live.

The Ten Commandments are the standard that God has given as an expression of his unchangeable moral law. They are a marker for those who are 'perfecting holiness out of reverence for God' (2 Corinthians 7:1). The first three Commandments are concerned with our relationship with God, because this relationship is absolutely essential. Society almost totally ignores this and focuses instead upon inter-personal relationships; it is thought that if only men and women could live in harmony then societies could do the same, and if societies could, then nations could also. The logic is sound but the theology is flawed. All the problems on earth stem from the original breakdown in mankind's relationship with God. This is why the first three Commandments are concerned with our relationship with God. They state the Creator's priority. God must come first.

We described the fourth Commandment as a transition, a bridge: it moves us from our relationship with God to our relationship with one another. Whilst it is primarily concerned for our relationship with God himself, we are to make sure that our relationships with others are right as well—for this reason the employer is to ensure not only that *he* has one day for worship and rest but that his servants and visitors have the same.

Why is this Commandment next?

If we were asked to unscramble the Ten Commandments and put them in some kind of order I have little doubt that most of us would get the first three about right. Depending upon our tradition we might put the fourth Commandment next—or last! But where would we go after the fourth commandment? Which one would follow?

Some would opt for the command: 'You shall not murder' because it is so fundamental. Murder is a direct attack on the image of God. Men and women were made in the likeness of God and by their human reason, conscience, morality and capacity to worship, they reflect their Creator. Murder is therefore an assault upon God's image in mankind and it involves the destruction of God's apex of creation.

Others would doubtless give a high priority to 'You shall not commit adultery'. That surely is an attack upon the very first relationship God created when he made the world—the relationship between a husband and a wife. God gave a man and a woman to each other in that unbreakable bond called marriage. That also would be a fair conclusion, because to violate this relationship is to strike at an important foundation of society. Besides, we must never under any circumstances commit adultery, but we cannot always and in every circumstance honour our parents. How could the daughter of Joseph Stalin honour her father in the light of his massive crime of genocide?

The fifth Commandment is probably not where we would place it, but it does happen to be where God put it—and that is at least intriguing, if not instructive. If God considered it ought to be the first check upon human relationships, then that must surely reveal something of God's ordering of society. Here is a relationship that in God's sight is so vital that he lists it before the relationship of a husband and wife and even before the sin of murder. But why?

FIRST, BECAUSE EVERYONE IS PART OF A FAMILY!

We may not live with our family, or like it or even know it, but we were born as part of it. We may not have a wife or a husband or children, but we all have parents, whether they are now dead or alive. There are no exceptions to this and there never has been, not even the incarnate Son of God avoided this. The relationship of child to parent is the one relationship—and the only one—that is true of us all. However brief or bad the relationship, it is a universal condition. For good or for ill we all have parents. So the child-parent relationship is the only factor common to everyone in society and to every society in human history. A marriage can exist without children, and children can exist without a marriage, but we all have to have a mother and a father to exist at all! That is true even in the age of surrogacy, IVF, AID, cloning and whatever else. There still must be a father and a mother. In the light of the uncertainty as to when Christ will come again we cannot even claim that we will all die, so there is nothing else that is true of everyone without exception.

Most governments acknowledge that the family is the foundational unit in society and many therefore make encouraging sounds about the importance of the family. Sadly, however, many are actively supporting the very measures that are rapidly eroding the fabric that should protect the family unit. Divorce is made faster and easier, disciplining children is likely to be taken out of the hands of parents if EPOCH (End Physical Punishment of Children) eventually has its way, the removal of Sunday protection now makes it an almost impossible family day for many households, mothers are enticed and intimidated back to work by generous provision of nursery care, and little is done to stem the tide of violence, filth and blasphemy that pours into our homes through the television. No wonder so many of our children have grown wild and uncontrollable. A politician who was watching the trends of the times wrote, 'Domestic life and domestic discipline must soon be at an end; society will consist of individuals no longer grouped into families; so early is the separation of husband and wife, of parents and children.' That was not published in a recent letter column of *The Times* but in the mid-nineteenth century by Lord Ashley—the renowned Earl of Shaftesbury.

The fifth Commandment establishes God's clear priority of the family as ideally the basic and most stable unit in our society. We have ignored this and are therefore reaping the whirlwind. The tragic statistics with which we opened this chapter did not include juvenile crime, but they certainly prepare the way for it. Sociologists may write of 'a web of relationship' when they really mean dysfunctional families. The truth is that the most serious moral decline in a nation is when parents lose control of their children and when children no longer respect their parents.

SECONDLY, BECAUSE OBEDIENCE TO PARENTS APPLIES TO THREE GENERATIONS AT THE SAME TIME

Faithfulness between a husband and a wife is vital but it applies to only one generation and for one life. Obedience to the seventh Commandment is between two people and no more; of course its breach affects many more than just the husband and wife involved, but the command is only addressed to two people of one generation. On the other hand obedience to parents is much wider in scope because it always affects at least three generations: grandparents, parents and children. In Bible times it could be many more. They are living generations: Children to parents and parents to the grandparents.

In the Old Testament there could be four or five generations alive at the same time; and again today we have an increasing number of great, great grandparents. This is therefore the largest and the longest human relationship. A couple were reported recently to be celebrating their seventieth wedding anniversary; that must be close to the limit! But the parent/child relationship can continue much longer than that. The husband/wife relationship is broken by death after half a century or a little more at the most. But even when one parent/child relationship is broken by death there is usually an ongoing relationship through the next generation of children and grandchildren.

In the Hebrew of the Old Testament there is no word for grandchildren, grandson, granddaughter, grandparents, grandfather or grandmother. For this reason the words 'father' and 'mother' can refer back a long way. In 2 Chronicles 29:2 we are told that Hezekiah 'Did what was right in the eyes of the LORD just as his father David had done.' In fact Hezekiah was fourteen generations down the line from David. So the only other way that relationship could have been described in the Old Testament was to say that

Hezekiah did what was right in the eyes of the LORD 'just as David had done seventeen generations before'. That would have been clumsy to say the least, so the word 'father' stands alone and the readers are left to fill in the gaps. Incidentally, the use of the word 'forefathers' in modern translations (and once in the *Authorised Version*) is simply a translation of the word 'fathers' when it refers to generations reaching into the past.

You can therefore see how big the phrase is. 'Father and mother' is more than a reference to the man and woman who were humanly responsible for bringing you into the world, though it will have a primary reference to them. In this Commandment God has drawn our attention to the longest, fullest and most lasting relationship in human experience. Even more so than the relationship of husband and wife. The fifth Commandment is not only a reference to parents, but it would remind the Israelite of the honourable line of his forefathers.

Significantly, although Hebrew has no word for the grandparent/ grandchild relationship, it is rich in words expressing the development of a child. There are no fewer than eight words to describe the growth of the young child from the baby in the womb and newly born (*yeleth*), to the suckling child (*yonek*), the child asking for food (*olel*), weaned (*gamul*), clinging to its mother (*taph*), becoming firm (*elem*), shaking itself free (*naar*), and finally the ripened one (*bachur*). God's deep and lasting concern for children and their relationship to their parents is revealed frequently, not least in Deuteronomy 6:4–9, Nehemiah 8:2–3 and 2 Timothy 3:15.

THIRDLY , BECAUSE THE HOME IS A CHILD'S FIRST ENCOUNTER WITH AUTHORITY
In the summer of 1996 a group of young elephants was taken from the Kruger National Park in South Africa to the reserve at Pilanesburg just twenty kilometres from Sun City. Before long the small herd had become delinquents—ripping trees, attacking tourist cars and even threatening the rangers. The reason for this aggressive behaviour, which led to at least one animal having to be shot, was the fact that they had been taken too early from their parents. If young elephants do not have a role-model in their adults they will become violent as they develop; the older animals will teach their siblings discipline and the rule of authority.

In the family God puts the husband as the head of the home (Ephesians 5:22–28; 1 Peter 3:1–7) and the parents jointly as head of the children (Ephesians 6:1–3). It is in the home that God expects basic Christian and moral teaching to be given (Deuteronomy 6:4–9 and 2 Timothy 3:14–15). When we are born we enter a world of authority and our first introduction to it is our parents. Clearly if this relationship goes wrong then our society goes wrong. This is precisely why we have a society today that is violent and disobedient. Disobedience in the home leads to a despising of authority in all its forms, and obedience in the home leads to respect for old age, respect for civil authority, and respect for Christian leadership.

The encounter of the child with the authority, or lack of it, in the home, leaves an indelible impression. God wants to teach the need for authority and submission to authority and he does so in the home through parents. God has made it clear that in the whole of society—in the family, the state, industry, the church, the school, in fact wherever we are—he has ordained authority; he has a line of relationship. This is all part of God's plan. Because men and women are sinful by nature there must always be those who lead and those who are led; those who obey and those who give orders.

A few years ago statistics revealed that in just under two thousand schools around the United Kingdom there were six thousand violent acts and thirty-seven thousand disruptions. Teaching is tougher today than it has ever been: children are no longer aware of the lines of authority and will respond to those in authority in a way that at one time would not have been tolerated. God starts with the parent/child relationship because this is the relationship in which authority begins. We should learn a lesson from the elephants: a role model in the family is vital for future stable development.

FOURTHLY, BECAUSE THE CHILD IS THE MAN

In a different context Samuel Taylor Coleridge wrote, 'In today already walks tomorrow.' If a child starts right, then there is a fair possibility that the adult will be right as well. And when that man or woman becomes a parent, then that parent will be right also. That is why in Proverbs 22:6 God gives a general principle to parents: 'Train a child in the way he should go, and when he is old he will not turn from it.' Though that general rule may sometimes be broken it is a principle that must always be followed.

Today one in every six young people in the United Kingdom lives in London—and many live alone because they have already turned their back decisively against the parental home. Children are born with a sinful nature and they behave sinfully. Any honest parent will agree with Proverbs 20:11, 'Even a child is known by his actions, by whether his conduct is pure and right.' Erasmus, the sixteenth century Dutch theologian, wrote to one of his students: 'Remember nothing passes away so rapidly as youth.' If we learn to respond to authority in infancy, there is a high possibility that we will follow through in childhood, teen years and in youth. But childhood and youth passes rapidly and the window of opportunity to instil the right principles into the lives of our children becomes smaller with each generation. A century ago a young man in his twenties or thirties would still defer to his father's opinion for such major decisions as marriage and career.

You can see why God places this Commandment first in his list of human relationships. It is a vital relationship. That brings us naturally to the next question.

What does it mean to honour our father and mother?
FIRST OF ALL 'HONOUR' MEANS TO VALUE OR RESPECT

There is nothing complicated about the word. The reference is to our natural parents or the guardian who stands in the place of our natural parents. Parents are to be given respect. God does not make any distinction. He does not say, 'Honour your father and mother if they deserve it.' God intends us to honour our parents because they are our parents. Even if their life cannot be copied, they are to be honoured.

In all his rules for ordering society, God never allowed the character of the leader to govern his right to lead, or the obligation of the subjects to obey him. That was just as true when Peter urged the Christians scattered across the Roman Empire through persecution to 'submit to every authority instituted among men... and honour the king' (1 Peter 2:13–17); the apostle was painfully aware that the 'king' was Nero—the 'mad butcher of Rome'—but Nero was nevertheless the legitimate head of state and only if he ordered the Christians to act contrary to their higher commitment to

God were his laws to be disobeyed. The same principle holds for the honour children should have towards their parents. In fact the daughter of Joseph Stalin did have a responsibility to honour her father, not for the evil that he committed, but for the fact that he was her father. Paul urged children to 'obey your parents in everything, for this pleases the Lord' (Colossians 3:20)—and he added no qualification.

I stood in the inevitable post office queue when an elderly man ahead of me was collecting his pension and that of his wife. The counter clerk returned the wife's book with an apology: 'I am sorry, your wife hasn't signed it'. The immediate response of the husband was: 'The silly old cow'. That went through me like a knife. If that was the way he spoke of her in public I dreaded to think what he said to her in the home. Exactly the same is true of the way children speak of their parents. And, remember, children may be of any age. Honour is shown in our attitude to our parents. It is the way we think about them, behave towards them and speak of them and to them. The young person who refers to his parents as, 'the old man' or 'the old woman' is betraying what he really thinks.

The cool business-man in the boardroom can be a monster in the home; the patiently smiling pastor can be irritably unkind to his family. The children of a manse revealed all when one of them suggested to their father as they prepared for church one Sunday morning: 'I know, let's do something really different today. Let's be ratty to them and nice to us.' And it is just because the home is the hardest place to maintain consistent respect for each other that God places the marker there. This value and respect should begin in the home because that is the hardest place of all to maintain it consistently. In the home we are all at our most vulnerable. Children generally behave worse in the home than outside, and so do parents! If children learn to honour their parents and grandparents by the example and discipline of the home then they will be well placed to honour all people in society. That is a vital lesson.

An elderly Christian friend of mine was openly mocked by his adult children; it was tragic for him but I believe it was even more tragic for his grandchildren since they grew up learning to hold their grandfather in total disrespect. This would inevitably spill over into their attitude to their own father and mother and beyond this into their attitude to others—especially the elderly. The lack of respect for age in our contemporary society is the direct result of a widespread violation of the fifth Commandment. Someone has described it as 'a decline in deference'.

It is in the home, and particularly in obedience to the fifth Commandment, that the value of all human life is learnt from the earliest age. The home where parents are dishonoured without discipline, and where ageing grandparents are ridiculed by two generations, is hardly likely to correct disparaging remarks about someone's colour, race, religion, occupation, or their mental or physical disability. Long before a child thinks about murder, contemplates the passing pleasure of adultery, understands the apparent advantage of stealing, learns to lie or yearns for the possessions of others, it struggles to break free from parental discipline. That is always the first relationship to be trampled upon and therefore the first one that a child must learn to value. From this Commandment flows an attitude to a thousand people.

SECONDLY, HONOUR MEANS OBEDIENCE

Honouring our parents will mean that we will listen to what they have to say. All wisdom is not locked up with grey hair, but there is a wisdom gained by age and experience that is not to be despised. Most young children think they know better than their parents and every teenager is sure that their parents are so out of touch with reality that they have nothing to teach a younger generation. This was doubtless the same in the Old Testament and certainly we have documents reaching back into the ancient dynasties of Egypt complaining that the younger generation is not what it used to be!

Nothing has changed. The older generation never thinks the younger generation is as good as they themselves were when they were young, and the younger generation has always dismissed the older generation as not being 'switched on' to reality. However, the biblical proverb has a wise word: 'Listen, my son, to your father's instruction and do not forsake your mother's teaching. They will be a garland to grace your head and a chain to adorn your neck' (Proverbs 1:8–9). Listening is honouring. We do not have to accept everything, believe everything or follow everything, but to listen and respect is a significant way of honouring our parents. The attitude of despising parental advice just because it is parental is sinful. There should be a respect for the views of an older generation even if we disagree with those views; but especially so of the views of parents who model their lives on Scripture.

With all the concern we have today, and rightly so, about child abuse, we are in danger of forgetting that God's first concern was for the abuse of parents by children. In his instructions to Moses, God majored on the relationship between children and their parents: 'Anyone who attacks his father or his mother must be put to death' (Exodus 21:15). But two verses later God refers not only to physical abuse but to attitudes: 'Anyone who curses his father or mother must be put to death' (v 17). The last six Commandments are all covered in Agur's instructions in Proverbs 30 but perhaps the most vivid language is reserved for the child who ridicules its parents: 'The eye that mocks a father, that scorns obedience to a mother, will be pecked out by the ravens of the valley, will be eaten by the vultures' (Proverbs 30:17). This is how seriously God views the child, young person or the adult who despises or curses their parents. God may not expect us to carry out such severe penalties now, but he has not changed his mind about the crime. There are many sins today that God 'overlooks' for the time being (Acts 17:30), but he will certainly bring them into his reckoning on the Day of Judgement. We should be in no doubt what God thinks about the breach of his fifth Commandment: 'A wise son brings joy to his father but a foolish man despises his mother' (Proverbs 15:20).

In Ephesians 6:1 (and similarly in Colossians 3:20) Paul takes up this commandment and applies it to the family relationship: 'Children, obey your parents in the Lord, for this is right'. The phrase 'in the Lord' has opened some discussion. When writing this, Paul most likely has in mind Christian children; after all, he would not expect to have access through his letters to many non-Christian children. So the phrase 'in the Lord' does not refer to the parents, but to the manner in which Christian children should be obedient to their parents. Whether or not the parents are Christians themselves, the Christian child should obey as one who is 'in the Lord'. Paul adds, 'for this is right'—it is both naturally and spiritually right. To the Colossians he goes even further and presses home obedience with the words 'in everything'. We are left with very few arguments that will enable us to avoid the mounting pressure of Paul's insistence in these two passages.

A significant sign of the degeneration of an age drawing close to the coming of Christ is the breakdown of relationships at this very level. In Matthew 10:21 Jesus is talking about the end of the age when he says that one of the signs is that 'children will rebel against parents.' Paul has the same to say in 2 Timothy 3:1–2 where he warns, 'There will be terrible times in the last days… People will be lovers of themselves, lovers of money, boastful, proud, abusive, *disobedient to their parents.*' Such things will get worse and worse as the time of Christ's return draws nearer. In Romans 1:30 disobedience to parents is included in a list of the typical sins of the 'depraved mind' of those who reject God (v 28).

All this is in marked contrast to the example of Christ himself who set us that perfect pattern of obedience: 'He went down to Nazareth with his parents and was obedient to them' (Luke 2:51). That brief statement summarises the larger part of Jesus' life. People have longed to know more about the childhood and the teenage years of Christ. For this reason, by the second century AD there were a number of made-up stories circulating concerning his childhood and youth. *The Gospel of Thomas* includes fanciful stories of Jesus making little birds out of clay and throwing them into the air so that they would fly away and entertain the children in the street. There is no historical basis in these stories, but people wanted to fill a gap. On the other hand, what we do know about his childhood is significant. It is as if God is saying, 'Do you want to summarise my son's youth? Then here it is, "He went down to Nazareth with his parents and was obedient to them."' That is all God tells us, but it tells us all.

The Old Testament describes an event that appears to be grotesquely unnatural: 'If a man has a stubborn and rebellious son who does not obey his father and mother and will not listen to them when they discipline him, his father and mother shall take hold of him and bring him to the elders of the gate of his town. They shall say to the elders, "This son of ours is stubborn and rebellious. He will not obey us. He is a profligate and drunkard." Then all the men of this town shall stone him to death. You must purge the evil from among you. All Israel will hear of it and be afraid' (Deuteronomy 21:18–21). If that dreadful punishment appears to be unnatural it can only be that God considers the sin committed as utterly unnatural. We do not take that action now, any more than we put adulterers to death, because God in his mercy has tempered his just anger by patience; in effect he says, 'I will wait, but my ultimate judgement for disobedience to parents will be even more severe.' There are children of all ages throughout the world who are just like this son in Deuteronomy, and God is waiting—he is giving more time. But if we are tempted to take the fifth Commandment lightly, and fail to recognise its importance in the plan of God for his world, then we should return to that terrible passage in Deuteronomy 21. God was determined that his covenant people would be 'holy'—different from all the nations around them. And in this respect at least they were to be remarkably different. They were to set an example to the world.

It cannot be without significance that the one Commandment that holds the greatest promise for its observance also carries a most frightening penalty for its breach.

Our emphasis on obedience to parents may present a problem. Some children may respond, 'It's all very well talking like that but you don't know my parents.' What if the parents are godless people who hate the word of God and force a child to do things that are contrary to God's law? The response to that is straightforward: there is a principle that the highest law rules. Let me give you an illustration. There is a law that says we must not drive beyond 30 miles per hour in a restricted area. But if we are rushing someone to hospital on a life or death journey we will not allow that law to stand in our way. We will break that law because there is a higher principle that governs us: the saving of life. That is why ambulances and fire engines break the law in an emergency; they don't have the law on their side when they jump the lights and 'skip' the bollards, but everyone agrees that they have an important principle on their side. Saving life is more important than obeying a rule. In the same way our obedience to God is paramount. That stands true in every leader/led relationship, whether it is the boss at work, the teacher in the classroom, the politician framing laws in parliament, the husband in the home or the child obeying its parents.

THE RIGHT TO DISCIPLINE

If obedience is part of the implication of the fifth Commandment then a natural conclusion must be the right of parents to discipline. Discipline should be expressed in the spirit of encouraging, comforting and exhorting (1 Thessalonians 2:11–12), with the goal of bringing up children in 'the training and instruction of the Lord', without 'exasperating them' (Ephesians 6:1–4). However, discipline there must be. The book of Proverbs lays significant stress upon the obligation of parents to train their children by discipline where necessary, see Proverbs 19:18; 22:15; 23:13–14. Our Lord reserved some of his most severe and damning words for those who cause a child to sin either by neglect or by positive bad example (Matthew 18:1–9).

In 1860 Chief Justice Cockburn defended the right of parents to use physical punishment in order to discipline their children: 'By the law of England, a parent or schoolmaster may, for the purpose of correcting what is evil in the child, inflict moderate and reasonable corporal punishment, always, however, with this condition, that it is moderate and reasonable.' This was confirmed in the Prevention of Cruelty to and Protection of Children Acts in 1889, and again in the Children and Young Persons Acts 1933. This right is under severe attack today; in 2001 it became illegal to smack a child under three in Scotland. During the passage of the Children Act 1989 several attempts were made to repeal these sections of the 1933 Act, and the United Nations Convention on the Rights of the Child (1989 and ratified by the United Kingdom in 1991) has already formed the basis for the campaign conducted by EPOCH (End Physical Punishment of Children).

A twelve year old boy recently took his mother and step-father to the European Court to prevent them from smacking him. How many more forms of discipline will be outlawed as we allow our children to run wild? Will a harsh word become 'psychological abuse'? Will the loss of privileges be called 'deprivation'? And will 'grounding' become 'forcible imprisonment'? Whoever decided that a sharp smack for insolent behaviour was more brutal than a cancelled outing? It is nothing short of disaster for our children when head teachers are unsupported in their discipline by school governors and when the media turn little thugs into national heroes.

If the fifth Commandment is to be applied, parents must have the freedom to exercise discipline that is both 'moderate and reasonable' without the interference of government. Our soft options in recent decades in our homes, schools and in society generally have led directly to the increase in the lawless and authority-defying behaviour of so many children in our nation.

THE THIRD APPLICATION OF HONOURING OUR PARENTS IS IN OUR CARE FOR THEM
In this connection there are two verses in the New Testament that require balancing. The first is 2 Corinthians 12:14, 'Children should not have to save up for their parents, but parents for their children.' That is a reference to the care of children whilst they are the responsibility of the parents. The parents have a duty to provide for them; it is a plain statement of parental responsibility. The other verse is 1 Timothy 5:4, 'If a widow has children or grandchildren (note that, unlike the Old Testament Hebrew in which the Commandments were written, New Testament Greek has words for grandparents and grandchildren) these should learn first of all to put their religion into practice by caring for their own family and so repaying their parents and grandparents for this is pleasing to God.' The pattern is therefore clear. Parents have a divine obligation to care for their children, but as the children grow up, slowly the roles begin to reverse: as the parents grow older and more frail, it is the children who have a responsibility to care for the parents. These two things are part of God's plan for society and it is equally sinful to overlook the one or the other. Our concern for 'child abuse' today has blinded us to the fact that God is equally concerned for 'granny abuse', and that may just as easily be by neglect as by positive action. The apostle Paul urged his readers to put their religion into practice. A bad or neglectful relationship with our parents, at whatever age they or we are, is sinful. Everyone with living parents or grandparents must ask the hard question about relationships.

When we are young we have a duty to value and honour our parents, not just because they care for us and provide for us, but because they *are* our parents. When they are old and senile, and when Alzheimers has begun to write its degrading graffiti across the closing years, then honour is even more significant.

We do not honour our parents in old age only because they have served their country with courage or cared for their family with love or worked for the community for half a century. That is the ethics of the racing stables where the successful horse is retired with honour and the failure goes to the knacker's yard! Honour for our father and mother is a commitment because of their value as people made in the image of God. Care for our elderly parents is not repayment for past favours but a response to the Commandment of the God who will have us remember the value of those he had made. And this care expresses the value not only of the cared-for, but of the carers themselves.

The two most powerful arguments against euthanasia are just here. In the first place the elderly are never to be given the impression that they are a burden to society. In this third millennium the number of octogenarians in the community will increase by fifty percent, and by the year 2010 they will form five percent of the entire population of the United Kingdom. But old age is a chronology, not a malady—no one dies of old age. The elderly are valuable to society because they are living people whose lives, however limited and sometimes contorted, reflect the image and likeness of God.

But the second argument against euthanasia lies in the value of children and of a society that learns to care. Currently there are six million family carers for the elderly or disabled and that is often seen as a tragedy rather than an opportunity. Of course there are incredible burdens and pressures upon carers in our modern society, but if the answer is a loving kiss and a shot of potassium chloride then we are all at risk sooner or later and the pressure from families and society will become intolerable. Of that there is no doubt. Obedience to the fifth Commandment implies that we must learn to support those who support the elderly, and the sick and disabled too, so that their burden is lighter and our society becomes caring and not careless. The tragedy of post-modernism lies in its passion for 'quick-fix' solutions. We dispense with unwanted children by fast abortions, inconvenient marriages by fast divorce, and we would like to off-load unwanted parents and 'sufferers' by a fast exit, all with the casualness with which we satisfy our appetite with fast food.

Societies grow in value as they learn to care and not as they become more proficient in dispensing with their 'problems'. That much the eugenics of Nazi Germany in the 1930s and 40s should have taught us.

The promise attached

This is the only Commandment with a promise: 'So that you may live long in the land.' When this law is repeated in Deuteronomy 5:16 a phrase is added, 'And that it may go well with you in the land.' It is one of the many general promises in Scripture. It is not a guarantee of certain old age for the obedient child. Similarly Proverbs 22:6, 'Train a child in the way he should go, and when he is old he will not turn from it' is a general promise that must be followed, but God is not held to it in every particular case. In the same way when Jesus invited his disciples: 'You may ask me for anything in my name, and I will do it' (John 14:14), what he was saying was that they must make sure that what they are asking for is within the context of his perfect will.

However, the promise here in Exodus 20:12 is still a promise. In Ephesians 6:3 the apostle quoted the command from Deuteronomy 5:16 and paraphrased the promise: 'that it may go well with you and that you may enjoy long life on the earth.' There are similar promises in the book of Proverbs. We read in Proverbs 1:8–9, 'Listen, my son, to your father's instruction and do not forsake your mother's teaching. They will be a garland to grace your head and a chain to adorn your neck.' And in Proverbs 4:1–4, 'Listen, my son, to a father's instruction; pay attention and gain understanding. I give you sound learning, so do not forsake my teaching. When I was a boy in my father's house, still tender, and an only child of my mother, he taught me and said, "Lay hold of my words with all your heart; keep my commands and you will live".' Again, Proverbs 6:20–22 reads: 'My son, keep your father's commands and do not forsake your mother's teaching. Bind them upon your heart for ever; fasten them around your neck. When you walk, they will guide you; when you sleep, they will watch over you; when you awake, they will speak to you. For these commands are a lamp, this teaching is a light, and the corrections of discipline are the ways of life.'

Only the parent who is a fiend encourages the child to abuse alcohol, take drugs, destroy their body with nicotine, or foul their mind with pornography. Only the parent who is utterly irresponsible would want their children to go down those paths. If parents give advice, their wisdom may save a child from financial disaster, physical injury, social failure, moral sin—and hell. Many of the children who run away from home each year never return: you can see them on the streets of our large cities. Not all are the product of careless parents; sadly, too often the passionate pleas and earnest counsel of a heart-broken parent have been rejected, and a young life is squandered in the cheap joints and on the cold pavements of a grey and callous city.

Every ten years of advance in medical science adds five years to the average life-span, but it does not 'go well with us in the land.' Suicide among the under twenty-fives is now the third cause of death for that age group after accidents and cancer.

Parents worthy of honour

A young man who committed suicide in New York City left a note which included the words: 'My parents brought me up to believe in God, and to believe that he doesn't matter.' Parents who dabble in Christianity without the serious intention of obeying God are no better than the atheist. In the autobiography of John Stuart Mill, the political economist, there is a very striking sentence which underlines two of the great dangers of life. His father educated the boy himself and crammed his head with knowledge so that John Stuart Mill became a brilliant academic. But his father, James Mill, had no religious faith at all and refused to allow any religion to be taught to his son. Years later when John Stuart Mill was a famous man he looked back on his education with a great sense of loss. He said his mind was filled with information but his soul was starved. He commented, 'I have found myself at the beginning of adult life with a well-equipped ship and a rudder but no sail.' In fact he was wrong, he did not have a rudder either.

The final two decades of the twentieth century saw a social revolution resulting from feminism and a scramble for more of everything: more money, more sex, more freedom. With the divorce rate in Britain the highest in Europe at four in every ten marriages, with more than half of our twenty-five year olds choosing to cohabit rather than accept the commitment of marriage, and with a third of our children born out of wedlock, the traditional and biblical pattern of the two parent family belongs to a strange and long-lost world to most of our children today. To millions of children in the western nations the idea of honouring and respecting two parents is less plausible than believing in Father Christmas—and a lot less attractive.

The influence of Feminist philosophy has a lot to answer for. Children require role models for every area of life but the biblical models of father and mother have been rejected as 'gender stereotyping'. Consequently a generation has grown into adulthood and parenthood without a good model to follow—or in modern parlance, without an adequate paradigm. In Western society the models of parenthood are as varied as autumn tints and almost as transient: the model may be an 'open marriage' where the children hardly know who their real parents are, a temporary 'shacking up' for convenience or pleasure, a homosexual model of bewildering mystery for a child, a violent storm-filled home of drugs and drink, a house where mother and father are rarely at home, or a feeding and sleeping centre where television rules and parents are 'distant'. And so the tragic catalogue of our twenty-first century 'homes' could continue.

After three decades of a philosophy that drove women out of the home and into the office and factory, it is slowly dawning upon politicians, sociologists and journalists that we have made a terrible mistake; unfortunately young people and parents have not yet come to the same conclusion.

Writing in *The Independent* in September 1994 Helen Wilkinson picked up the theme of the great feminist mistake: 'The baby boomers who espoused personal liberation in the Sixties have become the forty-something parents. Poll evidence suggests that many have turned conservative, becoming deeply worried about bringing up their children in a world marked by insecurity.' She is not alone. In the coauthored book *Brain Sex* (Mandarin Paperbacks) Anne Moir and David Jessel write, 'Many women have been brought up to believe that they should be "as good as the next man" and in the process they have endured acute and unnecessary pain, frustration and disappointment ... Some women feel that they have failed. But they have only failed to be like men.' Similarly Deborah Tannen published a best-seller, *You Just Don't Understand* (Virago Press) underscoring the necessary differences between men and women. (These last two publications are quoted in *Men, Women and Authority*. Day One Publications 1996).

A quiet revolution by sociologists and politicians is moving in the same direction, but whether or not it is too late to turn round the political correctness of society before a moral Armageddon overwhelms the West remains to be seen. One thing is certainly true; never in modern history has the fifth Commandment been so neglected and so necessary.

Some of the most terrible words of Christ on record are found in Matthew 18:6. In response to a question about priority positions in heaven, our Lord had a little child stand by him and proceeded to give his disciples a lesson on humility. But he went far beyond this. Christ used the opportunity to encourage those who care for their children: 'Whoever welcomes a little child like this in my name welcomes me' (v 5). To welcome a child is to treat it with dignity, respect and care; and this surely involves caring for its spiritual as well as its physical, mental and social life. However, it is what Christ went on to say that carries the greatest challenge: 'If anyone causes one of these little ones who believes in me to sin, it would be better for him to have a large millstone hung around his neck and to be drowned in the depths of the sea.' If there is one epitaph for millions of parents in our nation today it is this terrible verse. We feed our children with sufficient food, clothe them with the latest designer outfits and provide them with the most comprehensive education in history, but their souls are starved, their emotions are hurt and their minds are filled with violence. Our children are neither cared for nor disciplined and we have kept them in ignorance of the laws of their Creator.

An experiment has been launched in parts of the United States of America to hold parents accountable for the actions of their dependent children, even to the extent of giving parents the criminal record their children have earned. Similarly in the United Kingdom parents can be fined for some crimes that their young children commit. Alarming trends call for drastic solutions. At least it is having the effect of reminding both children and parents of their proper relationship to each other.

The fifth commandment alone reduces everyone to the level of a sinner: none of us has consistently honoured our parents, and this is why the law always leads to the gospel. It always takes us to the place of forgiveness and renewal called Calvary, where everyone who has broken the fifth commandment can find new life through the Saviour who died for those who break the laws of God. Not only does he take away the past but he gives us new life and new strength to be obedient in the future, to be more honouring to our parents and more worthy of the honour of our children. And his word provides us with the only model that can give our children a home to enjoy and a father and mother to honour.

The value of life

You shall not murder. Exodus 20:13

A quarter of all murders committed in our society are between husband and wife, mostly with the wife as the victim. Serial killing and terrorist killing have become part of our regular news reports and the horrific brutality and callous disregard for human suffering exhibited in so much premeditated murder is frightening. Added to this, spontaneous killing—murder in the course of rape, robbery, or as a result of 'road-rage'—is on the increase. It sickens us all. Children and young teens are too often the victims, or incredibly even the perpetrators, of what appears to be mindless killing.

But no murder is 'mindless'. Whenever a life is taken, deliberately or in a moment of spontaneous rage, that action betrays a mind-set that treats life cheaply. The lack of control that lashes out with fatal consequences and the carefully planned 'elimination' of an unwanted opponent are both the result of holding human life of small value compared with the satisfaction of getting revenge. All murders come from a mind that does not appreciate the value of human life and does not understand the significance of the Commandment: 'You shall not murder'.

In our modern age we look back in disgust at the butchery of the Roman arena, the burning of infants in the fires of Moloch, leaving unwanted children to die on the mountains and the savage slaughter of whole communities in ancient warfare. But we harden our minds to the fate of thousands in ethnic cleansing, and the pain of a quarter of a million babies killed in the womb each year. Our wilful hypocrisy is astounding.

Many words in Hebrew can be employed to describe killing, but the one used here in Exodus 20:13—*ratsach*—is significant; it refers to killing human beings and is never used with reference to an animal. For slaughtering animals, either for food or for sacrifice, the word used is the Hebrew *shachat*. In addition *ratsach* is almost always used in the sense of an unlawful killing, a rare exception to this being Numbers 35:27 and 30 where in v 27 the killing would be murder in all but the exceptional circumstance of the victim straying from the 'city of refuge', and in v 30 where the reference is to judicial capital punishment. In fact Exodus 20:13 is the first time the word is used in the Old Testament. Our modern translations have therefore quite properly changed the older rendering 'Thou shalt not kill' to 'You shall not murder'.

Murder, simply defined, is 'premeditated unlawful killing'. An older definition picks up the *Authorised Version* English and refers to 'malice aforethought'. However, the malice aforethought may include instantaneous rage, since a frenzied attack in spontaneous revenge is still murder. The fact that there is a sin called murder implies that there are certain occasions when to kill is not a sin.

Should we ever kill?

FIRST, GOD HIMSELF COMMANDS THAT ANIMALS CAN BE KILLED FOR RELIGIOUS SACRIFICE

The Hebrew word *shachat* is used exclusively for animal sacrifice, for example in Exodus 12:6 and 29:11. Whether the offering was a kid, lamb, heifer, bullock or two doves for the poor, it was God himself who set up the sacrificial laws. This Commandment did not prohibit the necessary shedding of blood in the regular animal sacrifices of Israel.

SECONDLY, GOD ALSO QUALIFIED HIS COMMAND BY ALLOWING ANIMALS TO BE KILLED FOR FOOD AND CLOTHING

God himself took the life of an animal to use its skin to clothe Adam and Eve (Genesis 3:21). By doing so he was saying to them: 'You are lords over all the world and that includes the use of animals for the purposes of food and clothing.' Later God gave his people a list of the animals they could and could not use for food, 'clean' and 'unclean' animals (Deuteronomy 14). Any Christian is entitled to be a vegetarian if they wish (Romans 14:6), but they must not take their stand upon the ground of 'animal rights' or 'cruelty', least of all of this Commandment. To do so would be to imply that we are more moral than God himself.

THIRDLY, FOR THE MANAGEMENT OF THE EARTH'S RESOURCES

In Genesis 1:26 and 28 we are told that God created man: 'to rule over the fish of the sea and the birds of the air, over the livestock, over all the earth, and over all the creatures that move along the ground.' Mankind has a responsibility to look after the world and to keep it in order. This means that in addition to using the birds, fish and animals for food and clothing we can control them as well, but only for the good of the world God has given to us. The wholesale slaughter of North American buffalo for 'sport' during the nineteenth century could never be morally justified; on the other hand if the rabbits or rats are getting out of control we have the right to cull their numbers. This is all part of mankind's right of rule. The fact that we have consistently abused that right does not negate our God-given authority over creation. However, God himself was the first to remind mankind of the importance of ecological values, as a thoughtful reading of Deuteronomy 22:6–7 will show.

FOURTHLY, GOD ALSO ALLOWS THAT LIFE CAN BE TAKEN AS A LEGAL PUNISHMENT FOR CERTAIN CRIMES SUCH AS MURDER

In 1969 Britain abolished the death penalty after eight hundred years of hanging criminals. Whatever society's views may be on 'capital punishment', it is clear that it was part of God's rule of law for murder. Whilst God himself did not take the life of the first murderer, Cain (Genesis 4:1–16), by the time of Noah God considered it appropriate to establish capital punishment as a proper response to one of the most violent crimes against humanity (Genesis 9:6). When we reach the giving of the Ten Commandments fifteen hundred years before Christ, it was sufficient for God to underline what was already common practice (Exodus 21:12 and Leviticus 24:17): 'If anyone takes the life of a human being, he must be put to death.' Similarly in Romans 13:4, Paul upholds the right of the state authorities to exercise capital punishment by referring to the fact that they 'do not bear the sword for nothing'—a phrase that affirms the right to execute. It is precisely because God holds human life as sacred that he demands the highest penalty for those who treat cheaply the image and likeness of God in others.

Looking back to the early sixties when the debate for abolition was at its height in Britain, George Gale, the editor of *The Spectator* commented, 'To be against the death penalty…was the normal, good, decent and fashionable thing to be. My friends and acquaintances were in no doubt about it. All of us were civilised and sensible. It was only the ignorant and the thugs who thought differently. And the police.' Twenty years later he had changed his mind entirely. Most of the debate had been conducted on the level of emotion and majored on cases of known miscarriage of justice. Virtually none of it referred to the plan of the Creator. That is still the case today.

Whatever else we may say about capital punishment, it cannot be wrong in principle since God himself instituted it; once again, we must not imagine that we are more moral than God. On the other hand it cannot be wrong to abolish it either! There were many other crimes punishable by death in the Old Testament, such as: the abuse of parents by children, kidnapping, criminal negligence, witchcraft, idolatry, sex offences, blasphemy and false prophesying. Few would argue to reinstate capital punishment for these. Compare this list with the fact that by the end of the eighteenth century there were some three hundred and fifty crimes in Britain punishable by death—which would certainly make Israel, three and a half thousand years earlier, more civilised!

The fact that we do not insist on the death penalty for all these crimes today is not because the Old Testament laws were harsh and uncivilised— they were not—but because, as we have seen before, the law was often softened by mercy. The clear example of this is our Lord's response to the woman taken in adultery (John 8). It would be perfectly right to re-introduce the death penalty if society realised that its comparative 'soft-option' for violent criminals was neither sufficiently expressing our disgust at the crime, nor adequately honouring the value of the life taken. It was this value of life that lay at the heart of capital punishment in the Old Testament. Even today there is a sense of bewilderment on the part of the husband who watches a man sent to gaol for a few years for killing his young wife in a drink/drive accident; the inevitable thought must be: is that how my wife was valued? It is this value of life argument that leads many to conclude that whilst capital punishment may be dropped for many crimes, it should be retained for murder.

However, in this subject of capital punishment God makes two provisos: first he places the judgement in the hand of the judiciary and second he allows for unintentional killing, or manslaughter (Exodus 21:13).

FIFTHLY, MEN CAN KILL IN WAR

God sent his people into Canaan with orders to destroy all the inhabitants of the land (Joshua 11:20) because of the vile sins being committed there. That does not allow any nation the right of wholesale genocide today, since no other nation is governed directly by the revelation of God as Israel was in the Old Testament. But to kill in defence of freedom and the security of the weak and defenceless, can be justified. There is such a thing as a 'just war', though Christian principles will severely limit what is and is not allowed even during such armed conflict.

No Christian can ever take the position of 'My country, right or wrong'. Similarly we should recognise all war for what it is: inglorious and evil. However just the cause, and however necessary the action—consider the consequences of otherwise allowing Hitler the fruit of his aggression in 1939— war is always to be hated. On the other hand, pacifism is not a biblical alternative. John the Baptist was preaching a message of radical righteousness when the soldiers asked, 'And what should we do?' John's reply, recorded in Luke 3:14, was hardly calculated to paralyse the Roman army: 'Don't extort money and don't accuse people falsely—be content with your pay.' None of the soldiers who met with either Christ or the Apostles were encouraged to resign their commission.

Why is murder wrong?

FIRST, BECAUSE MURDER TOUCHES THE IMAGE AND LIKENESS OF GOD

When a man or woman is killed, something unique is destroyed; a life that will never be repeated is eliminated. The uniqueness of men and women is their soul—their ability to communicate with God—and their capacity to think and reason; this is what is meant by God creating man and woman in his own image and likeness (Genesis 1:26–27). To destroy that is to destroy something God made like himself. It is to mock the Creator.

To enter a private art gallery and smash every picture to the ground, would not only be wanton destruction, it would destroy something that the artist had created—something unique; it would be an insult to the artist himself. To destroy a human being is to smash the image of God.

We cannot compare humans with the animal kingdom: animals are not humans and humans are not animals. There is something within human nature that is unique; that uniqueness is the image and the likeness of God. This is not a physical but a spiritual likeness. The Mormon understanding that God has 'A body of flesh and bones as tangible as man's' (*Doctrines and Covenants* 130.22) is a complete misunderstanding, since God is 'spirit' (John 4:24). Mankind has moral responsibility and value that animals do not have; if dog bites baby we destroy dog, but if baby bites dog…! The greatest sin about murder is that it touches the Creator's finest act of creation. It is an act of scoffing at the Creator himself; it is like smashing the artist's most perfect picture.

The Old Testament provided an elaborate ceremony for unsolved murder. We find it in Deuteronomy 21:1–9. If a man was found murdered in the countryside and no-one knew who had committed the crime, then the elders and judges were to measure which city was nearest to the place where the body was found. In a similar way today the police force responsible for the area in which the crime took place is brought in to solve it. The elders of that city would then take a heifer into a local valley that was barren and uncultivated but through which a river flowed; the Levite priests would slaughter the animal and the elders would wash their hands over the body of the sacrifice declaring as they did so: 'Our hands did not shed this blood, nor did our eyes see it done. Accept this atonement for your people Israel whom you have redeemed, O LORD, and do not hold your people guilty of the blood of an innocent man' (vs 7–8). They did not do the same thing if they stumbled across a goat that had died in the desert or a bird that had fallen from the sky; in such cases they were told only that they were not to touch the carcass because of the danger of infection. In other words the death of a man and the death of an animal were in entirely different categories. An elaborate declaration of innocence and a sacrifice had to be made on the discovery of a murder victim. Why was that? To drive home the seriousness of the crime, even if no-one was found to stand accused of it.

SECONDLY, MURDER IS AN ACT OF FINALITY THAT CANNOT BE UNDONE
This is not an argument against capital punishment, or God himself would never have allowed it, but it is an argument against murder. There is no way of going back on murder; it is a final act and what this Commandment in

effect says is: 'Before you act, think.' That is true of all killing. Before we kill anything we should stop and reflect for a moment: is this necessary? If people habitually thought like that then the act of murder would be unacceptable in all circumstances.

The cult of New Age has brought with it a resurgence of interest in reincarnation—the belief that the human spirit has more than one opportunity to live in an earthly body. The ancient Buddhist and Hindu belief is that successive lives provide more opportunity to better ourselves in the upward struggle for perfection. New Age, with its view that 'all is one' (monism), offers the hope that the great spiritual circle, or cosmic mind, of which we are all a part, will give us the opportunity to return into this world in some other form. The revelation of God is decidedly against such ideas. According to the Bible 'man is destined to die once, and after that to face judgement' (Hebrews 9:27). This is precisely why murder is condemned so clearly in God's word. If reincarnation is true then murder could be justified on the grounds that it may well be doing the victim a favour. If he is a bad person we can hurry him into the next stage of his existence before he 'downgrades' his future life even more; on the other hand, if he is a good person then we will be moving him into the next level of life while the going is favourable! I have not seen this argued by those who believe in reincarnation, but it is certainly a logical conclusion to an erroneous doctrine. The finality of death and the absence of a second chance is one strong reason why murder is so wrong.

THIRDLY, MURDER IS THE MOST FAR-REACHING ACT OF MAN TO MAN

Murder always affects more than just the person killed; whole families are involved. God speaks of bringing the guilt of bloodshed 'on your house' (Deuteronomy 22:8) since murder always brings at the very least shame and disgrace to a family. But it also affects society; we will see this in a moment, but significantly the media write and speak of the 'guilt of society' when some particularly horrific murder has been committed and it is followed by some passing, though shallow, soul-searching by the nation.

Murder particularly affects the murderer. How can a terrorist develop a mind-set that lets him plant bombs knowing that he may blow up babies, children, mothers or soldiers—and that it doesn't much matter to him who it is? The answer is that he began by killing someone. There was a moment in his life when he took a human being in his sights, crossed him and pulled the trigger; or when he placed a bomb carefully and deliberately in the waste-bin outside McDonalds. From that moment on it was easier to do the same thing again and then again. Killing hardens; it desensitizes. This desensitizing may begin by shooting rabbits just for the sport of killing. Across the world thousands of 'sportsmen' shoot many rare and beautiful birds on their migration; they are shot for no other pleasure than to see the creature fall out of the sky. That is an evil mind which is contrary to this command; it betrays the desire to kill, and killing trains the mind for cruel indifference.

Sociologists are concerned today at what they refer to as the 'desensitizing' influence of television violence. The first response to violence on the screen is shock; in the child it results in fear and disturbed behaviour. The second response is desensitizing when there is no more shock. This results finally in addiction, which is the enjoyment of violence. God's prohibition against murder is far reaching in its scope.

What is prohibited?
FIRST, THE COMMANDMENT REFERS ESPECIALLY TO PREMEDITATED KILLING
We all know this as murder. It is referred to in Exodus 21:12,14, 'Anyone who strikes a man and kills him shall surely be put to death... If a man schemes and kills another man deliberately, take him away from my altar and put him to death.' That means he cannot be allowed to find a safe haven anywhere; he must be brought to justice.

Nowhere, however, does God make a distinction between premeditated and aggravated or provoked murder. We may have every sympathy for the abused wife who reacts in bitter anger, but her action is still murder. It is precisely that kind of personal revenge-murder that our Lord condemns in his claim: 'You have heard that it was said "Eye for eye, and tooth for tooth". But I tell you, do not resist an evil person...' (Matthew 5:38–39).' Many then, and now, believe they have the right to 'take the law into their own hands' and to get even. It was the misuse of Exodus 21:23–25 that our Lord opposed; the penalties of the Old Testament legal system were to be given by the magistrates and no one else. Extenuating circumstances may, and always could, limit the severity of the punishment, but we must never let people believe that it can be socially acceptable for an abused wife, child, husband, employee, citizen—the list could be endless—to take the law into their own hands. Murderers are not heroes or heroines, whatever the provocation. The beaten wife, spurned lover, or cheated businessman should all have access to justice, but not to the personal satisfaction of murder. Human life is too significant for that.

A misleading argument has too often crept into the debate over whether capital punishment is justified or not. In their anger over the murder of police officers who are killed in the course of their duty, some have argued in favour of the death sentence for certain categories of murder. This line of argument reveals a false view of the value of life. Significantly, in the passage in Deuteronomy 21 referred to earlier, the elders were to plead that they were not guilty of the 'blood of an innocent man' (v 8). This does not suggest that any man is wholly innocent, nor that the murder victim was not necessarily guilty of some crime against his attacker, but that he ought not to have died in the way he did, and in that sense his was 'innocent blood' (compare v 9 with James 5:6). In other words, the lives of all are protected by the sixth Commandment and to suggest that the murder of a police officer is in some way more heinous than the murder of a young mother is insulting to the life of that young woman. Murder is murder and must be equally outlawed irrespective of the character or occupation of the victim. There is no partiality with God.

SECONDLY, MURDER THROUGH CARELESSNESS

In Deuteronomy 22:8, God urges his people to live in such a way that they cannot be the cause of the death of another person: 'When you build a new house, make a parapet around your roof so that you do not bring the guilt of bloodshed on your house if someone falls from the roof.' The way we build our house, drive our car, walk our dog or sell our produce can be the cause of the death of others; that may not be our intention, but it can still be the direct result of our actions. This Commandment forces us to consider that possibility. We have fire and safety regulations in all areas of life because we take seriously the value of human life and acknowledge that we must not be responsible for the death or injury of someone else. As Leviticus 19:16

reminds us: 'Do not do anything that endangers your neighbour's life.'

Exodus 21 describes an incident of an ox goring a man to death. When that happens the ox is put to death, just as we destroy a dog that savages someone; the owner does not suffer the same fate. However, according to Exodus 21, if the ox has been aggressive in the past and the man was warned but took no action, then both the ox and its owner must be put to death. Does that appear harsh? But how else could the laws of Israel uphold the sacredness of human life in the face of a man who clearly considered the economic value of his ox of more importance than the potential safety of his neighbour? There is an important lesson here for the negligent and often greedy directors of industry, drug companies and food manufacturers. Those who hazard human lives for financial gain are guilty of a breach of this sixth Commandment. When death results from something like this today the courts can record a verdict of 'death by unlawful killing'—that is murder by another name.

God also gave his people laws to limit the force we may use to protect our property. In Exodus 22:2 God told his people that if a man broke into a home during the daytime the householder had the right to use some degree of force against the intruder; however if the robber broke in during the night time, greater force could be used. If in this instance the defence of the family or property resulted in the intruder's death then the householder was not guilty of murder, whereas he would be if it happened during the day. Why was this? We must understand the teaching here in the context of a society where people lived in close communities and where homes would be left unsecured during the day. If a thief was found at night he must have broken in and the danger was all the greater. This rule of reasonable protective force is enshrined in all civilized statute books today. It is another way of recognising the significance of human life. If my neighbour's children climb over the fence and steal a few strawberries, I do not have the right to blast off with a shot-gun. I may protect my property by putting a fence round it, but if I electrify the fence with a sufficient voltage to kill, then that is unreasonable protection.

God also recognises that there are times when something happens that was not expected to happen and 'manslaughter' tragically occurs: 'However, if he does not do it intentionally, but God lets it happen, he is to flee to a place I will designate' (v 13). God provided a number of cities in Judea, called 'cities of refuge', so that those accused of manslaughter could find a safe haven from family revenge. An accidental death would not be considered as murder; an example of this is in Deuteronomy 19:1–7.

THIRDLY, THE SIXTH COMMANDMENT CONDEMNS ABORTION, EUTHANASIA AND SUICIDE

In his popular commentary on the Ten Commandments, *God's Good Life* (Inter-Varsity Press 1992), David Field introduces the subject of abortion with the following story: Some medical students were attending a seminar on abortion when the lecturer confronted them with a case study. The father of the family has syphilis and the mother tuberculosis. They have had four children already. The first is blind, the second died, the third is deaf and dumb, and the fourth has tuberculosis. The mother is now pregnant with her fifth child and is willing to have an abortion if that is what you suggest. What would your advice be? The students overwhelmingly voted to terminate the pregnancy. To this the lecturer responded, 'Congratulations, you have just murdered Beethoven'!

Evangelical Christians are united in their opposition to abortion. But why? Simply because of the risk of eliminating another Beethoven? Of course not! We believe life is valuable from the moment of conception and that the child in the womb expresses consciousness, pain and humanness at a very early time in its development. It cannot be without significance that in the Hebrew of the Old Testament there is no word for foetus. The same word (*yeleth*) is used for the child in the womb and for the new-born child. The familiar verse in Isaiah 9:6 reads, 'To us a child is born', and the word *yeleth* is used. The same is true for the New Testament where the Greek word is *brephos*—this word is found in Luke 1:41 and 2:12. Clearly the biblical teaching is that from conception on, that which is carried in the womb is a child.

In the Old Testament, God presents a scenario that illustrates this clearly. In Exodus 21:22–23 we read of a possible incident in which two men are fighting; in the course of the scuffle a pregnant woman intervenes, is injured, and 'gives birth prematurely'. Since there is some debate over this important passage we must turn our attention to it for a moment.

The phrase 'she gives birth prematurely' is literally 'if her children come out'. The plural of the word *yeleth* is used. In other words, if a woman is pregnant she has a child (a *yeleth*)—or children—in her womb. Remember that there is no word in Hebrew equivalent to our 'foetus'; that which is in the womb is always referred to as a child. Unfortunately some versions of the Bible translate this phrase 'if her children *come out*' with the word 'miscarriage'. But that is a bad translation. The Hebrew word used in v 22 is not the word for miscarriage at all. You can find the word for 'miscarriage' in Genesis 31:38 where Jacob tells his uncle Laban that in his care none of Laban's sheep 'miscarried'; that is a different word altogether. The word used here in Exodus 21 literally means 'to go out' and in this context refers simply to a premature birth. The *English Standard Version* translates literally at this verse: 'When men strive together and hit a pregnant woman, *so that her children come out....*' A premature birth and a miscarriage are not the same thing. The word is used also in Genesis 25:25–26 when Esau and Jacob 'came out' of their mother's womb—that was certainly no miscarriage!

The *New International Version* and *New King James Version* translate Exodus 21:22, 'If men who are fighting hit a pregnant woman and she gives birth prematurely but there is no serious injury, the offender must be fined whatever the woman's husband demands and the court allows. But if there is serious injury, you are to take life for life, eye for eye, tooth for tooth, hand for hand, foot for foot, burn for burn, wound for wound, bruise for bruise.' This passage refers not to a miscarriage but to a premature birth. If the child survives then there is a fine, but if the child dies or it is seriously damaged then the punishment is a life for a life etc.

Notice that the passage in which Exodus 21 occurs is referring to penalties for murder. If the focus in v 22 is on the woman, then we do not need to be told that she is pregnant since the same penalty would be due if harm came to her whether or not she was pregnant. The focus of attention must be the child in her womb. If as a result of violence to her, the baby 'comes out' but there is no serious injury to it then a fine will be levied, but if the child is dead or injured then the punishment is life for life.

What this instructive passage teaches us is that a deliberate act that causes the death of an unborn child is considered to be murder. What then does God think of the doctor who deliberately kills an unborn child? This is not the place to consider the complexities of this whole debate, but the value of human life and God's refusal to concede that the child in the womb is anything other than truly human, should settle the principle of whether or not it can be right to terminate the life of a child in the womb. Our society may choose to refer to abortion as 'a retrospective method of fertility control' but it is directly condemned in the sixth Commandment of God's Law. Once we have accepted the biblical principle that human life starts at conception, to break this principle—however heartrending the reason may be—is to add murder to our action.

We considered two arguments against euthanasia under the previous Commandment. The significant arguments put forward then were the need to ensure that the elderly are never made to feel a burden either to society or the family, and the value of children and society learning to care, rather than to 'offload' those they consider to have come to the end of a useful life.

We can now add a third and more important argument against euthanasia. Apart from the exceptions listed earlier in this chapter, God has nowhere given us the right to take life. To bring an ageing, suffering, or what we consider to be 'useless' life to a premature close can only be called murder in biblical terms. It is all too easy to take the most extreme and heart-rending cases and try to build a principle on those; but the legal warning that 'hard cases make bad laws' is never more appropriate than on this subject. Whether someone is suffering 'unbearably', or has little or no 'quality of life', or 'cannot face the future' are all subjective judgements—either on the part of the sufferer, those who are caring, or more often on the part of society. Despair is no solution to the problems of life, but continuing care certainly is.

When a court gave permission in 1993 for the life-support system of Tony Bland to be switched off, it accepted the arguments that the victim of the tragic Hillsborough Stadium disaster was unconscious and had no quality of life. Three years later the *British Medical Journal* for 6th July 1996 carried a report from specialists at the Royal Hospital for Neurodisability that forty-three percent of patients referred to them between 1992 and 1995 as being in Persistent Vegetative State (PVS) were mis-diagnosed. In fact these patients were conscious and could communicate. This raises serious questions over the treatment of Tony Bland—who was starved to death—and others like him.

However significant this report may be, the Christian response to euthanasia does not start there. In the same way, the discovery that even very young children in the womb can react to pain, is not where the argument against abortion begins. Euthanasia and abortion are wrong because they are as much forms of murder as the wanton destruction of children and the disabled in 'primitive' civilizations. The value of life is not based upon the ability to feel pain or to communicate but on the fact that every human being is created in the likeness of God and he alone controls both life and death.

It was the eugenics philosophy of the first half of the twentieth century that gave rise to the widespread view that the poor and ignorant were unfit to propagate and should therefore be sterilised in the interests of society generally. The atheistic philosopher George Bernard Shaw concluded, 'There is now no reasonable excuse for refusing to face the fact that nothing but a eugenic religion can save our civilization from the fate that has overtaken all previous civilizations.' In 1905 H G Wells wrote in *A Modern Utopia:* 'There is only one sane and logical thing to be done with a really inferior race, and that is to exterminate it'. At the same time Sidney Webb, founder of the London School of Economics and an influential political thinker at the beginning of the twentieth century, declared that it was a primary duty of governments 'to determine which kind of fitness shall survive.'

The word 'eugenics' means 'well-born' and refers to the ideology that only healthy adults should be allowed to reproduce so that only healthy children should be born. Prior to the Second World War, the eugenics crusade was supported by politicians, the British Medical Association and many educationalists. It grew directly from the evolutionary biology of Darwin and was enthusiastically taken over by Hitler and his Nazi party in Germany during the 1930s and 40s. The terrible 'Final Solution' that led to the genocide of millions of Jews, gypsies, homosexuals, communists, elderly, the mentally and physically disabled and anyone else Hitler took a dislike to, carried to its logical conclusion the agenda of 'applied biology' set by the British, European and North American eugenicists. The scale was horrendous—but no more so in numerical terms than the massive abortion crusade over the past three decades with almost a quarter of a million prenatal babies being killed annually in the United Kingdom alone.

Eugenics lies behind all abortions of children that may be born with some deformity, however mild or severe. But beyond this is the sinister mind-set that makes economic and other 'quality' judgements on the lives of the mentally disabled, the senile and the suffering. The Creator who cares for the poor, the widows and the orphans does not give us the right to make such judgements when the intention is to terminate a life. The Hospice Movement is a Christian response to suffering, Exit and the National Hemlock Society in America is a remedy of despair. The sixth Commandment forbids euthanasia.

Suicide is the third most common cause of death among those under 25, after accidents and cancer—teenage girls are particularly at risk. Suicide has always been met with aversion in civilised societies, and so it should be. It has often been seen as 'self-murder' and as such comes under the same condemnation. We may have every sympathy for the victim whose mind could not cope with the problems of life, and even more for their family; but whilst it may be right to remove suicide from the category of crime, there is a significant danger in giving the impression that to live or to die is simply a matter of personal choice. It is not. Of all the incidents of suicide recorded in Scripture not one is applauded and all were of sinful men in despair: Saul (1 Samuel 31:4,5), Ahithophel (2 Samuel 17:23), Zimri (1 Kings 16:18) and Judas (Matthew 27:5). Good men may long for death, as did Elijah (1 Kings 19:4), Simeon (Luke 2:29) and Paul (2 Corinthians 5:2,8 and Philippians 1:21–23) but none is recorded as having attempted to take their own life.

Contrary to contemporary thinking, our life is not our own; we hold it in trust from the Creator who gave it—whether we acknowledge that or not. Just as it is a lie to suggest that a woman has sole right to determine whether her child in the womb should live or die, so it is a deceit of modern society to pretend that everyone has the right to choose the time of their death. That belongs to God—and to him alone.

FOURTHLY, THE SIXTH COMMANDMENT CONDEMNS VICARIOUS MURDER

It has been estimated that by the time the American teenager is eighteen years of age he will have watched forty thousand killings and murders in his own lounge. Whilst some researchers do not accept that television creates violence in the mind of the child or adolescent it is agreed by all that it certainly 'stamps it in'. Seneca, the Roman philosopher and tutor for the emperor Nero, concluded his expression of disgust at the violent and cruel butchery of the arena with these words: 'Come now, can't you people see even this much—that bad examples recoil on those who set them?' (*Moral Epistles* VII.2). By encouraging a generation of children and teenagers to watch hours of gratuitous violence we are simply 'stamping in' a love of killing, and desensitizing their conscience to the horror of murder, assassination and war. War toys can have the same effect and for that reason should be discouraged.

There is an unhealthy enjoyment in the act of killing expressed in our modern society. The bloodier the conflict, the more macabre the murder, and the media revel in the details for days or months. The fact that the 'public' watch, read and listen with avid interest betrays a society that takes pleasure in surrogate murder—we can 'enjoy' the fruit of someone else's crime. This is what I mean by 'vicarious' murder.

An addiction to violent novels, films or war-games in which some degree of pleasure is experienced in reading, watching or re-enacting the slaughter of others must surely be an offence to a holy Creator for whom war, though at times unavoidable, is always inglorious and one of the great tragedies of the Fall into sin by mankind. The Command: 'You shall not murder' is intended to stamp into our minds the horror of killing in all its forms, and the news that we are fed daily by the media should fill us with loathing and disgust; when we find any kind of gruesome interest or pleasure in vicarious killing then it is time for repentance.

FIFTHLY, THE SIXTH COMMANDMENT CONDEMNS PASSIVE AGGRESSION
Christ is the best interpreter of the Commandments and in Matthew 5:22 his application is both plain and close, 'I tell you that anyone who is angry at his brother will be subject to judgement. Again, anyone who says to his brother: "Raca" is answerable to the Sanhedrin. But anyone who says "You fool!", will be in danger of the fire of hell'. Our Lord's introduction to that was simply: 'You have heard that it was said to the people long ago, "Do not murder"….' He then applied that text. We can defame a character, despise a person, slander them and spread malicious gossip, and in doing so we

break this Command. Leviticus 19:17 warns, 'Do not hate your brother in your heart.' That is a form of murder.

The reason why God warns that passive aggression is a form of murder is because hatred hurts us just as murder does; it hurts our relationships, twists our mind and ruins our life. But there is another reason: every action starts with the mind—as we think, so we behave. The New Testament has much to say about the danger of the tongue and the necessity to guard our mind, simply because we can do untold harm to ourselves and others when our tongue reveals our bitter or angry mind. Once again, Christ put it plainly: 'The things that come out of the mouth come from the heart, and these make a man "unclean". For out of the heart come evil thoughts, murder, adultery, sexual immorality, theft, false testimony, slander. These are what make a man "unclean"' (Matthew 15:18–19). It is clear that our Lord had the Commandments in mind in this list.

Another way of expressing this passive aggression is by passive intention. To plan and scheme to kill is an offence that is punishable in law; but we can wish someone dead and only God knows. However, God *does* know. The disciple of Christ who was once described as a 'son of thunder' wrote these words in old age: 'Anyone who hates his brother is a murderer, and you know that no murderer has eternal life in him' (1 John 3:15). We can wish someone dead in order to make a way for us into promotion, to provide us with a much coveted legacy, to relieve us from the burden of caring, or for revenge on their mean and spiteful behaviour. Whatever the reason, a momentary desire for the death of another as a means of achieving benefit for myself is an act of mental murder. It is time for repentance.

SIXTHLY, WE CAN BREAK THIS COMMAND BY PASSIVE INACTION
There have been some disturbing accounts recently of people being attacked in public whilst onlookers do nothing; of people in London abducted at knife-point with crowds watching passively. Of course in this brutal society we are aware of the dangers of interfering, but at least some action is demanded in defence of others. The same can happen internationally and nationally and that is why we earlier defended the concept of a just war. We should not stand by passively whilst the atrocity of genocide is committed by one nation against another. When Robert Hussein stood condemned to

death in Kuwait in 1996 for the 'crime' of converting from Islam to Christ, the Western nations had a duty to make strong protests backed by political pressure. To avoid the issue on the basis of diplomatic and economic expediency is to be an ally in the threat of murder. And this scenario is all too common among aggressively religious governments in the world today.

There are times when right has to be defended and the praiseworthy desire to avoid killing can actually be a breach of this Commandment if we simply stand back and watch while evil men continue with a free hand. National and international policing may at times need to be severe in order to save lives. It was only when, in 1995, the United Nations took strong action against the Serbian forces in the former Yugoslavia that the widespread genocide and 'ethnic cleansing' was halted. In 2001 a coalition of nations went to war against the Taliban and al Qa'eda terrorists in Afghanistan in an attempt to stem the indiscriminate murder of civilians by the forces of terror. In each case, lives were taken in order to save the lives of the 'innocent'. At times to do other than this is culpable murder.

Finally

In one way or another, to a greater or lesser degree, by action, inaction or intent, we have all broken this Commandment. But remember: where there is law there is gospel. When Christ was on trial, Pilate was desperate for his release. The governor had been looking at every possible way to let this man go free. Finally the Governor played his last card. It was a custom that he should allow the Jews to claim one prisoner to be set free at this particular festival. Pilate tried to dupe them into giving the right answer. He offered them the release of Barabbas who was, 'a notorious prisoner... who had committed murder in the uprising' (Matthew 27:16 and Mark 15:7) or Christ whom he knew to be innocent (Matthew 27:13).

The choice should have been obvious, but they clamoured for the death of the King of kings. Barabbas the murderer was released and so Christ died to save the life of a murderer. But something more wonderful was to happen on the cross. Crucified beside the Saviour were two common criminals; they too were guilty of great crimes, possibly robbery and murder. Christ's dying words offered hope to one of those men: 'Today you will be with me in paradise.' Christ died to rescue and forgive murderers.

Marriage matters

You shall not commit adultery. Exodus 20:14

A notice hangs in the office of every Superintendent Registrar throughout the country. It reads: 'Marriage according to the law of this country is the union of one man with one woman voluntarily entered into for life to the exclusion of all others.' That simple, legal definition of marriage was set out by Lord Penzance in 1866 and we can hardly expect to find a better definition in law. Marriage is the union of one man and one woman, not two men or two women, to the exclusion of all others. Adultery is the inclusion of others. It is the act of breaking out of a marriage or breaking into a marriage; of separating a husband and wife by turning their affections away from their marriage partner.

The Old Testament has a fairly specific approach to sexual sins. Adultery (Hebrew *na'aph*) is the common word and it always refers to the violation of a marriage, even when it is a symbol used to describe spiritual apostasy from God; this was a society where marriage at a fairly early age was the norm, and the only other possibility was prostitution—either cultic or social. This alternative was clearly wrong, but it was the violation of marriage that struck at a fundamental relationship in society and it was this that God especially targeted in the seventh Commandment.

Fifteen hundred years later, pagan society had developed a wide range of sexual perversities, and so the New Testament writers alerted their readers to the dangers facing Christians during the first century after Christ. The usual Greek word for adultery is *moichao*, but there is also a far wider and all inclusive word, *porneia*, from which our word 'pornography' is derived. The *Authorised Version* translates *porneia* as 'fornication', whilst the *New International Version* settles for 'marital unfaithfulness' (Matthew 5:32 and 19:9) and 'sexual immorality' (Galatians 5:19). Two more words are used in Galatians 5:19 to refer to 'impurity' and 'debauchery'; in reality they are excessive words that would be best translated by the stronger 'profligacy' and 'licentiousness'. The two passages in Matthew's Gospel which deal with divorce each use *moichao* and *porneia*. If anyone divorces his wife 'except for *porneia*, he causes her to commit *moichao*'. *Porneia* can refer to any form of sexual unfaithfulness. A marriage can be violated by any of the sexual sins that God condemns: homosexual practices (Leviticus 18:22; 20:13; Romans 1:26–27, 1 Corinthians 6:9 and 1 Timothy 1:10), bestiality (Deuteronomy 27:21), transvestism (Deuteronomy 22:5), or other sexual perversions.

Clearly then, God's plan was to confine sexual relationships to the loving commitment of marriage; this was certainly his expressed purpose at the beginning (Genesis 2:24 and Matthew 19:5). Any sexual experience outside of that is either adultery or sexual immorality. God does not list all possibilities since every generation and each society will invent its own. Tragically the list would be endless. The seventh Commandment: 'You shall not commit adultery' is an abbreviation banning all sexual diversions and perversions; that is, everything that falls outside the relationship of one man and one woman in the social bond known as marriage.

One man and one woman only

It has become fashionable and politically correct today to applaud homosexual relationships as a normal and healthy alternative to heterosexual marriage. Even professing Christians, and incredibly supposed 'evangelicals' among them, have endorsed the view that a committed and caring same-sex relationship is good in the eyes of God. But God's command against adultery is set firmly in the context of heterosexual marriage—of this there is no doubt. In fact the clarity and straightforwardness of this command is in itself a divine defence of heterosexual marriage. In spite of all the attempted justification of practising homosexual relationships today such liaisons are wrong for three reasons:

First, homosexual relationships are *unbiblical*. In the plainest terms possible God decreed, 'Do not lie with a man as one lies with a woman; that is detestable' (Leviticus 18:22). Some have tried to argue against this by suggesting that it is conditioned to the culture of the day or that it refers to cultic prostitution. There is not a shred of evidence for such conclusions. The whole chapter (and see also Leviticus 20:13) is concerned with sins, and especially sexual sins, that are detested by God, and verse 22 stands between a warning against child sacrifice and bestiality; are these also tied to the culture of Moses' day only? The New Testament reinforces this position in, for example, 1 Corinthians 6:9 where Paul refers to both 'male prostitutes' and 'homosexual offenders'. How more plain does Paul need to be?

Secondly, homosexual relationships are *unnatural*. This much cannot be denied, however acceptable such practices may become in our modern society. Homosexuality is unproductive and sterile and the organs simply do not 'fit'. It clearly does not conform to the plan of 'nature', and in this sense is unnatural. Even those who believe that evolution explains the origin and progress of all things must accept this; even in the natural world, homosexual sex is absurdly crazy, to say the least.

Thirdly, homosexual relationships are *unreasonable*. An essay by Charles Krauthammer in *Time* magazine (22 July 1996) asks the question: 'Do gay-marriage advocates propose to permit the marriage of, say, two brothers, or of a mother and her (adult) daughter? If not, by what reason of logic or morality?' The writer then points to the inevitable conclusion that society, including gay-marriage advocates, will not allow polygamy or incest, but he adds, 'The point is *why* they won't allow it. They won't allow it because they think polygamy and incest wrong or unnatural or perhaps harmful… (or) psychologically or morally abhorrent.' In other words Krauthammer is forcing the gay lobby to answer the question why it is right to have gay sex and wrong to support incest and polygamy. Such a distinction is unreasonable and even illogical. The conclusion must be that without the law of God to guide us, all forms of sex between consenting adults are, logically, free to all.

In the order of God's human relationships in which he protects his image in mankind from humanity's wilful destruction, this Commandment is third in line. The first is the child/parent relationship, the second is the value of life and the third is the relationship between husband and wife. The importance of this third relationship is underlined by its inclusion in the tenth Commandment: 'You shall not covet your neighbour's wife'.

An edition of the *Authorised Version* of the Bible published in 1631 earned the printer the significant fine of three hundred pounds, imposed by Archbishop Laud, for the error of omitting the word 'not' in the seventh Commandment; that edition became known as 'The Wicked Bible'. Today, such an oversight might well be rewarded. We live in an age when marriage vows are being tailored to suit our preference for hasty contracts, short relations and easy dissolution. We are encouraged to believe that relationships outside a marriage are good things and that divorce may be the most constructive achievement in the life of many people. So why does God spoil it all with a Commandment like this?

Why is adultery so significant?
FIRST, BECAUSE SEX MATTERS
There is no doubt that sex takes centre stage in our modern society. Remove it from the films, songs, advertisements and conversation of every-day life and there would not be too much left! But that is nothing new. When archaeologists dug out the city of Pompeii, buried for nearly two thousand years beneath the ash and lava of Mount Vesuvius after its eruption in AD 79, they discovered crude murals decorating the walls of the homes of those unfortunate citizens. Sex is the most powerful emotional force in the human body. Controlled and used as God intended it is one of his greatest gifts, allowed to take control it becomes a tyrant that degrades and destroys.

The very existence of this Commandment assumes that sex, in its proper place, is good. In the plain language that Paul never hesitated to use in his letters to enforce an important point, the apostle described to the Corinthian Christians just what sexual intercourse means: 'Do you not know that he who unites himself with a prostitute is one with her in body? For it is said, "The two will become one flesh"' (1 Corinthians 6:16). Paul recognised that the beautiful promise of God in Genesis 2:24, that a man and woman become 'one flesh' when they come together as husband and wife in the sexual union, was capable of being distorted by the same physical union of a prostitute and her client. Both lead to the experience of 'one flesh'.

You can have a true marriage without sex, but you can never have true sex without a marriage. As far as God is concerned, 'Marriage should be honoured by all, and the marriage bed kept pure' (Hebrews 13:4), and that is the end of the matter. Nothing else will do. The various Bible words for sexual immorality include all sex that stays outside of marriage and all sex that strays outside of marriage.

It is impossible to read the Bible and come to the view that sex is 'dirty' for the Christian. Perverted sex most certainly is, but sex as God intended is not. The human race has made sex dirty, not God or the Bible. Arguably the greatest love-song ever written is found in the Bible in The Song of Songs, but the cheap use of sex is always condemned in Scripture.

SECONDLY, BECAUSE MARRIAGE MATTERS

God planned that there should be order in society; anarchy forms no part of his plan. Over a nation he gives a government and within the nation he provided for masters and servants (employers and employees); in the church there is leadership (elders) and in the home God provides a headship and order; he places the husband as head of the home and the husband and wife as head over the children. This is the most basic unit that God has ever given to society—the home and family. To commit adultery is to shatter God's foundational unit for society.

The first human relationship that God created was between a man and a woman in marriage, and when he looked for a human relationship that would best mirror the relationship between himself and his chosen people, God used the picture of marriage. He was the loving and faithful husband, and Israel was married to him (Isaiah 54:5–8); her spiritual apostasy was described in the harsh terms of adultery (Ezekiel 16:32), and most vividly portrayed in the experience of the prophet Hosea (Hosea 1–3). The same picture is drawn in the New Testament where Christ spoke of the Church as a bride looking forward to the great wedding celebration at the end of the age (Matthew 22:1–14).

No sexual relationship that by-passes the marriage bond between a man and a woman is ever countenanced in the Bible. Even polygamous marriages—that were never God's perfect plan for mankind (Genesis 2:24) but which were permitted by God through much of the Old Testament as a concession to human weakness—were bound by the commitment of marriage. God more than once warned against polygamy (e.g. Deuteronomy 17:17) and almost all stories of it in the Old Testament illustrate the tension that results. Strict laws governed the equal care of wives and no man could simply dispense with a wife he no longer wanted (Exodus 21:7–11). For the New Testament church a higher standard was clearly expected and a Christian leader must be 'the husband of but one wife' (1 Timothy 3:2). Literally this verse can be read, 'A one-woman man'.

When Christ confronted the attitude of easy divorce and easy remarriage he did so deliberately. The Jewish man was able to divorce his wife merely by announcing to her three times that that is what he was doing. In this way he considered himself free to take a new wife without the stigma of adultery. At least one school of Jewish teachers considered that the wife who spoiled her husband's dinner gave him sufficient grounds for divorce! When the Pharisees asked, 'Is it lawful for a man to divorce his wife for any and every reason?' (Matthew 19:3), our Lord seized the opportunity by reminding them of the plan of God that marriage was intended to be unbreakable. Divorce was the tragic and unavoidable end in some cases, but the only cause of a marriage breaking up that allowed the partner freedom to re-marry was 'marital unfaithfulness'—a phrase that translates the Greek word *porneia* meaning sexual immorality of any kind (v 9). Casual divorce and remarriage would be adultery. The response of the disciples: 'If this is the situation between a husband and wife, it is better not to marry' (v 10), was precisely what Christ wanted to hear. At least this was one group of men who would take their marriage commitment seriously!

THIRDLY, BECAUSE CHILDREN MATTER

In the year 2000, Judith S Wallerstein, a senior lecturer at Berkeley in America published her best-selling, *The Unexpected Legacy of Divorce: A 25 Year Landmark Study*. In it she identified the tragedy that trails the lives of children from broken homes: delinquency, depression, low educational attainment and so on. Two years later in January 2002, E Mavis Hetherington, a professor of psychology in Virginia, published her own report with contradictory conclusions, *For Better or for Worse: Divorce Reconsidered*. However, anyone in the world of education, social welfare or crime control will not require academic studies to conclude that, as a general rule, children from broken homes are at a significant disadvantage. In England and Wales more than thirty thousand children a year under the age of five are the victims of parental divorce.

Most marriages that break-up do so because of sexual immorality of one form or another, and the separating of husbands and wives in consequent divorce causes all kinds of emotional and psychological trauma for children. Half the children caught up in divorce believe the separation to be only temporary and five years later one in six long for their parents to be reconciled. The emotional cost to children and the financial burden to the state are enormous.

But there is something far more significant than either of those two factors. When a husband or wife is unfaithful to the marriage bond, they shatter a child's respect and honour for its parents. Adulterous parents cause the child to break the fifth Commandment; and we have already seen that our Lord's most serious warning was reserved for those who cause a young child to sin (Matthew 18:6–9). Unfaithful parents set an example to their children, and children from a broken home are at a higher risk of their own marriage ending in divorce. Remember the lesson from the African elephants referred to in chapter eight! Children who have no parents on which to model their lives are liable to become wild in their own lifestyle. Through the prophet Malachi, God reminded Israel that he wanted 'godly offspring', and that faithfulness and love within marriage was the most certain way for this to be accomplished (Malachi 2:15).

FOURTHLY, BECAUSE EMOTIONS MATTER

There is no relationship in life more intense and emotional than the relationship of a man and a woman; and that is why God placed it in the relatively secure context of a marriage commitment. To shatter this shatters lives. Sexual unfaithfulness is the root cause of most shattered marriages today, and the emotional trauma of a devastated partner and bewildered children is profound. Statistics show that the lost efficiency of an employee involved in divorce is estimated to cost the employer as much as five thousand pounds. Divorced women are three times as likely to develop lung cancer and divorced men are three times as likely to die from a stroke. In 1993 six hundred million pounds was spent on treating illnesses relating to divorce. And none of this takes into account the numerous homes where adultery destroys relationships and trust, but where somehow the marriage drags on.

Some years ago one of my sons reported a conversation with a school friend. The young friend admitted that he often lay awake at night wondering who he was; so many 'uncles' came and went that he could not be sure who his real father was. A young woman confided that even years after the event she considered the most miserable day of her life was when her mother burst into her room and joyfully announced the completion of the divorce. This happens in over four hundred homes *every day* in the United Kingdom. Adultery tramples over the emotions of others as if they were irrelevant.

The book of Proverbs carries more warnings against the sin of marital unfaithfulness than against any other sin. The outrage felt by such a betrayal is clearly portrayed in the following passage: 'A man who commits adultery lacks judgement; whoever does so destroys himself. Blows and disgrace are his lot, and shame will never be wiped away; for jealousy arouses a husband's fury, and he will show no mercy when he takes revenge. He will not accept any compensation; he will refuse the bribe, however great it is' (Proverbs 6:32–35). In our society it is sadly true that there appears to be little shame in adulterous relationships, but apart from that, the passage clearly reveals the human emotions of anger and fury that are still felt by children and 'innocent' partners when their trust and love are so carelessly destroyed.

FIFTHLY, BECAUSE LOVE MATTERS

When Paul taught about the relationship of husbands and wives, he referred to the example of Christ and exhorted husbands to love their wives: 'As Christ loved the church and gave himself for it' (Ephesians 5:23–32). In Romans 7:1–4 Paul claimed that only on the death of one partner would the other be free to re-marry. The apostle's jealous care of the church at Corinth is expressed in a vivid metaphor: 'I promised you to one husband, to Christ, so that I might present you as a pure virgin to him' (2 Corinthians 11:2). The same picture is taken up in Revelation 21:2,9 and 22:17.

Proverbs 5 presents a serious warning against adultery—and it is always the husband who is in view here. The first fourteen verses are a plain description of the danger of this sin and the miserable results of it; those verses are not hard to understand. However, from verses 15 to 19 the preacher portrays the benefit of 'enjoying the wife of your youth' under the picture of running water; he describes enjoying your own marriage as drinking 'from your own well'. The intense love and sexual joy must never be shared with others or become a public thing: 'let them be yours alone, never to be shared with strangers'. A wife loved by a faithful husband is described as 'a loving doe, a graceful deer' and the preacher concludes, 'may her breasts satisfy you always, may you ever be captivated by her love.' This is not passing and erotic love, on the contrary it is the secure love of a faithful husband who will never abandon the wife of his youth, but will be 'ever captivated by her love.' God loves the love of a faithful husband and wife.

In the last book of the Old Testament the prophet describes the people's complaint that God was no longer paying attention to their worship. The reason was that so many of the men had 'broken faith' with 'the wife of your youth'. In a powerful description of the importance of marriage, God declares that he makes the husband and wife 'one' and that he hates divorce (Malachi 2:13–16). In the New Testament Peter urges honour and respect within marriage 'so that nothing will hinder your prayers' (1 Peter 3:7). Nothing has changed. There can be no healthy spiritual life where there is no absolute faithfulness in marriage.

SIXTHLY, BECAUSE ADULTERY MATTERS

The results of a Gallup poll conducted in July 1996 revealed that almost half the population thinks adultery is wrong 'in all circumstances', whilst forty-four percent consider that it can be 'frequently justified'. The first figure would be encouraging if the second was not so discouraging! Not far short of half the population of Britain believe that adultery doesn't matter.

God reserved his strongest and his crudest language to condemn adultery. Whether he is referring to physical or spiritual adultery is beside the point, here is God through Jeremiah complaining bitterly about the life of the inhabitants of Jerusalem in the eighth century before Christ: 'Why should I forgive you? Your children have forsaken me and sworn by gods that are not gods. I supplied all their needs, yet they committed adultery and thronged to the houses of prostitutes. They are well-fed, lusty stallions, each neighing for another man's wife. Should I not punish them for this?' (Jeremiah 5:7–9). And further: 'I will pull up your skirts over your face that your shame may be seen—your adulteries and lustful neighings, your shameless prostitution! I have seen your detestable acts on the hills and in the fields. Woe to you, Jerusalem! How long will you be unclean?' (13:26–27). If that language offends, it is only because God intends it to! That is what he thinks of our national pastime, our family sport—flirting and adultery.

The punishment for adultery in the Old Testament was death (Leviticus 20:10); and although God reserves the right to soften this with mercy (John 8:1–11) and often has done, as in the case of David (2 Samuel 12:13), the severity of the punishment clearly reveals the seriousness of the crime. Nothing has changed from the viewpoint of the Creator.

SEVENTHLY, BECAUSE PROMISES MATTER

It is an odd statistic that in the same Gallup poll that revealed that nearly half the population of Britain considered adultery to be 'frequently justified', three quarters believed it to be unacceptable to lie to a husband or wife. We can only assume that there are some very open marriages in our nation where partners freely and immediately admit their extra marital affairs!

The serious promises that are made in both secular and religious marriages in this country are never meant to be broken. Rightly or wrongly I have always refused to marry those who have no interest in a genuine Christian commitment; my reasoning being that I do not believe anyone can make promises to a God they do not believe in. A secular marriage is more appropriate for them. However, whether a marriage is religious or secular, God expects our word to be kept (Matthew 5:37). One of the greatest casualties of adultery is that trust is blown apart. By the one act of unfaithfulness we rubbish all we ever promised to our partner and neither they, nor anyone else, has a reason for trusting us in the future. Trust is the steelwork that holds all of society together, and the relationship of marriage above all.

These are the reasons why God says, 'You shall not commit adultery'. There are to be no exceptions and no excuses. The Commandment is clear and categorical. We can search the Bible and we will not find one exception that God allows on this. And yet it is one of the most common sins of our nation.

How does adultery happen?

FIRST, THE PRESSURE AROUND US

More than one third of those happy occasions last week that brought a smiling young man and woman together in marriage will end in the divorce court. To be precise, one in every 2.8 marriages will fail.

A significant responsibility for this lies with the media. Tremendous pressure today is exerted against keeping the marriage bed pure (Hebrews 13:4). Our minds are constantly pummelled with the idea that this is a relationship that doesn't matter. Marriage is the butt of jokes and adultery is the theme of so many soaps, novels and radio plays. Adultery is assumed to be normal and right, even healthy and invigorating. It has become the one contract that doesn't matter and it is a fun thing to break it. A few years ago I heard a statement by the guest on a radio programme say, 'The wife who does not flirt grows old prematurely. The husband who has no affairs loses confidence in himself.' That is precisely the thinking of our age. Some years ago, around Christmas time, the following advertisement for diamonds appeared: 'Isn't it time you flirted with your wife; other men do?' Adultery is assumed, approved and practised in millions of homes.

The eldest daughter of a family I stayed with found herself and a friend the only two girls in the class who were living with their two natural parents; what was even more tragic than this was the fact that the rest of the class thought it quaintly comic! This is hard to square with statistics published in *Sexual Behaviour in Britain* (Johnson, Penguin 1994) that young people in the 16 to 24 age group overwhelmingly considered adultery to be wrong—eighty-one percent of males and eighty-five percent of females. Perhaps we have trampled upon the emotions of our children so successfully that we have seared their consciences, soured their hearts and desensitized their feelings, so that whilst they think they know what is wrong, when the temptation comes to them personally they will simply follow the herd.

Little by little the thinking of society begins to take possession of our minds, even Christian minds. In August 1993 a canon at Westminster Abbey, writing in *Theology*, suggested that, in order to keep in step with society, the Church of England should be more lax on those who engage in extra marital affairs and who live together without marriage in a loving union. What we watch and read, and the way we talk, has a certain effect upon all of us. We are bombarded with the idea that adultery is romantic, exciting, clean and fulfiling. Sin is always made to look attractive: 'Stolen water is sweet; food eaten in secret is delicious. But little do they know that the dead are there' (Proverbs 9:17–18).

In their book *Divorce: How and When to Let Go* (Prentice-Hall 1979) John Adams and Nancy Williamson write, 'Yes, your marriage can wear out. People change their values and lifestyles. People want to experience new things. Change is a part of life. Change and personal growth are traits for you to be proud of, indicative of a vital, searching mind. You must accept the reality that in today's multi-faceted world it is especially easy for two persons to grow apart. Letting go of your marriage, if it is no longer good for you, can be the most successful thing you have ever done. Getting a divorce can be a problem-solving, growth-oriented step. It can be a personal triumph.'

The assumptions here are glaring: marriages are by definition temporary things; change is inevitable, but we need not worry because values change as our preferences change; and my preferences, ('if it is no longer good for you'), presumably take precedence over the interests and emotions of my marriage partner. Losing our marriage is positive, not negative; it is a mark of success and not failure; it is evidence of personal strength and not weakness; it is something of which to be proud and not ashamed. Nothing is said of the Creator's wisdom, or of the shattered lives of a faithful partner and innocent children. Less is said of the statistics which show that second and third marriages generally have a lower success-rate than first marriages. We appear to learn nothing by experience.

The guest on a Radio 4 phone-in programme in August 1993 advocated the value of 'open marriages' where each partner is free to follow their own 'affairs' providing the other partner agrees and is kept informed! Almost all callers to the programme agreed, and when one reminded listeners of the value of keeping promises he was dismissed with the comment that his view was a commendable ideal, but that this was not an ideal world. I listened to a woman defending her newly-formed dating agency for married people. She claimed that such liaisons would enrich the marriage; and so they might—with about as much chance as falling from a tower block will enrich life! Significantly the same woman admitted that if her husband tried such an agency she would throttle him!

The story of Joseph is told in Genesis 39. Here was a young man more vulnerable to this particular temptation than most. He had been violently snatched away from his home and sold into slavery. The Bible tells us that he was tall, strong, good-looking and he served in a position of trust in the home of Potiphar, the captain of the bodyguard of the Pharaoh of Egypt. He was also single, lonely, and a servant. Day after day Potiphar's wife tried to seduce him. It is not hard to imagine how this woman in Egypt dressed and made-up whenever she went to invite him to have sex with her. She invaded his mind and emotions relentlessly.

That is exactly what we are faced with in the office, factory, workshop and classroom. We cannot escape it any more than Joseph could. To enter a monastery would not help because we would take our sinful hearts there with us, as the monastic movement found to its cost. We can easily identify with the daily temptation that Joseph was faced with. Godly people have had to live in this sort of society ever since the Fall of Adam and Eve. In Colossians 3:5–8 Paul reflected on the society around the young Christians at Colossae; among other things he wrote of 'sexual immorality *(porneia)*, impurity, lust, evil desires and greed', and reminded them that this is how they used to live; but now they were to be 'renewed in knowledge in the image of the Creator' (v 10). In other words obedience to the Commandments of the Creator is one of the most significant ways in which we find true human personhood: dignity, fulfilment, value and meaning. Whilst the world is busy encouraging men and women to animal behaviour, Christ and his word are turning animal behaviour into the image of God.

SECONDLY, THE PRESSURE OF OUR OWN FANTASY

Our watching, listening and reading leads us often to conclude, 'I want my experience to be like that.' The soaps and novels rarely portray the reality of marriage. They never tell us of the miserable, messy and mundane times, because the world finds such things almost impossible to romanticise; and it is no part of its interest to remind us that marriage is sustained more by loyalty, faithfulness and commitment than by heady romance. In the tough context of the real world everyone loves to fantasise. We dream of becoming a sporting idol, a top professional, a talked-of success. Dreams are no bad thing. But fantasy is dangerous. It allows our minds to become idle and we lose a grip on our emotions and on reality.

King David of Israel lost his grip on reality in the tragic story recorded in 2 Samuel 11. One season when kings went to war, David stayed at home. He sent his commanders and his army to the front and he idled his time in fantasy. Wandering on the roof of his palace he saw a beautiful woman bathing. He looked. But that was not all. Instead of turning away immediately, he watched—and lost control of his mind and his emotions. David sent a servant to bring Bathsheba into his house and there he fulfilled his fantasy. To cover his crime David arranged for her courageous husband to be killed in battle. The king committed not only adultery and murder, but he brought dishonour to the nation.

A second look can be disastrous. According to Christ, to look at another person 'lustfully' is to commit adultery in the heart (Matthew 5:27), and what our Lord goes on to say about gouging out an eye or cutting off a hand is picture language meaning that nothing is too much of a sacrifice in order to get out of the way of adultery. Adultery always begins with a look either with the eyes or in the mind: 'Do not lust in your heart after her beauty or let her capture you with her eyes' (Proverbs 6:25). When a married partner looks at someone else or a single person looks at a married partner and the heart misses a beat, alarm signals should be ringing. This is forbidden territory. Again, Proverbs wisely warns us: 'Above all else, guard your heart, for it is the wellspring of life' (Proverbs 4:23).

Beware of the arranged meeting; the subconscious desire to be near someone else's husband or wife. When we deliberately or subconsciously 'arrange' to sit with someone in church, or fall into conversation in the entrance lobby or call often, for any reason, at the house, the warning is there. There is an incredible slackness among Christians today, a naivety that can only be the result of a mind captured by the world. Christians engage in opposite sex counselling, regularly give lifts to the partners of another marriage, 'call by' for a cup of tea and a chat, watch videos and films and read books and magazines that depend heavily upon the alluring excitement of marital infidelity, and in a thousand ways we lay ourselves open to the sin of David.

There is a wise word that Peter slips into his first letter and which unfortunately some translations slip out. In 1 Peter 3:1 the apostle actually says, 'Wives... be submissive *to your own* husbands'. Paul makes the same point in 1 Corinthians 7:2. No woman should ever place herself under the spiritual authority of another man to the detriment of her relationship with her own husband, whoever that man may be and whatever his position.

Mental comparison is another disaster area. To compare our husband or wife unfavourably with another—or what is worse to make love to our marriage partner with someone else in our mind—is to commit adultery in our heart. Flattering attention may be good for our ego but is disastrous for our marriage—or that of someone else.

When Jesus warned in Matthew 5:28, 'I tell you that anyone who looks at a woman lustfully has already committed adultery with her in his heart', he was well aware that some sins never progress beyond our heart and mind, but when they enter the heart and mind they must be dealt with immediately. This is what our Lord warned about in Matthew 15:17–20, 'Don't you see that whatever enters the mouth goes into the stomach and then out of the body. But the things that come out of the mouth come from the heart and these make a man "unclean". For out of the heart come evil thoughts, murder, adultery *(moichao)*, sexual immorality *(porneia)*, theft, false testimony, slander. These are what make a man "unclean"'. Christ was talking about the Pharisees who were so concerned about ceremonial "cleanness" and yet harboured so much evil in their heart. Jesus was teaching his disciples that what we want begins in our heart, travels from heart to mind and from the mind to action. I want, I will, I do. My heart, my mind, my action. That, says Christ, is how you commit adultery.

Adultery does not just happen, it is planned—even amongst Christians. Some people foolishly and ignorantly try to excuse themselves with the response: 'We couldn't help it'. Of course they could help it. Monkeys, dogs and rats can't help it; but people plan it. Adultery is always planned, it never simply happens. King David planned and schemed to get what he wanted. There were reasons but no excuses. It is no excuse to blame a failing marriage, a coldly distant partner, or even an unfaithful spouse. How often we hear the pathetic defence: 'We shouldn't be too hard on her; after all, he was unfaithful first'. Is that a defence for murder and theft as well?

How can we guard against adultery?

THE FIRST THING TO DO IS TO THINK

In the story of Joseph we have an impeccable example of dealing with the temptation to adultery. Alone and vulnerable, the temptation must have been almost irresistible. A wealthy Egyptian wife, seductively dressed, alluringly perfumed and with the bedroom carefully prepared would make an exciting lover; and she would ensure that no-one ever knew. Besides, his family had treated him badly and, he might have reasoned, his God had apparently abandoned him on the wrong side of the Red Sea. How else could Joseph satisfy his manly emotions, and anyway, this kind of liaison was happening all over the land of Egypt—doubtless Potiphar had his own little thing or two.

But Joseph stood firm. He had sufficient understanding of the requirements of his God and sufficient sound sense to stop and think. He knew that his sin would surely find him out (Numbers 32:23)—a lesson that many politicians and others in public office seem strangely in ignorance of. Joseph reasoned that he was in a place of great trust and that even though Potiphar might never know, the all-seeing God he worshipped most certainly would. He would break his commitment neither to his master nor to his God, and he told the seductress just that 'My master has entrusted everything he owns to my care ... (and) has withheld nothing from me except you, because you are his wife. How then could I do such a wicked thing and sin against God?' (Genesis 39:8–9). That straightforward lesson in morality was not appreciated—it rarely is!

Joseph was clearly aware that Potiphar had taken notice of his faith in the Lord (v 3,5) and that he was the sole representative of the true God in the entire land of Egypt. If the Egyptians were to learn anything of Yahweh and of his moral code then they would only learn by watching Joseph. Perhaps many *were* watching. This man with a strange foreign religion lived a remarkably honest and clean life. For Joseph to betray his master would be bad enough, but by the same action he would betray his God to the ridicule of the Egyptians, whose sun-god and sacred bull would appear no better or worse than Joseph's deity. Joseph thought about this. King David did not. Adulterers never sufficiently consider the consequences. The professing Christian who fails at the seventh Commandment drags the reputation of Christ down into the world's gutter.

Blinded by passion and lust, few men and women stop to think until it is too late. Joseph could not have known the biblical Proverb: 'Can a man scoop fire into his lap without his clothes being burned?' (6:27), but he certainly understood its meaning. When the sight of someone hits us in the stomach it is time to think first—and fast. Joseph thought about the consequences of such an action; he thought of all who would be damaged and he thought of his God. Doubtless he thought of the kind of woman who was tempting him. Anyone who is prepared to break up a marriage for the lustful pleasure of a moment's romp, or even for the long excitement of an illicit liaison, can never be trusted. How often we have heard the plaintive wail of those whose secret endearments have been made public by the one they trusted in the bedroom!

Potiphar's wife is perfectly described in Proverbs 5:3–6, 'The lips of an adulteress drip honey, and her speech is smoother than oil; but in the end she is bitter as gall, sharp as a double-edged sword. Her feet go down to death; her steps lead straight to the grave. She gives no thought to the way of life; her paths are crooked but she knows it not.' The warning follows to the man who is ensnared by her: 'At the end of your life you will groan, when your flesh and body are spent' (v 11). Those who go on this road will find themselves, at the end of it, the most miserable of all.

THE SECOND THING TO DO IS NOT TO THINK

Joseph clearly did not fantasise on this woman as he attended to his duties. Having made his decision, as far as was humanly possible he put her out of his mind. When our mind is clear that God condemns a possible course of action, we must then put out of our mind that which is tempting and testing. Don't look, don't touch and don't talk about it. Don't pray about it either! After all, there is nothing to pray about since God gave his clearest word on the subject to Moses on Sinai.

Significantly we are told of Joseph that he refused 'even to be with her' (Genesis 39:10). That was brave of him—and difficult. He was only a slave and she was his master's wife; she could order him to do anything. But Joseph could be a scheming man too, and he organised his lifestyle so that he would not be near her unless it was absolutely unavoidable. If orders came that the master's wife wanted something, Joseph would make sure that somebody else took it to her. The fact that she had to scheme carefully to trap him only proves what a wise man he had been. Her cunning continued after Joseph had fled from the house and she called the servants to see Joseph's cloak not in her hand, which would have betrayed her guilt, but 'beside' her (v 18). Certainly Joseph, and the reputation of his God, suffered temporarily, but the ultimate vindication of both is plain before the story of this man of integrity closes.

We must come to that point where we scheme to run away from that which is tempting us into this sin. Nothing matters more than the total commitment of a man or a woman to their promises in marriage. There are many men who play into the hands of an adulteress by choosing the wrong secretary, travelling in the wrong car, or establishing the wrong business contact. An 'open marriage' should not be as defined today, in which each is allowed their own 'affairs', but a marriage in which total loyalty leads to total trust and a total absence of even the hint of 'secret' relationships.

Moralizing?

It is incredible how sensitive society becomes when any comment is made about sexual sins between consenting adults. We condemn mugging and murder, child abuse and rape, theft and fraud; against these most will unite in opposition. But if we condemn adultery we are told not to judge the actions of other people. The explanation for this paradox is that we imagine adultery, like homosexual practice and a host of sexual sins, concerns only those involved, and providing they are consenting adults then no harm is done. It is not for us to interfere with our 'moralizing' judgements.

The 'blind spot' in this reasoning lies at the very point of believing that any such action 'concerns only those involved'. No behaviour between two people ever concerns them alone; others are always involved sooner or later. For a husband and parent, everything he does affects his family—for good or ill. There is no such thing as an action that is morally or socially neutral. The horrific effects of the HIV virus are witness to the impossibility of promiscuous sex being morally or socially neutral. The 'affair' of a married partner always rebounds on children, parents, spouse, friends, employers or employees, work colleagues and society in general.

This is surely what is meant in Numbers 32:23, 'You will be sinning against the LORD and you may be sure that your sin will find you out'. It is in the context of these Ten Commandments that God introduced the warning of sins being punished 'to the third and fourth generation' (Exodus 20:5). When looking at that expression in chapter four we commented that this is not an arbitrary decree of a vengeful God, but that by the law of cause and effect future generations are inevitably hurt by the sins of previous generations. The tragedy of the junkie's new-born baby going 'cold-turkey'—or worse, dying painfully from inherited AIDS—and the asthmatic child of the chain-smoking mother, are obvious examples of this principle of the children being punished for the sins of their parents (Exodus 34:7). In the same way an emotionally scarred child, reared by a mother who is herself scarred by the selfish adultery of an undisciplined man, may himself grow up to be weak, undisciplined and resentful; in turn he may bring all that to his own marriage with similarly disastrous consequences. Paul makes the same point in Romans 14:7, 'None of us lives to himself alone....' Clearly the apostle has in mind our responsibility to the Lord in everything, but the context is care for another man's conscience. Remember the African elephants!

Society quickly insists upon moral judgements when someone steals a car, breaks into a home, or simply plays loud music into the early hours; but adultery is apparently our own business. Every society has to make moral judgements, but without God's word we have no sound base to start from. This is why apparently it would be unthinkable in our modern society to frame a law against adultery, and yet few objected to the law that compels me to wear a seat-belt in my car. Presumably breaking my publicly declared vows to my wife is of less significance than breaking my head on the windscreen!

It was the task of the priest in the Old Testament: 'To teach my people the difference between the holy and the common and show them how to distinguish between the clean and the unclean' (Ezekiel 44:23). That is the purpose of God's word in general and of the Ten Commandments in particular: to teach us to distinguish what is right and wrong, clean and unclean, holy and sinful in the sight of God. Adultery is always, everywhere, unclean and sinful.

Universal guilt

Not one of us can stand before God and claim that on this Commandment we have been perfectly clean in thought and heart even though we may have been innocent in action. For some, this chapter may have been painful reading. Perhaps it awakened memories of experiences that you had hoped to forget, or it may have upgraded a sin you had been trying to minimise. Often God needs to hurt before he can heal. The writer of Proverbs appeals to the man in temptation: 'Why be captivated, my son, by an adulteress? Why embrace the bosom of another man's wife? For a man's ways are in full view of the LORD, and he examines all his paths' (5:20–21).

Jeremiah 17:9 sums up all of us: 'The heart is deceitful above all things and beyond cure. Who can understand it?' That is in fact one of the most encouraging verses in the whole Bible although it may not appear that way at first reading. Nobody really understands the human heart because it is the most deceitful thing on earth—and its deceit is beyond human cure.

Untold millions of men and women have sincerely promised an undying love to a husband or wife, only to shatter the covenant a few years later. Men have preached powerfully and convincingly against adultery and yet in a moment of thoughtless lust, or worse in calculated deception, have ruined their family, their church and their ministry. Even King David, the composer of the greatest hymns ever written in praise of God, committed adultery. There is no human cure for adultery. It does not become less offensive to God because it goes on for a long time. Nor does it become less offensive because society condones it, the media exploit it, royalty practises it or the church goes soft on it. It does not even become less offensive to God if you are living faithfully with a new partner, or your adultery was provoked by a failure of your first marriage.

Adultery can never be paid for. Unlike idolatry, blasphemy, Sabbath breaking, dishonouring parents, stealing, lying, and coveting, adultery—like murder—is an act that once committed can never be uncommitted, paid for, or even adequately apologised for. Even love will not cover it. It is the most serious breach of trust that anyone can commit. It is beyond human cure.

Is there therefore no cure? Of course there is. Wherever there is law there is gospel. Wherever the law of God thunders, 'You shall not', the cross of

Christ opens wide the arms that say, 'I can forgive'. There is no human cure for adultery, but through his cross Christ can forgive any sin and reconcile us to the Father—and to the partner we have offended. Christ carried our sin, all of it, on the cross. 2 Corinthians 5:21 tells us that Christ became all our sin and in exchange we can become all his righteousness.

Commenting on Galatians 3:13, 'Christ redeemed us from the curse of the law by becoming a curse for us, for it is written: "cursed is everyone who is hanged on a tree"', the sixteenth century German Reformer, Martin Luther, wrote, 'Christ is innocent as concerning his own person, and therefore he ought not to have been hanged on a tree: but because according to the law of Moses every thief and malefactor ought to be hanged, therefore Christ also according to the law of Moses ought to be hanged, for he sustained the person of a sinner and a thief, and not of one, but of all sinners and thieves... For he being made a sacrifice for the sins of the whole world, is not now an innocent person and without sins, is not now the Son of God born of the Virgin Mary; but a sinner which has and carries the sin of Paul, who was a blasphemer, and oppressor and a persecutor; of Peter, who denied Christ; of David, who was an adulterer, a murderer, and caused the Gentiles to blaspheme the name of the Lord: and briefly, who has and bears the sins of all men in his body, that he might make satisfaction for them with his own blood.'

Luther knew better than to believe that Christ, even on the cross, was ever less than the eternal Son of God, but he was concerned to emphasise the full depth of the sin-bearing sacrifice of the Saviour. He 'became our sin' and Luther could think of no better way of explaining that terrible mystery. That is what justification means: Christ taking my sin so that I can be set free and be declared not guilty; he took both the guilt and the punishment of our sin upon himself. All he asks for is a repentant heart with an unqualified admission that I am wrong.

David committed murder and adultery, but in Psalm 51:3 he prayed, 'I know my transgressions, and my sin is always before me.' For eighteen months he had had his sin before him. It was always in front of his mind. When he slept it was nagging at his conscience, and when he woke up it was still there. Heaven was closed and worship was impossible. Then one day the prophet Nathan convinced David of his sin and the broken king began his journey back to God: 'Against you, you only I have sinned' (v 4). We may disagree by responding, 'Oh no David, you are wrong, you sinned against Bathsheba, against her husband, against Joab the commander of the army, against the nation'. But David knew all that when he declared his guilt before God. The difference between Joseph and David was just at that point. Joseph feared to sin against God, and David, in that moment of lust, lost his fear of God. Adultery is easy when we lose our fear of offending God.

Until we feel like that, the gospel has nothing to say to us. When David cried out, 'Blot out my transgressions. Wash away all my iniquity and cleanse me from my sin… Create in me a pure heart, O God, and renew a steadfast spirit within me' (Psalm 51:1–2,10) there was an immediate response from God.

Elsewhere the Psalmist declared, 'As far as the east is from the west so far he has removed our transgressions from us' (Psalm 103:12) and Isaiah the prophet promised, 'I have swept away your offences like a cloud, your sins like the morning mist. Return to me, for I have redeemed you' (Isaiah 44:22). Similarly God promised through Jeremiah: 'I will forgive their wickedness and will remember their sins no more' (Jeremiah 31:34). Thank God that although there are some sins *we* cannot either forgive or forget— God can do both.

Property rights

You shall not steal. Exodus 20:15

The Home Office estimates that more than eight percent of the people visiting a large store are likely to be stealing. Doubtless some of those will try to justify their action on the grounds of poverty, though for most it is simply their way of life. However, we cannot assume that the other ninety-two percent would disapprove of the shoplifter's action, since a recent poll showed that more than a quarter of those questioned believe that it is acceptable to remain silent if a superstore undercharges them. Our confused double standards are seen in the fact that the figure is cut by a half if it is a small corner shop that undercharges. Presumably the fat-cats are fair game. Whilst stealing is generally disapproved of in society, we are not always sure why. For that matter we may not even be sure what stealing is.

Agur, the wise man of Proverbs, appears to have been well acquainted with the Ten Commandments, for in one powerful poem he includes the substance of at least seven of them. Here is the way in which he refers to four of the Commandments: 'Keep falsehood and lies far from me (9th); give me neither poverty nor riches, but give me only my daily bread. Otherwise, I may have too much and disown you and say, "Who is the LORD?" (3rd). Or I may become poor and steal, and so dishonour the name of my God (8th). Do not slander a servant to his master, or he will curse you, and you will pay for it (9th). There are those who curse their fathers and do not bless their mothers…'(5th). (Proverbs 30:8–11).

The eighth Commandment: 'You shall not steal' should be a simple Commandment to understand. Stealing is to take without permission that which rightly belongs to another person. Our first opportunity is probably in the play-group when our friends are chosen for us and their toys are decidedly more attractive than our own. In every society there are some laws of property that are generally understood and agreed, and punishment is reserved for those who violate the law. No society can survive for long without laws that forbid stealing.

Why is it wrong to steal?

FIRST, STEALING IS SIN BECAUSE IT VIOLATES THE GOD-GIVEN LAW OF PROPERTY

When God put Adam and Eve in a beautiful garden, he told them to 'work it and take care of it', but he placed a prohibition against taking fruit from one particular tree in the garden that did not belong to them (Genesis 2:15–17). This was the first law concerning property. All through the Old Testament God taught his people the distinction between owning and stealing. The law of property recognises that some have more and some have less, but that we all have something. This principle is clear from Acts 5 where Peter reminded Ananias that whilst he owned the property he was free to dispose of it as he wished. The sin was not that he kept some of the money for himself, but that he lied to God (Acts 5:3,4). Many of our Lord's parables were based on property rights. God has recognised that in this world almost everyone owns some property, however little, and to take that away is violating the God-given right of people to possess what they own. Owning property is part of the responsibility of working and taking care of the world in which we live. David Field in *God's Good Life* helpfully describes us as caretakers rather than owners.

Some ownership may be wrong if we gained it illegally or immorally, if we have too much or if we make it our god. This was the problem of the young man who heard from Christ more than he bargained for when he asked the way to eternal life (Mark 10:17–31). But even if not all ownership is right, stealing is always wrong. Redressing the balance, by means of those who have less stealing from those who have more, is a violation of the eighth Commandment.

SECONDLY, STEALING IS SIN BECAUSE IT BETRAYS A GRASPING SPIRIT

Stealing is the desire to get something for nothing, entering into the labours of others free of charge. One of the earliest thefts recorded in history is found in Genesis 14:11–12. Four Kings seized all the goods of Sodom and Gomorrah and carried them off, including Abraham's nephew Lot and his possessions. That was a large scale theft.

Jeremiah 49:9 reminds us of something that is very obvious, especially if you have had the misfortune to be burgled in your home: 'If thieves come during the night would they not steal only as much as they wanted?'

Unlike the fox who will kill all the hens whether he can eat them or not, thieves are normally selective. Friends of mine have discovered valuable camcorders left behind simply because the burglars were targeting only jewellery. There is in all of us a grasping spirit; in our coveting—the prelude to theft—we target what we would like and then we want some more.

Stealing always betrays that spirit of wanting and wanting. It is the spirit that we read about in Proverbs 30:15, 'The leech has two daughters. "Give! Give!" they cry.' Agur goes on to compare this insatiable greed to the grave, the barren womb and fire—none of which is ever satisfied. Stealing is sin because it betrays a grasping spirit that says, 'Give! Give!' Stealing is society's leech; it takes the waiting out of wanting!

THIRDLY, STEALING IS SIN BECAUSE IT ENCOURAGES VIOLENCE

Criminal law distinguishes between theft, burglary and aggravated robbery. The second always involves some form of breaking-in whilst the last is accompanied by violence. In the New Testament James summarises this perfectly: 'What causes fights and quarrels among you. Don't they come from your desires that battle within you? You want something but you don't get it. You kill and covet but you cannot have what you want, you quarrel and fight.' That theft in Genesis 14 was accompanied by violence. The four kings did not enter Sodom and Gomorrah and simply invite the population to join them! Their visit was accompanied by fire and sword. All wars are caused by greed, whether for power, property or principle; we want, and are prepared to fight to get it (James 4:1–2). Very few burglars are totally unarmed; they are ready to fight if necessary. Today nations and sections of society are confronting each other violently simply because of greed.

But violence is also the *response* to stealing. Our first reaction when we arrive home from holiday to find our house 'cleaned out' by an unwanted visitor is probably: 'If only I could get my hands on them!' Human nature being what it is we respond to stealing with at the least the *thought* of violence. This is why we have laws in our society that limit the aggression of the man who is defending his own property. The same was true in the Old Testament as we saw in chapter nine (e.g. Exodus 22:2). God had to put a check on the violent reaction that stealing draws out from most of us.

This principle is the same for the international response to theft also. During 1990 an alliance of nations took back the tiny kingdom of Kuwait from the greedy hands of Saddam Hussein, the despotic ruler of Iraq. Some response was essential because international theft is no more tolerable than individual theft. What caused concern to some, however, was the sheer weight of the reaction. Powerful nations moved vast armies and spent many weeks pummelling the life out of the people and the military in Iraq. This raised the whole question of the appropriate level of response to aggression. No violent reaction to aggression can be considered good, though it may be necessary. Similarly, when the United Kingdom despatched a large armada to retake the tiny Falkland Islands from the Argentinian invaders, some response was necessary to uphold the rule of international law; however, it would have been indefensible for the British government to have dropped nuclear bombs upon the Argentinian mainland! The evil of the response would have exceeded the evil of the theft. Once again, stealing invited an aggressive response. The violent theft recorded in Genesis 14 prompted a violent reaction. Abraham buckled on his sword, called out his three hundred and eighteen trained servants, and in a decisive night attack routed the plunderers. Violence to steal, violence to regain. That is why God says stealing is sin.

Is it always wrong to steal?

After a punishing Atlantic crossing, the Pilgrim Fathers landed at Cape Cod in New England in November 1620. They arrived weak and dispirited, without a home, with very little food and faced with wild animals, deep forests, freezing weather and unseen but hostile Indians. They believed it to be the providence of God when they stumbled across Indian corn supplies hidden in the ground. That probably saved the life of the early settlers. They took the corn, but because of the eighth Commandment, they solemnly pledged before God that they would pay back to the Indians after the first harvest—and they kept their word. They had wives and children waiting on the beach whom they had to keep alive through a dreadful winter. The Pilgrim Fathers took the food to keep themselves and their families alive, but this commandment forced them to say, 'In the sight of God it is a sin to steal, though it would be a greater sin to allow our families to die when food is available, so we will pledge ourselves to replace it though the Indians know nothing of it.'

Of course stealing is wrong when it betrays greed, but can circumstances change this command? Is it wrong to steal if the alternative is starvation? Apparently the wise man in Proverbs thought so: 'Keep falsehood and lies far from me, give me neither poverty nor riches, but give me only my daily bread. Otherwise I may have too much and disown you and say, "Who is the LORD?" or I may become poor and steal and so dishonour the name of my God' (Proverbs 30:8,9). As far as Agur was concerned even to steal in his poverty would dishonour the name of God; but he appears to acknowledge that nevertheless, extreme circumstances may compel him to break one of God's laws.

During the middle of the nineteenth century the evangelical philanthropist, Lord Shaftesbury, attended an unusual meeting. Late one night he met with some four hundred members of London's toughest criminal fraternity. A London City Mission worker set up the meeting because the missionary knew the men well and had their confidence; they all knew of Lord Shaftesbury as the only man of influence who appeared to be interested in doing anything to help people like them. Here they were, crowded into a cold, dimly-lit room, four hundred of the worst criminals on the streets of London. Shaftesbury talked with them and urged them to give up their violence and aggression and to adopt a different way of life. The 'Lord of the great unwashed' as he was later nicknamed, wrote in his diary that many of the men were in tears when they admitted that they had no alternative but to steal. Either they stole or they and their wives and children would starve to death. Shaftesbury added, 'What a spectacle! What misery! What degradation! And yet, I question whether we fine, easy, comfortable folks, are not greater sinners in the sight of God than are these poor wretches.' Why did he say that? Because he was concerned for the fact that it was the luxury of so many that drove these men into poverty, and forced them into violent theft simply to remain alive.

Does the guilt involved in stealing lie at the door of those who force the poor into starvation? In the Old Testament God provided a law for 'gleaning' (Leviticus 19:9 for example). When the farmer sent his servants into the field to cut the corn they were not to harvest close to the edges;

similarly, what fell from the sheaves would be left and not picked up. The poor had the right to 'glean', or gather that which was left over. The same was true in the vineyard. We should ask whether any of our actions contribute to the poverty of others and force them into theft; and if so, what we should do about it. With all the Commandments we have a responsibility not only to guard against breaking them ourselves, but to ensure that we are never the cause of others breaking them.

Another wise man in the book of Proverbs reminds us that, 'Men do not despise a thief if he steals to satisfy his hunger when he is starving. Yet if he is caught he must pay sevenfold, though it costs him all the wealth of his house' (Proverbs 6:30–31). The point is that we may understand the extreme reasons that lead a man to steal, and we may sympathise with his tragic dilemma, but even in such circumstances the preacher recognised the justice of punishment for stealing. Stealing is sin, whatever the reason, though it may sometimes be the lesser of two evils; and for that reason the punishment may be tempered with mercy. Equally guilty, as Shaftesbury recognised, are those who, by their own greed or negligence, force others into theft. This is why we need both the tenth and the eighth commandments. The tenth commandment is against coveting, and that will compel us to check our motives. But the Pilgrim Fathers and many of the 'footpads' of Georgian and Victorian London were not motivated by covetousness, they simply needed to keep themselves and their families alive.

This Commandment allows no exceptions. Stealing always and in any circumstance is sin. That may be a hard conclusion to grasp, but if we take another position then anarchy rules and it will be easy to justify almost any standard that an individual cares to set. Shoplifting in France is described as a national sport; supermarket barons are seen as parasites on the community and so it is 'fair game' to steal from them. On the same basis we may deplore the indecent 'fat-cat' salaries paid to the management of companies and utilities and therefore justify fiddling our meters or stealing items from work. But is that how God sees it? To justify stealing a few nails from work on the basis that my wages are ridiculously poor compared with the MD's salary and perks, allows a poorer man than me to burgle my home with impunity.

What kind of stealing?

FIRST, THEFT BY DIRECT STEALING

This may range from the robbery of gold bullion worth millions to petty pilfering where only a few pence are involved. In the United Kingdom half a million shoplifters cost the nation over ten million pounds every day. In 1994 Marks and Spencer alone spent twenty million pounds in security costs and still lost thirty million in stolen goods. A documentary featuring a woman who boasted she could make thirteen hundred pounds a day by shoplifting went straight to the top of television ratings. Perhaps millions admired her, forgetting that they were the ones who paid for her life-style.

Human nature has a great ability to justify sin in ourselves and condemn the same thing in others. In 1983 Dr Gerald Mars, a Cambridge sociologist, claimed that fiddles at work increase job satisfaction, raise work rates and lead to greater economic production! That sounds an impressive justification of stealing in our modern society, and one that we may be surprised Paul did not use for the poor exploited slaves in the congregation at Ephesus. Instead, he wrote, 'He who has been stealing must steal no longer' (Ephesians 4:28). Even if Dr Gerald Mars' facts are correct and it could be proved that fiddles at work did increase job satisfaction, raise work rates and lead to greater economic production, stealing would still be wrong; and it would be healthier for us to have less satisfaction, lower work rates and smaller economic production, and remain obedient to the command of God. When someone burgles your home it may give him great satisfaction, but it doesn't make it right. Stealing is sin.

However, Christians are sometimes not far behind the world in stealing, though the issues may be far more subtle. Unregistered software on PC's, unlicensed spiritual songs on acetate, and unpaid copyright for sheet music are all contemporary forms of theft by those who deplore the thousands who cheat on their road tax and television licences.

The Commandment is clear and the New Testament simply underlines the clarity. Paul ensured that the young converts, slave or free, knew perfectly well the plain standards expected of the Christian.

When he wrote to Titus at Crete during the early sixties AD, Paul had a relevant word for the slaves. A little role-play will help us to appreciate the impact of Paul's letter: You are a first century slave. You own nothing, not even your wife and children; your master is living in splendid luxury and you are keeping him in that comfort for virtually no return at all. Among all your fellow slaves it is 'accepted practice' to steal as much from your master as you can get away with. They are simply redressing the balance a little here and there; you join with them, of course, and in the evenings you boast to one another of the day's 'takings'. One day you become a Christian and when you attend the meeting place on Sunday, Titus is reading from a letter that Paul has sent to him as the group leader. Almost the first words you hear are these: 'Teach slaves to be subject to their masters in everything, to try to please them, not to talk back to them, and not to steal from them, but to show that they can be fully trusted, so that in every way they will make the teaching about God our Saviour attractive' (Titus 2:9–10). That is radical! This kind of far-reaching morality will become the gossip of the great house and it will soon catch the attention of the master himself. You will not find it easy or popular when you explain your changed lifestyle to your fellow slaves. But change you must.

SECOND, THEFT BY DECEITFUL DEALING

This may be 'insider dealing' and corporate dishonesty or fiddling the tax, VAT or expense accounts; it may be adjusting things a little or conveniently forgetting something. God commands, 'Give everyone what you owe him: if you owe taxes, pay taxes; if revenue, then revenue' (Romans 13:7) and we may add 'if Value Added Tax, then pay Value Added Tax'. The VAT office and our big corporations are in open warfare on this single issue, and tax evasion is currently big business.

Stealing can also include offering a false age to reduce costs or silently accepting a miscalculation when it is to your advantage. A few years ago I purchased a PC notebook and printer from an international corporation. I brought the hardware home with me and a few days later a second set arrived by post! I now had two computers and printers for the price of one! I phoned to report the error, but two weeks later I still had the extra goods. I phoned again to remind them but no action resulted. After a few more weeks I wrote to say that if they did not collect the surplus equipment within two weeks I would assume the company was happy for me to keep it. Within a few days there was a knock on the door! Some would say I was crazy to try so hard; besides, a vast company like that would hardly miss one set, and who knows whether it was ever returned to the company or was simply 'lost' somewhere in the paper work. But none of that was my business. The eighth Commandment allowed no juggling with the truth. I simply had no option.

Within a two-and-a-half hour period on one January day, British Rail Transport Police detained one hundred people on Victoria Station in London travelling without a ticket. That is stealing—even though the polls indicate that fourteen percent of the population consider this to be morally acceptable.

When I was at college in London we shared the premises with the office of a well-known furnishing company. The typing-pool above us would frequently lapse into a time of chatter when the typewriters fell silent—this was well before the days of word-processors! We students could always tell when the boss walked into the office because there would be an instant clatter of typewriters as work resumed in earnest. Stealing time by extended breaks and slack work is deceitful stealing. The Colossian slaves were reminded, 'Obey your earthly masters in everything, not only when their eye is on you and to win their favour...' (Colossians 3:22). To slacken off when no one is looking is stealing.

In principle all this 'petty' stealing is no different from corporate fraud or insider dealings. The amount of time wasted or money stolen, either directly or indirectly, only makes the sin more or less notorious, not more or less sinful. God does not rate the severity of a breach of the eighth Commandment according to the sums involved.

THIRD, THEFT BY DELAYED PAYMENT

We live in a world of contracts. Many have a mortgage on their house and this is a contract. The Building Society or bank lend the money and I repay at an agreed rate at specified times. We all have another form of contract with the utility companies such as gas, water, electricity, and the telephone. We agree to pay on receipt of a bill for the facility we have been using. Some people consider it smart to pay only when the red reminder comes through the door. That is stealing. To delay to pay is theft. In the face of the threat of legal action it is no defence to boast of our judicious use of money by delaying payment for as long as possible. This robs a company of money that is rightly theirs and of the interest on that money. If a creditor asks for his money by the 30th of the month, on the 31st you are a thief. 'Let no debt remain outstanding' could hardly be more clear (Romans 13:8).

When a cheque bounces and a debt, however small, remains unpaid we are stealing. It is time many Christians put their financial house in order. Paul was not wide of the mark when he accused the Jews of their guilt because they boasted that they were a privileged people because they alone had the laws of God, and yet they consistently broke the very laws they thought marked them out as different: 'You who preach against stealing, do you steal?' (Romans 2:21).

When Paul writes, 'Let no debt remain outstanding' he refers us to the Commandment: 'Do not steal' (Romans 13:8,9). But he then gives another reason: 'Love your neighbour as yourself'. It doesn't matter if the whole world refuses to pay out until threatened with legal action, Christians are supposed to be salt and light; which means that we are not to be sucked down with the world but we are to show a far better way and to lift the standards of the world up. On this subject 'pay as you would be paid' should be the motto of every Christian. I am ashamed when business men tell me that they dislike dealing with Christians because they are so slow to pay. That is disgraceful. Thousands of small firms go out of business each year for this very reason— because debtors delay payment for so long that the company cannot pay its own bills. Any Christian who is at the beginning of that chain is breaking the eighth Commandment and brings dishonour on the name of his Lord. Pay as you would be paid. The world will notice that. It is radical.

FOURTH, THEFT BY DISHONEST CHARGING

In a society governed by market forces it is not always easy to determine what a fair price for an item should be; but the Christian must seriously consider the fact that an item is not always worth what the market is willing to pay. The political economist may disagree, but what if the market pays because it is unaware of the real value, or unable to choose? Even our secular Government recognises this fact and that is why we have a Monopolies Commission. There is such a thing as Christian integrity in charging. I have met craftsmen who, aware that they could charge more for their work, are nevertheless satisfied that they are receiving a fair rate for the job. It is no excuse to hide behind the claim that 'the market can bear it'—perhaps it can, but many may find the charges crippling. Greed is the motivation that grasps for everything it can.

To sell anything at a price we know to be well above the true value is a violation of the eighth Commandment. 'Fixing' an unreliable vehicle for a quick sale, selling an item that will never give service, or talking up a product or facility far beyond its real worth are all forms of dishonesty.

Stealing from God

Some years ago I preached a sermon on the eighth Commandment and during the following week only one person came and asked me if I intended saying anything more on the subject of stealing, or whether I had said everything I thought necessary. I knew what they had in mind and I could assure them that there was one important issue still to be covered. It is to that subject that we now turn.

According to the *UK Christian Handbook* for 1996/97, British church-goers give around 1.8 billion pounds each year to Christian organisations. That doesn't sound too bad until we realise that it is approximately two percent of their average income! Since virtually all Christian churches, missions and organizations believe that they could achieve more if their income increased, it could well be that Christian people today are robbing God. But is that really possible?

There is a passage in Malachi that is of great significance today. The historical context is found in the books of Ezra and Nehemiah. Some five hundred and thirty years before Christ, through the decree of Cyrus, king of the Medio-Persian Empire, the Jews had returned from exile and had commenced rebuilding their temple in Jerusalem. It was not long, however, before the work came to a halt. There were two reasons for this: first, because the people were terrified by the threats of their enemies, and second because of their selfishness; they found it safer and more comfortable to get on with their home extensions rather than bother with the work of God. The prophet Haggai whipped the people back to work by his uncompromising preaching, but not long afterwards, even though they now had a brand new temple, their spiritual activity became slovenly and careless. The prophet Malachi arrived on the scene to address this state of affairs.

Malachi turned his attention to four things in particular. First of all he complained against their inferior sacrifices; they were looking for the worst possible animals among the flock and concluded, 'That will do for the LORD'. Secondly, Malachi pointed to their inferior lives; they were not living like the people of God ought to live. He then drew attention to their inferior leaders; the leaders were not setting the right example to the people and were prepared to say whatever the people wanted them to say. But fourthly Malachi complained about their inferior giving. They were holding back the tithes.

Through the prophet, God set up an imaginary dialogue with his people, suggesting their questions in response to his challenges. Here is part of the debate:

'"Return to me, and I will return to you," says the LORD Almighty.

"But you ask, 'How are we to return?'

"Will a man rob God? Yet you rob me.

"But you ask, 'How do we rob you?'

"In tithes and offerings. You are under a curse—the whole nation of you—because you are robbing me. Bring the whole tithe into the storehouse, that there may be food in my house. Test me in this", says the LORD Almighty, "and see if I will not throw open the floodgates of heaven and pour out so much blessing that you will not have room enough for it"' (Malachi 3:7–10).

Clearly, to fail to give God what he expects us to give is to 'rob God', and that must be a violation of the eighth Commandment. It is possible to be scrupulous in avoiding any offence in the ways we have discussed so far in this chapter, and yet to steal from God.

Tithes and all that

Although the tithe was one tenth of the income of the Israelite, the Old Testament pattern for giving was not as straightforward as that simple statement may appear.

The first reference to the tithe is found in Genesis 14:20, where we read of Abraham giving a tithe to a strange figure that appears and disappears rapidly from the stage of the Old Testament. His name was Melchizedek. Some believe that he was a pre-incarnation appearance of Christ upon earth, but whether or not that is true need not concern us here. The fact is that Melchizedek was a priest of the true God and Abraham gave him a tithe, just as the Israelites were later commanded to support the Levite priests in the same way. Four hundred years after Abraham, God gave Moses this law recorded in Numbers 18:21, 'I give to the Levites all the tithes in Israel as their inheritance in return for the work they do whilst serving at the Tent of Meeting.' From Leviticus 27:30–32 Israel was reminded that a 'tithe of everything from the land, whether grain from the soil or fruit from the trees... the entire tithe of the herd and the flock... belongs to the LORD; it is holy to the LORD.' If a man wished to convert his tithe into cash, he had to add a fifth to the value (v 31). The tithe belonged to the Lord and to no one else. However, Old Testament laws on giving did not end there. A poll-tax, or ransom, was to be paid at the time of a national census (Exodus 30:11–16), and sacrifices, special gifts, vows, firstfruits, redemption of the first-born, and free-will offerings were all in addition to the tithe (Deuteronomy 12:6 and Exodus 23:19).

By the time of Christ, the Pharisees were so legalistic in their thinking that they counted out every small seed to ensure that they gave God his tenth—and no more (Matthew 23:23). Christ did not condemn their care for the tithe, but their neglect of far more important issues. He told them that they should practise the tithe without neglecting 'justice, mercy and faithfulness'.

In chapter two I recalled how we dealt with this matter of the tithe in a teens and twenties discussion. When we started from the Old Testament law of giving it was not too easy to apply the various details to our modern situation, particularly when we discovered that the Jews actually spent some of their giving on the sacrifice, part of which they ate! But when we began again and searched for information in the New Testament another approach opened up. From 2 Corinthians 8 and 9, 1 Corinthians 16, and Mark 6 we gathered a list of words to describe Christian giving: sacrificially, joyfully, willingly, spontaneously, proportionately, abundantly, secretly, humbly, regularly, trustfully—that was all the result of grace. At this point the young people asked for a biblical pattern, a rule by which to measure our giving. The tithe gave us our pattern. To insist upon the exact proportion of the tithe and to make it a mark of spirituality would be legalism, but Christian freedom may lead us there willingly.

A positive approach to this subject is found in the record of the most significant Old Testament revival. During the reign of King Hezekiah, seven hundred years before the birth of Christ, spiritual revival affected the worship of the nation and the personal holiness and evangelistic enthusiasm of the people. But there is another area that is always touched when the Spirit of God comes into our lives in a powerful way. As the nation 'returned to their own towns and to their own property' (2 Chronicles 31:1), the king ordered them to give the appropriate contribution for the support of the priests. We are told, 'As soon as the order went out, the Israelites generously gave the first-fruits of their grain, new wine, oil and honey and all that the fields produced. They brought a great amount, a tithe of everything... They piled them in heaps' (2 Chronicles 31:5–6). So much came in, that storehouses were built, but still more came in. Law called for a tithe, but grace gave more, much more.

Nothing discovers our true value more than our attitude to 'our own property'. It was this very thing that Haggai was complaining about nearly three hundred years after Hezekiah—the people had a wrong attitude to *their own* property precisely because they considered that it was their own. They had money, but because they spent it all on themselves it was like putting it in 'a purse with holes in it' (Haggai 1:6), they never had enough. In our Lord's parable of the rich man and Lazarus, that which found out the rich man better than anything else and showed that he lived like an atheist who had no interest in God was his attitude to his own property (Luke 16:19–20). The young man who came to Christ and asked, 'How can I inherit eternal life?' revealed his heart commitment when our Lord touched his personal property (Luke 18:22–24). In one of the stories Jesus told, a farmer built bigger barns containing the great harvest he had reaped that year. But the real state of his heart was seen in his utterly self-centred attitude to his wealth (Luke 12:19).

Perhaps the saddest story of all is that of the husband and wife who lied about their giving to God. They wanted at the same time a reputation for spiritual health and yet to keep a firm hold on their earthly wealth; the story in Acts 5 demonstrates that a strong grip on both is not possible. In the same way Demas was once a keen follower of the gospel but his true self was one day found out by his attitude to his own property—he loved the world most of all (2 Timothy 4:10).

Whenever the Holy Spirit comes into our lives he touches our pockets. He loosens our hold on our own possessions. In 1839 in St Peter's, Dundee, Robert Murray McCheyne remarked upon the generosity of the giving of his people for the work of the gospel overseas—it was a time of revival in Dundee. In his valuable book *Lectures on Revival* (1832) William Sprague had this to say, 'It is in the midst of effusions of the Spirit of God that men are trained to engage actively and efficiently in the great enterprise of Christian benevolence. Here they are to have their hearts and their hands opened on behalf of those who are sitting in the region and the shadow of death.' When God comes into our life, he concentrates our mind on eternity and loosens our hold upon time. If it is true that 'expenditure increases to absorb income' then it is time many Christians faced the challenge of 'pegging' their standard of living so that they do not rob God.

As you read through the Old Testament you will discover that there are two barometers of the life of the people. The first is whether they kept the Sabbath day holy, and the second is whether they gave to God what belonged to him. By reading these barometers you can tell whether the people are up or down spiritually.

Giving generously

Since it is possible for us to steal from God, and since we have at least a model of giving set for us in the Old Testament, how should we give?

In 2 Chronicles 31 the people gave so generously that they actually gave more than the priests knew what to do with! Arguing over such issues as to whether we should tithe our gross or net income, whether we should give from legacies or other gifts, and how much we can give when we are on a small income, misses the whole point. It is like the debates over what we should and should not do on Sunday. On none of these issues can we make laws or be the conscience of another, but the Bible abounds in principles to guide us.

In 2 Corinthians 9:6 and 7 Paul is writing about giving and he says, 'Remember this: Whoever sows sparingly will also reap sparingly and whoever sows generously will also reap generously. Each man should give what he has decided in his heart to give, not reluctantly or under compulsion, for God loves a cheerful giver.' Now notice these words and phrases in the verses that follow: verse 10 'increase, enlarge', verse 11 'generous, generosity', verse 12, 'overflowing', verse 14 'surpassing grace'. These are all large and expansive words. Some of them refer to our giving to God and some of them refer to God giving to us. That is exactly how it should be. When God planned the way of salvation he was not meagre in his giving, and my giving should reflect that. Dr James Kennedy built Coral Ridge Presbyterian Church in America from 40 to 5,000 members in twenty years, and he speaks of tithing 'the second time round'. That is a church with a multi-million dollar budget, and providing that was not made a law for the members, it is an example of generous giving. Should we be extravagant or mean? How many of us are stealing from God?

I have never heard Christians arguing about how they can give more. I only ever hear them arguing about how they can avoid giving as much as they think they should. Tithing is not the issue; that is simply an Old Testament model or template, and many Christians would want to exceed this under the law of grace. Paul says 'not reluctantly or under compulsion'. God would rather we give nothing if we do not want to give anything. Whenever we put up our arguments about the different culture today, and about taxes by central and local government, we have forgotten the joy of giving generously. There is a spiritual gift that I have never yet heard anyone praying for, it is the gift of 'contributing'— perhaps we don't pray for it because Paul adds the rider: 'Let him give generously' (Romans 12:8).

Giving cheerfully

There are some who talk about giving as if we can barter with God. We give to God and he will make us wealthy in return. That is a false and dangerous message because it is not the teaching of the New Testament. It is true that the New Testament encourages us to believe that if we give to God he will ensure that we will have more, but it is more that we can give. God is not concerned for our wealth, but for our ability to go on being generous: 'You will be made rich in every way so that you can be generous on every occasion' (2 Corinthians 9:11).

'God loves a cheerful giver' (2 Corinthians 9:7). Not what we can spare, but what we dare, is more in keeping with God's generosity to us. Whenever it crosses my mind what else I could do with that money, I will be giving grudgingly to God.

Giving regularly

We all plan our finances in a way that suits us best. Some budget weekly, others monthly, and still others quarterly. We give in cash, by cheque, or though standing order. Some covenant, use Gift Aid, or avoid both. The details do not matter. I have often watched Christians pass the offering by in church. I know why; they are giving well and regularly by cheque. But I cannot help wondering what the new convert or unbeliever is thinking, 'Don't these Christians give anything at all?' It is surely not hypocritical to give a small token during that act of worship.

When Paul encouraged the Corinthians to give regularly and proportionately in 1 Corinthians 16:2 the phrase 'in keeping with his income' is not only in proportion to the income but in keeping with my appreciation of God's kindness to me. Our giving is always a measure of our love to God. More especially, however, our giving should be a measure of God's love to us. For this reason our children should be encouraged to give from their own money. Parents should never give their children money for the offering as they leave for church; that teaches them nothing about giving to God. Two pence from a child's pocket money is infinitely more valuable than a pound coin from dad; only in this way will they learn why and how to give. A child will never ask questions if he is given the offering by parents, but when the money comes from his own box he will soon be asking, 'Why?'

Finishing the job

When Churchill called to America for assistance in Britain's struggle against German aggression in 1941, he pleaded, 'Give us the tools and we will finish the job.' Almost everywhere, Christian work is held up through lack of funds. We hear of missionaries and pastors living on subsistence levels, working with out-of-date and inefficient equipment. The Christian gospel deserves better than this. It is an incredible mission. We have the task of caring and evangelising. Caring so that the world will take notice and remark on the character of a God who motivates his people to care for a careless world (Matthew 5:16), and evangelising so that the whole world will know the good news of the Son of God who loved us and gave himself for us (Galatians 2:20). We say we are concerned for evangelism, but in the modern world even evangelism costs money.

If everyone who named Christ as Saviour and Lord would give proportionately, regularly, cheerfully and generously from their income, not motivated by duty but by a purposeful enthusiasm and a heart full of love for God and his gospel, then nowhere would gospel advance be hindered by lack of funds. To keep a pastor in poverty is robbing God, to deny an evangelist the tools for the job is robbing God, and to curtail a good and necessary work through a lack of finance is robbing God. And all this is breaking the eighth Commandment.

If we break this Commandment by failing to give to God, how can we expect to be blessed spiritually? It doesn't matter whether we earn a little or a lot, we can still give proportionately. God doesn't write in figures, he says give from your heart. As in everything God himself sets us the example. In Luke 6:38 we are encouraged to 'Give, and it will be given to you. A good measure, pressed down, shaken together and running over, will be poured into your lap. For with the measure you use, it will be measured to you.' This is not a wealth and happiness text; it must be translated into spiritual blessings, and that is surely what we want more than anything else. Is this why God holds back spiritual blessing on a large part of his church today? Is two percent sufficient as an expression of my gratitude to the God who gave me such grace in the gospel of Christ and Calvary's love?

Have you ever bought flower bulbs from a store where you pay so much per bag? How long have you taken pushing bulbs in and arranging them to get the maximum number possible into a paper bag? It is incredible how many will fit when our motivation is high! That is exactly what Christ is talking about in Luke 6. God tells us that that is how we are to give.

We can rob God in a thousand ways. Take the hours in a week that are left over after we have completed our daily work, our sleeping and eating and the necessary household duties; What remains is our 'free time' and there is more of it than we may think. But how much of our free time is employed for God? The equation can be worked another way: add up the time you spend with your radio, television, hobby or relaxation, your magazine or newspaper and then add up the time you spent last week in worship and working for Christ. How do the two figures compare? Are you stealing time from God? Some of us give God only half as much time as we give to our hobby and relaxation. If every Christian gave more time to God, then there would be less to do for those who are doing most.

The translation of Ephesians 5:16 has not been improved since the time of William Tyndale in 1526: 'redeeming the time because the days are evil.' *The New International Version* offers a rough paraphrase: 'making the most of every opportunity.' But 'redeeming the time' emphasises that there is a cost involved and that we are answerable to God for the time that we waste. That is robbing God. If every careless word has to be accounted for (Matthew 12:36) then surely every careless moment will have to be accounted for as well.

But is that all? What about our gifts and our energy? Writing in Romans 12:6 Paul reminds us that we have 'different gifts according to the grace given us.' We hear much about gifts today— but only a few of them. We hear too little about the most important gifts of all. What are you doing with what God has given you? Your mind, your time, your abilities. You may not be a public speaker, but can you care, encourage, organise? Whatever gift God has given you, if you are not employing it you are robbing your fellow Christians and you are robbing the church—and that means you are robbing God.

In every area of our Christian life we will discover that the measure we are using to judge our giving will be the measure God uses to determine how to bless us with all spiritual blessings in Christ Jesus. Through Malachi he promised, 'Bring the whole tithe into the storehouse...and see if I will not throw open the floodgates of heaven and pour out so much blessing that you will not have room enough for it' (Malachi 3:10).

I would hate to stand before God as a thief, having robbed God of my money, my time and my gifts. 'You shall not steal' has taken on a new dimension.

Lies and more lies

You shall not give false testimony. Exodus 20:16

Ten words account for nearly a quarter of all the words that we use in the English language, fifty more cover half our needs and a thousand would be sufficient to provide nearly ninety percent of our conversation. In spite of the fact that there are almost half a million words available to us, most of us have a total vocabulary of less than six thousand words. However, the way we use our comparatively limited vocabulary can be either encouraging or devastating to those who listen to us. Just a few words can destroy a heart, a home, a business or a reputation. The pen may be mightier than the sword, but the tongue is more powerful than both. When children respond to a taunt with: 'Sticks and stones may break my bones but names will never hurt me', every adult knows that it is far from reality. In the fifth century, Augustine of Hippo wisely commented that no physician can heal the wounds of the tongue. Cruel words can kill.

It is hardly surprising, therefore, that having challenged us to consider our attitude to himself, his day, our parents, the value of life, our emotions and to property, God should now direct our attention to the tongue. In the New Testament in vivid and unforgettable language James writes about taming the tongue: 'The tongue also is a fire, a world of evil among the parts of the body. It corrupts the whole person, sets the whole course of his life on fire, and is itself set on fire by hell' (James 3:6). I doubt whether anyone has ever written a more powerful warning about the tongue than that. Every politician knows that a 'slip of the tongue' can end his career overnight, every physician has learnt that an unguarded comment can leave a patient in a torment of anxiety, and every husband, wife and parent has experienced the 'unholy' row that followed a thoughtless word.

The word that is translated 'false testimony' refers not just to falsifying the evidence, though that is included, but to speaking what is worthless, useless or unfounded. It can refer to speech that is empty of value, pregnant with dark innuendos, or a blatant lie. This ninth Commandment is God's way of making us think about the way we talk, and not just the way we talk about our neighbour. Besides, who is our neighbour? The expert in the law who came to 'test Jesus' was well aware of this Commandment, and the one recorded in Leviticus 19:18, 'Love your neighbour as yourself' when he asked, 'And who is my neighbour?' Our Lord's reply in the parable of the good Samaritan settles the question once for all—everyone who comes across my path is my neighbour (Luke 10:25–37).

Lies and more lies

Whilst the prohibition against lying is not the whole meaning of this Commandment, it is certainly included. In Colossians 3:8–9 Paul is writing to the young Christians at Colossae and he reminds them of the way they used to live and of the radical change that has to take place in the life of the Christian. He commands them: 'You must rid yourselves of all such things as these: anger, rage, malice, slander and filthy language from your lips. Do not lie to each other, since you have taken off your old self with its practices.' Before the Colossians were converted they had lived a life of lying. It was commonplace for them and they conducted their business and handled their relationships on the basis of lies; in fact lies came off their tongue more easily than truth. The Apostle reminds them that relationships were then built upon distrust and suspicion, but now that they are Christians, all this has changed. They put off the old practices of their life when they put on Christ. Everything is now different.

That is not far removed from the way millions live today; many people are so accustomed to lying that they will lie even when there is no need to. Much of our social and business life is based upon the art of lying. A plain lie avoids an unwelcome social invitation, achieves an occasional day off from work, and denies our involvement in the spread of gossip. It may be true that business depends upon trust, but many trade on that. Lying becomes easy once we assume that the managers of our respected banking institutions, merchants who have been knighted for their service to commerce, and men and women who attended prestigious schools and universities can always be trusted. Politics has been described as the art of lies, and with almost half our marriages ending in divorce, there are sadly too few homes where the word of the husband or wife can be taken at face value. Our national life is groaning under the loss of truth and trust.

This Commandment is equally violated when we are 'economic with the truth'—what Churchill once referred to as a 'terminological inexactitude'. To give a false impression by offering only the select information we choose to give is to deceive. The media are guilty of this above all. Truth can be stood on its head by a slanted report, a misquotation or part quotation, or an edited sequence. Whilst it is undeniable that the press, radio and television have not infrequently done a great service by providing society with information that governments or businesses wished to conceal, trial by journalism is one of the great dangers we face in our instant society. In a half-hour documentary a character can be assassinated, a business ruined, or a national leader destroyed. Journalists must be held to account when they give 'false testimony'.

An expanded application of this Commandment is found in Exodus 23:1–3, 'Do not spread false reports. Do not help a wicked man by being a malicious witness. Do not follow the crowd in doing wrong. When you give testimony in a lawsuit, do not pervert justice by siding with the crowd, and do not show favouritism to a poor man in his lawsuit.' Clearly God does not believe in positive discrimination! We are not to show favouritism to a poor man in a lawsuit just because he is a poor man (see also Leviticus 19:15). Positive discrimination can be just another form of breaking the ninth Commandment. Some would say that if a man is poor then he should always be right, even if that is unjust.

'Liberation theology' argues along these lines. The poor must have justice even if through unjust means. But God will never allow that sort of argument. Never does God encourage us to dispense with justice. We must show honesty and truthfulness at all times. If the rich man has right on his side then we defend him; if the poor man should be vindicated then we side with him. Neither poverty nor riches should persuade us away from truth; to do so would be to 'Give false testimony against your neighbour'.

One of the most serious breaches of this Commandment is the lie on oath. Every day in hundreds of courts across the country men and women perjure themselves in front of judges, magistrates, juries and witnesses. God will not treat lightly those who publicly pledge their honesty and then proceed to tell lies and more lies either to defend themselves or to incriminate others. The inveterate liar probably does less damage than the man of general integrity who lies massively on a few occasions. The first man has little credibility and is therefore distrusted by all; the second has a reputation for honesty and takes advantage of it. Most people would deplore the criminal who perjures himself in court, but we have become accustomed to politicians, business men, journalists and sportsmen who lie to cover their poor judgement, insider deals, bent informers or drug taking. A society can never be healthy or secure when lies form part of its unwritten code in politics, economics, the media, sport—or religion.

But can it ever be right to lie?

The answer is, 'No', but sometimes it is essential!

In times of war, in order to protect allies, defend the innocent, or to mislead an enemy, false information will be leaked—or to put it bluntly lies will be told. Churchill called deception in war: 'A bodyguard of lies'. The cause can never make a lie right in the sense of it being a morally and spiritually good action, but it is justified on the basis that in a particular situation to tell the truth may be a greater evil than to tell a lie. Is that distinction biblically valid? I believe it is.

Towards the end of Israel's four hundred years in Egypt, their numbers had increased to the alarm of the Pharaoh. As a method of population control he ordered the midwives to kill all male children born to the Israelite women. To stifle at least one generation would limit the expansion of the Jews. The Hebrew midwives, Shiphrah and Puah, refused to obey Pharaoh's command and, in order to defend themselves, they invented the story that, unlike the Egyptian women, the Israelite mothers gave birth before the midwives could attend to them (Exodus 1:19). There is no evidence that that was true. However, the biblical record states two significant things in this episode: First, Shiphrah and Puah 'feared God' (v 17) and secondly that 'God was kind to the midwives' (v 20). We may think that they should have told the truth and taken the consequences, but apparently God did not expect that of them. Their lie was justified by the alternative—infanticide.

In 2 Samuel 17 we are introduced to a very different situation. David's son Absalom had usurped his father's throne and had taken over Jerusalem. As so often happens in a time of war David had left some undercover agents in the city, Hushai the Archite, and Zadok and Abiathar who were priests; these men were actually assigned to Absalom's court. Two young men were to act as couriers, and a servant girl would carry information to the couriers from David's agents. The couriers, Ahimaaz and Jonathan were staying at En Rogel but unfortunately someone recognised them and informed Absalom who despatched troops to arrest them. Ahimaaz and Jonathan managed to withdraw to Bahurim before Absalom's men caught up with them, and they hid in a well. The householder's wife scattered grain over the cover of the well and when challenged she told a direct lie: 'They crossed over the brook' (2 Samuel 17:20). In telling this lie she protected a vital channel of information flowing back to David, and so contributed towards saving the king's life.

The point about these two stories is that although lying is condemned by God's law, there are times when the alternative to a lie is a greater evil than the lie itself. This is the same principle that we applied to the Commandment against stealing. This does not mean that we have an excuse to tell lies to other people and then justify ourselves because we think we have served a greater purpose. We must tread a careful line, it is a rare thing for a lie to be justified and it always needs to be forgiven. Fear may make us lie, but fear does not make it right (Genesis 18:15).

The delight of gossip

'The words of a gossip', says the preacher, 'are like choice morsels; they go down to a man's inmost parts' (Proverbs 18:8).

Gossip is passing on news and rumour for no better purpose than the satisfaction of doing so; usually it is detrimental to the character and reputation of the person spoken of. Remember, 'false testimony' is that which is worthless, useless or unfounded. Unlike lies, gossip can be true reporting—but for an evil or an idle purpose. It is no defence to say, 'This isn't gossip because it's all perfectly true.' It may well be true, but the jawbone of an ass was a killer in Samson's time—and it still is! There is a law of human nature that ensures that a story passed on in gossip always increases in its ridicule and condemnation and never decreases.

In 1867 Charles Haddon Spurgeon, the popular Victorian preacher, spoke at the induction service at Thetford in Norfolk of one of his students, a Mr Welton. Many years later Mr Welton referred to what Spurgeon had said in that sermon: 'I want you to go under an operation before you leave the college and go into the church. I am going to put out one of your eyes, stop up one of your ears and put a muzzle on your mouth. And then you had better have a new suit of clothes before you go and you must tell the tailor to make in it a pocket without a bottom to it. Do you understand my parable? There will be many things in your people that you must look at with the blind eye, and you must listen to much with the deaf ear, while you will often be tempted to say things which had been better left unsaid; then, remember the muzzle. Then all the gossip you may hear when doing your pastoral work must be put into the bottomless pocket.'

In Romans 1:29 the apostle Paul comments that gossiping is typical of the world. The Greek word for 'gossip' is very expressive. Transliterated it reads *psithuristes*. Try saying that aloud and you will see why it carries the meaning of a 'whisperer' or 'tale-bearer'. Sadly, everyone loves a whisper, a piece of 'tittle-tattle', the choice morsel of gossip. Gossip reaches parts that golden words never touch; that is human nature. In 1 Timothy 5:13 Paul links gossips with busybodies and idlers. We all like to tell a little bit more than we received from the person who told us the story in the first place. When Paul sets out a list of what we may call bad talk, he says, 'I fear there may be quarrelling, jealousy, outbursts of anger, factions, slander, gossips, arrogance and disorder' (2 Corinthians 12:20).

In his final sermon before he left Northampton, New England in 1750 after twenty-three years as minister, Jonathan Edwards warned the congregation: 'A contentious people will be a miserable people'. He was right, and gossip is the false testimony that fuels contention.

The book of Proverbs contains many references to gossiping and they tell us three things in particular that gossips do: First, 'They betray confidences' (11:13). The gossip always says too much. How often have you come away from a conversation conscious that you said more than you should, and you are now worried that you may have betrayed a confidence. The gossiping tongue never knows when to stop. Secondly, 'It separates close friends' (16:28). By a little word of gossip you can so easily turn somebody against his or her friend. I have known ministers 'play-off' members against each other in that way. Thirdly, 'It fuels a quarrel' (26:20).

Never pass on second-hand stories. I not infrequently hear of something that makes me so angry; but when I check back to its source the issue is often nowhere near as bad as was reported. I am left wondering how anybody could fuel a quarrel like that. Do you know how to stop a quarrel? Stop talking—it's as easy as that; it is very difficult to quarrel when nobody speaks! Again, the preacher says it plainly: 'Starting a quarrel is like breaching a dam; so drop the matter before a dispute breaks out' (Proverbs 17:14).

Contrast all this with Christ who was firm and true in his criticism but gracious, just and fair in all his words. He never spoke unadvisedly, never spoke out of turn, and never had to retract anything he said.

Malicious slander

In his ninth century laws, King Alfred, King of Wessex and England, reserved some of the most severe penalties for slander. The slanderous tongue was to be cut off. If you think that is a little too harsh, so did Alfred! He therefore gave the guilty man the opportunity of saving his tongue by redeeming it with a payment. The payment was a proportion of the *wergild*—the ransom price of a man's whole life. In other words, if the slanderer wanted to redeem his tongue and prevent it from being cut from his mouth, he had to recognise that he must pay a proportion of the ransom price for the whole life. That reflects the gravity of slander in the court of King Alfred.

Naboth refused to give up his family inheritance to the greedy whim of King Ahab of Israel. Jezebel, the king's scheming wife, hired scoundrels to bring false charges against Naboth. They lied, 'Naboth has cursed both God and the King' and in consequence the reputation of a godly man was ruined and he was taken outside and stoned (1 Kings 21:9–14). Slander led to murder. Gossip is often true, but idle. Unlike gossip, slander is always false and deliberately hurtful. Slander is a false report maliciously spread to damage another person.

Actually the line between exaggerated gossip and slander is so fine that we often do not bother about the difference. The prophet Zechariah offers sound advice on this issue: '"Speak truth to each other and render true and sound judgement in your courts. Do not put evil against your neighbour and do not love to swear falsely. I hate all this", declares the Lord' (8:16–17). When John the apostle wrote his third letter he referred to a man called Diotrephes, a man who, John said, always 'wants to be first'. That was neither gossip nor slander but in 3 John 10 we learn how this man betrayed himself: 'Diotrephes is gossiping maliciously against us'. Gossiping maliciously is slander. Literally John writes, 'Diotrephes is doing evil, unjust words against us'. Slander always feeds our own ego and pride by unfair words against others.

Do you know someone who is always ridiculing other people? That person is very insecure and needs to slander others in order to feel adequate. They must lift themselves up by putting other people down. Our exaggerated descriptions of events or of someone's character, in order to place another person in a bad light is false witness and slander. Our refusal to see any good in those with whom we disagree is false testimony. James urged his readers: 'Brothers, do not slander one another' (James 4:11). Similarly Peter had to charge the Christians, 'Rid yourselves of all malice' (1 Peter 2:1)—malice is speaking against someone in an evil way. That is slander. The enemies of the prophet Jeremiah condemned themselves when they decided, 'Let's attack him with our tongues and pay no attention to anything he says' (Jeremiah 18:18). Not content to ignore the word of the Lord, they determined to slander the character of the prophet.

A quarrelsome spirit

There are some who love nothing better, or so it seems, than a good religious row! They are brave crusaders for their cause and consider that they alone have the truth. They will either spend their time being provocative in order to create disagreement, or they will criticise all who do not agree with them precisely. They are argumentative, quarrelsome, suspicious of everyone, dismissive of anyone, and malicious in their 'spiritual' innuendos. In fact they are thoroughly objectionable! But, sadly, they are neither a rare nor a dying breed.

Writing to Timothy in the ministry at Ephesus, Paul warned against false teachers who have 'an unhealthy interest in controversies and arguments that result in envy, quarrelling, malicious talk, evil suspicions and constant friction...' (1 Timothy 6:4–5). The danger is that they may not be 'false teachers' on everything; in fact they may be champions for the truth at some points, but their 'unhealthy interest in controversy' does little to preserve the truth, advance the gospel or build up the church. Those who spend their time 'quarrelling about words' (2 Timothy 2:14) are not only misrepresenting God, but they 'ruin' those who listen; the Greek word used by Paul in this verse is *katastrophe*—which speaks for itself!

But our handling of Scripture can come under the same judgement. We are not to 'peddle the word of God for profit' (2 Corinthians 2:17)— twisting Scripture to suit our own prejudice. If I open the Bible and claim that my understanding is what God says, when that is not what God is saying, then I am giving false testimony. This cannot be far removed from the false testimony that denies the truth of the Bible at any point, whilst pretending to teach a congregation about God. That is the most serious lie that could be told. We looked in detail at the various forms of blasphemy in chapter five, and this included misrepresenting God.

Hasty words, coarse joking and flattery

The word translated 'false testimony' refers also, as we have said, to that which is worthless, useless or unfounded; it covers speech that is empty of value.

Nabal was a surly and mean sort of man; he was wholly unreasonable and churlish and none of his servants dared to try to talk sense into him. He was very wealthy and very stupid; in fact the only redeeming side to the man was that he had a beautiful and intelligent wife—Abigail. For years David and his band of tough outlaws were holed-up in the wilderness close to where Nabal's shepherds grazed their flock. Far from stealing the sheep, David actually protected them from harm. The day came when David asked for a return favour in the form of some supplies for himself and his men. Nabal's hasty and thoughtless reply brought him and his entire household to the brink of destruction; only the wise and swift intervention of Abigail saved the day (1 Samuel 25). Nabal 'hurled insults' at David without a thought (v 14). That hasty response illustrates the worthless and unfounded accusations that are too often the thoughtless reaction in a moment of anger. The ninth Commandment warns as strongly against that as it does against direct and blatant lies.

Among the list of sins that were typical of the unconverted behaviour among the Colossians, Paul lists: 'anger, rage, malice, slander (literally 'blasphemy') and *filthy language* from your lips' (Colossians 3:8). Writing to the Ephesians, the apostle is even more direct. He refers to 'obscenity, foolish talk (and) coarse joking, which are out of place' (Ephesians 5:4). Perhaps Christians need those two verses more today than ever before.

The most popular forms of comedy, are those that play upon *double entendre*, where one meaning is almost certainly indecent. This is exactly what is meant by 'coarse joking', literally 'easy turning'—words whose meaning can be turned at least two ways. This sort of entertainment is as old as the Fall; and it comes from a mind soaked in sex. I am often saddened to hear Christians playing this same game, or enjoying the wit of those who do. It cheapens sex, and degrades serious conversation. The 'filthy language' referred to in Colossians is also obscenity, innuendo and suggestive speech. Even when the conversation is not directly related to sexual innuendo, coarse and cheap joking is 'out of place' for the Christian.

Flattery and hyperbole are condemned by this Commandment also. We have all suffered from those who 'flatter others for their own advantage' (Jude 16)—and sadly we have probably all indulged in the same thing ourselves. Flattery may even tell the truth, but its purpose is selfish. The psalmist complained bitterly that he often felt alone: 'Help, LORD, for the godly are no more', and that 'Everybody lies to his neighbour; their flattering lips speak with deception' (Psalm 12:1–2). More often than not flattery exaggerates to ingratiate.

Hyperbole is a gross exaggeration. When this is done for effect as a form of speech everyone understands. No one disciplines the child for claiming, 'there were millions at the meeting today'. But when we exaggerate to impress, it is wrong. We are probably all familiar with those people whose report about anything will be increased in excitement, importance or urgency by at least a factor of four. We learn how to 'read' their story. But exaggeration can easily become a breach of the ninth Commandment when we convince others of the 'truth' of our 'false witness'.

Many people find it convenient to do their shopping at a catalogue store where items can be chosen from a picture in a book, the bill paid, a slip passed across the counter, and the merchandise is ready for collection within minutes—at least that's the theory! Whether or not it is a cheap way to shop, the great appeal is that almost all things can be bought in one store without walking miles of floors and escalators. It is certainly a lazy way to shop! One such store, Argos, is known in most households, but few people realise that the word *argos* is Greek for 'lazy'! However, *argos* also carries the meaning of 'idle' or 'useless'. In the New Testament it is used of the unemployed men in the market place (Matthew 20:3,6), of the Cretans who are described as 'lazy gluttons' (Titus 1:12), and of certain widows who can find nothing better to employ their time than going from house to house as gossips and busybodies (1 Timothy 5:13). I am sure that the founders of the Argos stores did not intend this negative connotation! However, our Lord used the same word when he warned that on the day of judgement 'every careless (idle) word' will have to be accounted for: 'For by your words you will be acquitted, and by your words you will be condemned' (Matthew 12:36–37).

Those words should make us think seriously about the deeper meaning of the ninth Commandment. The phrase 'careless words' does not ban light conversation, or for that matter every conversation that is not 'religious'; nor does it preclude humour or a time of verbal fun. But it does warn us of the conversations or humour that are useless, hurtful, or coarse. All this is included in the warning not to give false, or empty, testimony.

The silent lie

We can lie without uttering a word or speaking an untruth. When someone is being falsely accused, or a slur is made that could easily be corrected, and we remain silent and offer no counter evidence, we are guilty of sin. Sometimes it suits us to allow the false assessment or exaggerated report to 'go the rounds'. Our silence is seen either as agreement or as indicating that we have no information to counter-balance the gossip. Our silence speaks eloquently; but the deceit of silence can be a lie.

It is perhaps equally deceitful to remain silent when an issue is discussed that demands a clear Christian or moral defence. A great many people are intimidated by what is 'politically correct' and when, for example, the virtues of homosexual practice are applauded or the value of life-long marriage is downgraded, it is all too easy to opt out of controversy by silence. But silence can imply agreement. Similarly to remain quiet when the character of Christ and his cross are under debate is actually a false witness when, in fact, we could make a positive stand for truth. Peter's presence in the courtyard at the trial of Jesus implied that he had nothing to do with the man accused. His silent deceit was forced into an open denial when his casual conversation betrayed him (Matthew 26:69–75).

Holy lies

The most serious breach of the ninth Commandment must be false testimony in the context of worship; this involves the honour of God. This subject was covered in chapter five when we looked at the third Commandment, but it can be touched on briefly here.

There are many warnings in the Old Testament against those who claim to speak on behalf of God, when God has not spoken. God never says the false prophets are simply mistaken, he says they are liars. An example of this is Jeremiah 5:31, 'The prophets prophesy lies ... my people love it this way'. Again, in chapter 27:15, 'They are prophesying lies in my name'. Thirteen times in the book of Jeremiah the prophet warns against the lies of these prophets. In Zechariah 13:3 God has a strong word of judgement against the prophets who prophesy lies: 'You must die because you have told lies in the LORD's name'. Well-meaning or not, a 'prophetic lie' was punishable by death (Jeremiah 14:13–16; 28:16–17; Zechariah 13:3).

Spiritual lying comes under a far greater condemnation from God than any other kind of lying. In the same way those who profess to teach others will be judged more strictly (James 3:1). This is the age of instant everything and, not content with the task of applying God's revelation in Scripture to the issues of today, many want prophecies and revelations that are new and immediate. Some are offered in the first person as if God himself is speaking. Most of it is undoubtedly false, and that is a serious matter because it stands condemned by this Commandment: 'You shall not give false testimony against your neighbour.' It is one thing to offer our thoughts about the future course of events, but quite another to claim divine authority for our own imagination.

There is a serious warning against false counselling in the story of Job. In response to his suffering, three friends gathered round him to offer pastoral advice. They advised him psychologically, emotionally and theologically—and they were well off-target. Job, knowing that they had grossly misdiagnosed his case, dismissed them with this rebuke: 'You, however, smear me with lies; you are worthless physicians, all of you' (Job 13:4). Those who offer counsel will be well advised to acknowledge that sometimes 'to be altogether silent' would be wisdom (v 5). To misdiagnose a case, or to misapply God's word may be giving false testimony.

Christian testimonies break this Commandment more frequently than we care to imagine. Those who add a little here and there to their story, in order to bring excitement to what they consider is an otherwise colourless testimony, are doing no service either to themselves or others, for God cannot own a lie. It is incredible how bad we can make ourselves out to be under the misguided idea that a little lie will honour God.

If Sunday is the best day for a lie-in, it is also the best day for lying! The sin of Ananias and Sapphira was that of giving a false witness to the Holy Spirit (Acts 5:3). That is our very real danger also. We can pretend to one another a spirituality that we do not really possess; but we can pretend to God as well. We can look a lie, pray a lie, and promise a lie. It has been wisely commented that Christians don't tell lies, they just sing them in their hymns! We can pray lies with beautiful prayers that do not bear any resemblance to the reality of our lives. We can talk lies when we pretend all is well when it is not.

Jephthah made a hasty promise to God. In a rash moment of spiritual zeal he promised, 'If you give the Ammonites into my hands, whatever comes out of the door of my house to meet me when I return in triumph... will be the LORD's, and I will sacrifice it as a burnt offering' (Judges 11:30–31). Fine words and a spiritual sentiment—but it was his own daughter who came out to greet him on his return! A little thought would have told Jephthah that it was very likely to be a member of his own household who would fulfil his vow, and this would make it a promise that he could not possibly keep to the letter.

Solomon warns us of this: 'Guard your steps when you go to the house of God. Go near to listen rather than to offer the sacrifice of fools... Do not be quick with your mouth, do not be hasty in your heart to utter anything to God. God is in heaven and you are on earth, so let your words be few... It is better not to vow than to make a vow and not to fulfil it. Do not let your mouth lead you into sin.' Perhaps the most significant commentary on so much of our church life and worship today is found in the next phrase of the king: 'Much dreaming and many words are meaningless. Therefore stand in awe of God' (Ecclesiastes 5:1–7). Job, whose sensitive conscience made him a man without equal in the sight of God, could plead his cause with his Maker by daring to claim, 'Would I lie to your face?' (Job 6:28).

What's wrong with lying?

A little lie to keep relationships smooth or to protect a friend from trouble is surely no bad thing? But God did not create men and women to be deceitful. Lies are an offence against our Creator because they deface his image in us; according to Christ it is behaviour more suitable to those who belong to the devil than to God (John 8:44). But lying also breaches trust. As we said earlier, a society cannot be healthy if it is built upon dishonesty, because human relationships depend upon integrity. It is essential in the home, the school, the workplace and the boardroom. The wife whose husband has betrayed her and his marriage vows by adultery will never be sure of him again; there will always be an uneasy suspicion in that home. The same result will follow in every area of life. Lies always hurt others.

However, breaking this ninth Commandment inevitably hurts ourselves also and stores up problems for later. Whilst a lie may settle an immediate problem, it almost always requires intrigue to maintain it: 'What a tangled web we weave when once we practice to deceive'. An extreme example of this is the story of the Amalekite who brought news to King David that Saul had been killed in battle. Thinking that he would gain favour with David, the messenger lied that he personally had been responsible for Saul's death. His reward was execution for daring to destroy 'the LORD's anointed' (2 Samuel 1:14)! Honesty would certainly have been *his* best policy!

The parents who lie to their children, the doctor who lies to his patient, the politician who lies to his constituent, the husband who lies to his wife, the boss who lies to his work-force, and the shop-steward who lies to his employer, may all neatly resolve an immediate problem, but they have perjured themselves, breached their integrity and shattered the image of God. Lying is always a sin. We may make 'a lie our refuge and falsehood our hiding place' (Isaiah 28:15) but they will not defend us for long; a lie is a broken reed in the time of trouble.

Truth speaks

With God there is no colour coding for lies. White lies are like white magic, they are evil because they come from the same source who is the 'father of lies' (John 8:44). Children lie by nature; we are all born liars and that reveals our true parentage. Those in the teaching profession will certainly have met parents who are sufficiently naive or stupid to defend their child—who has been caught blatantly lying—with: 'My Freddy never lies, he always tells the truth.' If that is so then Freddy should be pickled and exhibited in the Natural History Museum in London as soon as possible. In this way he will never be able to blemish his record, and subsequent generations can admire this unique specimen! Children can lie without batting an eyelid. With chocolate all over their hands and face they can declare they had nothing to do with the missing sweets; they have not yet learned the art of lying. Sadly, as we get older we become more artful and most of us can lie fairly effectively. So we have to guard our tongue against lies and deceit in all their forms.

God has never spoken a lie (Titus 1:2; 1 John 2:21). His word is truth and his promises all stand for ever. This is one reason why we can trust our Bible as a book without error. It is inconceivable that a sovereign God, who was able to create this incredible world, should nevertheless be incapable of giving us his instructions in a way that can be trusted. So, if God is a God who does not lie and whose word can be totally trusted, and if we are commanded to be like him in the way we live, then deceit must never be part of our life.

How then should we talk? The answer must be: like Christ. The people were amazed at his words (Mark 10:24) because they were gracious (Luke 4:22), full of grace and words of love and eternal life (John 6:68). He never said anything out of place, or spoke harshly or unjustly. He could criticise, speak sternly, rebuke and condemn, but never unkindly, or as gossip or slander. He could call people 'whited sepulchres' and 'a generation of vipers', but he always did it to their face and in truth. And he always substantiated what he said to the people to whom he said it. This is why the people were amazed at his words.

Even at the cross whilst the soldiers hammered nails into his hands and feet Christ could pray, 'Father forgive'. Listen to him again on the cross: 'Today you will be with me in paradise.' Words of cleansing, transformation and hope. When he was insulted by lies and false charges he did not retaliate, instead: 'He committed no sin, and no deceit was found in his mouth' (Isaiah 53:9 and 1 Peter 2:22). That is our example.

Paul has the last word for us: 'Do not lie to each other... Let your conversation be always full of grace' (Colossians 3:9 and 4:6).

All in the mind

You shall not covet. Exodus 20:17

In our Western society there appears to be a pathological neurosis about what we eat. We analyse, sterilise and idolise our food until it becomes a highly dangerous activity to eat anything! We are not sure what to eat or drink because just about everything is certain to give us heart disease, cancer or Creutzfeldt-Jakob Disease. As a result there are vegetarians, vegans, and even fruitarians who think that vegetables are dangerous. I read recently of 'breatharians'—people who claim to live just by breathing the air, although to be fair the writer did admit that he had never actually located a successful follower of that cult! We are troubled by chemical disposal, nuclear waste, toxic fumes and acid rain.

But none of this is our real problem. It is not what goes into our mouth that spoils us but what goes into our mind. As Oliver Cromwell told the British parliament three hundred and fifty years ago: 'The mind is the man.'

Conflicts begin long before the first shot is fired or the first punch is thrown; they commence with the coveting, greedy or angry heart that is fed by an undisciplined and evil mind. However important 'green' issues may be, they are trivial in comparison with the problem of the human mind. Holes in the ozone layer and spilled oil in the oceans are infinitely less of a threat to humanity than the sewage that drains into our minds through the media each day. The Bible Christian is a first-cause person, always concerned for the big issues.

The last of these ten timeless and changeless Commandments is inescapable in its application: 'You shall not covet your neighbour's house, you shall not covet your neighbour's wife or his manservant or maidservant, his ox or donkey or anything that belongs to your neighbour.' The five previous commandments have to do with our actions rather than our attitudes; the things we do against one another. Here in the last Commandment we are forced to take a look inside.

Coveting is not what we do, it is what we plan to do, what we want, what we dream about. It is the last Commandment but not the least. In many ways it is a 'catch-all' Commandment because all kinds of evil spring from coveting. Every action starts in our mind. Animals act without thinking and reasoning but men and women always do what they have already thought and planned to do. 'I want, I plan, I do' is the invariable order of human activity. This is why the Bible lays such significance upon guarding our mind (Psalm 26:2; Romans 8:6,7; 12:2); only the mind can stand effectively as a buffer between the lust for more, and the action to grab the more that I want.

It is for this reason that God closed his basic instructions on the note of coveting. If we understand and obey what that word means then it will be impossible for us to break some of the other commandments; we will never get that far. It is exactly this that Christ is referring to in Matthew 15:11 when he warned, 'What goes into a man's mouth does not make him unclean, but what comes out of his mouth, that is what makes him unclean.' Christ continued, 'Out of the heart (the wanting), come murder, adultery, sexual immorality, theft, false testimony, slander. These are what make a man unclean' (vv 19–20). But in that quotation I have omitted a significant phrase that our Lord added between 'out of the heart' and the list that follows. The missing words are: 'evil thoughts'. In other words we never go straight from the 'heart'– our wanting—to evil actions; in between the two come our thoughts. Our thoughts are either 'evil thoughts' which provide a bridge, over which the wanting crosses into actions, or they are powerfully good thoughts which act as a barrier to evil actions.

What is coveting?

The Hebrew (*kamath*) is an interesting word. It is not always used in a bad sense because it simply means 'to desire or delight' in something. On many occasions it is used very positively.

In the book of the Song of Solomon the beloved says of her lover: 'I delight to sit in his shade' (2:3). Every fellow and girl who knows what love is can at least guess the meaning of a phrase like that. But that word 'delight' is also the word for 'covet'. In fact the young girl goes on in 5:16 to claim that the one she loves is 'altogether lovely'. That is literally 'altogether delightful or desirable' and it is the same word. There is nothing wrong with that. It is a strange girl who does not think like that about the guy she loves.

There are many things in life that we can delight in, and it is quite proper for us to want them. When in Psalm 19:10 the writer claims that God's words are 'more precious than gold', what he actually says is that they are more to be desired or coveted than gold. This is exactly the sentiment that Peter urges upon Christians when he tells them to '*crave* pure spiritual milk, so that by it you may grow up in your salvation' (1 Peter 2:2). Paul encourages a young man to '*set his heart* on being an overseer (elder)' (1 Timothy 3:1). Ambition and vision, if the motive and method are God-centred and not selfish, are excellent in Christian service.

Martin Luther King was not wrong when he declared, 'I have a dream'. His dream was honourable and his motive was pure. To long for something and to reach out for it is the hallmark of Christian perseverance. Christ commanded his disciples to 'Seek first the kingdom of God and his righteousness' (Matthew 6:33), and Paul encouraged the Christians at Philippi to 'Strain towards what is ahead' (Philippians 3:13). The Olympic athlete, throughout those long months of rigorous, self-sacrificing and often painful training, will all the time be 'going for the gold'. That is a longing desire without which no athlete would ever last the course. Very little would be achieved in this world without ambition and vision. But there is another side to all this.

Over the years, our English word 'covet' has taken on a consistently negative use. However, in the Bible there is no single word that can only be used in a bad sense. The Greek word that Paul uses in Romans 7:7 when he quotes from this Commandment is also used in Hebrews 6:11 to explain the longing that a Christian leader has to see his converts grow in diligence; and in 1 Peter 1:12 it even describes the attitude of the angels who 'longed' to understand the full significance of the Old Testament prophecies. On the other hand, there is no denying the fact that whatever word is used, both in the Old and New Testament, there is such a thing as sinful desiring and longing—and we are wise to reserve the word 'covet' for that sense. Proverbs 6:25 reads, 'Do not *lust* in your heart after the beauty of the prostitute'; the word 'lust' is this word for 'covet' in Exodus 20:17. The difficulty is that the line between a proper desire and sinful coveting is sometimes finely drawn.

Did you ever read of a war that was started because of what somebody ate? As a matter of fact all war and suffering began as a result of precisely that! Eve saw that the tree was 'good for food and pleasing to the eye and also desirable for gaining wisdom' (Genesis 3:6). None of that needs to be coveting. To enjoy gourmet food, a beautiful arboretum or a college lecture is not sin. What then was so wrong with what Eve did? First, her action was sinful because the fruit was forbidden by the command of God (Genesis 2:17). But her action was also sinful because she listened to the voice of Satan that whispered, 'You will be like God' (3:4), and she wanted a wisdom that would make her like her Creator. On both counts Eve wanted forbidden fruit. That is a simple definition of coveting: longing for forbidden fruit.

The warning here in Exodus 20:17 is not against wanting, but against wanting what belongs to someone else or what I ought not to have. Remember that our neighbour is anyone who crosses our path and comes within our sphere of knowledge.

Here in the final Commandment, God covers the main areas of a person's life. You must not covet your neighbour's house, that refers to *security*. You must not covet his wife, that refers to *marriage;* a breach of the seventh Commandment involves this first: a longing for another person's marriage relationship. You must not covet his servants; since they enabled him to live at ease, this must refer to his *leisure*. You must not covet his ox or donkey; in ancient times a man's wealth was measured by the number of his animals; the more beasts he owned the greater his trading capacity; this refers to his *wealth and his status*.

God covers almost the whole world of our experience: security, marriage, leisure, wealth, work and reputation. Nothing much has changed in the past three and a half millennia; these are still the six main areas of life that cause most envy and strife in our society. One great problem of our western life-style is not that we don't have, it is just that other people have more. Generally speaking the division is not between the haves and the have-nots, but between the haves and the have-mores. We are brainwashed to want and want: the marketing agencies pour billions of pounds a year into convincing us that we need more of everything. Coveting is not necessarily wanting some, but wanting some more.

When God led his people into the promised land they would not find billboards offering the well-marketed products of Canaan.com. God knew that the temptation to covet is often more subtle than that, so he said, 'The images of their gods you are to burn in the fire. Do not covet (desire) the silver and gold on them, and do not take it for yourselves, or you will be ensnared by it, for it is detestable to the Lord your God' (Deuteronomy 7:25). Notice the way God words that. He does not simply warn them against coveting the idols that are covered in gold, he says, 'you must not even covet the gold that is on the idols'. In other words it is not enough for Israel to take the idols and burn them in the fire so that the wood in the idols is completely gone, and then to use the gold. God says you must not covet their idols or the gold covering the idols. It took considerable self-discipline to destroy both gold and silver coverings; and not all possessed such discipline.

One man in particular broke that Commandment. His name was Achan and he assessed his own problem; it is recorded in Joshua 7:21, 'When I saw in the plunder a beautiful robe from Babylonia, two hundred shekels of silver and a wedge of gold weighing fifty shekels, I coveted them and took them.' I saw, I wanted, I took—and for that Achan and his family died. Coveting is fixing our ambition upon those things that are forbidden fruit. I deliberately use the word 'fixing'. We may have to glance at some things because we simply cannot avoid them, but it is the second glance that is so dangerous. Forbidden fruit may not be wrong in itself, just as silver and gold is not evil in itself, but it becomes forbidden fruit when it is clearly not ours to have.

As with all the Commandments, there is more in this one than meets the eye initially. We must dig a little deeper to discover what warnings God is giving us here.

Coveting clings to what it owns

In Charles Dickens' A Christmas Carol, old Marley's ghost lamented a life of clinging to money: 'My spirit never walked beyond our counting house—mark me—in life my spirit never roved beyond the narrow limits of our money changing hole.' In real life, the closing years of Howard Hughes typified this same spirit. When the American tycoon died in 1976 he left an estate of $2.3 billion, yet his latter years reveal him as a tortured, troubled man who wallowed in self-neglect, lapsed into periods of near-lunacy and lived without comfort or joy in prison-like conditions. His life closed, as one report described it, 'Sunless, joyless, half lunatic… a virtual prisoner walled in by his own crippling fears and weaknesses.'

Two and a half thousand years earlier the preacher in Ecclesiastes knew this only too well: 'Whoever loves money never has money enough; whoever loves wealth is never satisfied with his income. This too is meaningless' (Ecclesiastes 5:10). It was certainly meaningless for Howard Hughes.

Whilst coveting is significantly to do with looking out at what others possess, it always betrays a wrong attitude to what we ourselves own. It is a grasping and selfish spirit. The covetous man is never a generous man, because coveting holds firmly to what it has and will not open its hand to give. When Paul reminded Timothy that 'the love of money is a root of all kinds of evil…' (1 Timothy 6:10), he had in mind not simply the evil that results from wanting more, but the evil that results from clinging at all costs to what I have.

Coveting longs always for more—and lands in debt

One thing history has proved beyond doubt is that gaining more is not a cure for coveting. For this reason the psalmist warns, 'Though your riches increase, do not set your heart on them' (Psalm 62:10), after all, 'As goods increase, so do those who consume them' (Ecclesiastes 5:11). C. Northcote Parkinson expressed it another way: 'Expenditure increases to take up our income', and Lucius Seneca, the Roman philosopher who was born within a year or two of Christ, insisted that 'Money never made anyone rich.' We know this is all true, but we just don't believe it. We all want to be a millionaire!

We covet by day-dreaming how we would spend that million pounds if we had it. One of the big lies of Satan is to convince us that we would know exactly what to do with a fortune if we inherited it. If God knew I could handle it wisely he might well give it to me. Perhaps we have what we have because God knows we can just about handle that—and no more.

We covet by envying the lifestyle or income of those more affluent than ourselves and by longing to be where they are and to have what they have.

Most of us deplore the salaries of the 'fat-cats' of industry, but few would turn down the opportunity to be one. It is this attitude of mind that lies behind the great epidemic of gambling that has hit our nation in recent years. In January 1996 a roll-over Jackpot offered £40 million on the National Lottery; that week ninety per cent of eligible citizens in the United Kingdom decided to 'play the game'. All gambling is the result of a coveting mind.

George Washington, the first President of the USA, once commented, 'Gambling is the child of avarice, the brother of iniquity and the father of mischief.' He was right—yet he kept a careful diary of his own gains and losses at the card table! Was this kind of thing in Christ's mind when he spoke of 'the deceitfulness of wealth' (Matthew 13:22)? The business tycoon, Sir Hugh Fraser, once the boss of Harrods, was ruined by gambling. He died at the age of fifty and left two million pounds in trusts, shares and property and just two hundred and fifty two pounds in the bank. On one occasion he lost one and a half million pounds at roulette in a single night. Augustine was surely correct when, sixteen hundred years earlier, he claimed, 'The devil invented gambling.'

But millions who do not express their greed in gambling, covet by allowing the phantom pleasures of television adverts and soaps to soak into their minds, so that they become absorbed by that lifestyle and conclude, 'If only I could have that.' It is that kind of day-dreaming that wrecks marriages more than anything else. When a husband and wife are going through a tough time in their marriage the world readily offers, 'Here's the kind of marriage you could have.' But it is a phantom marriage that is on offer.

We covet by window-shopping that disturbs our contentment. What once we were satisfied with, no longer satisfies us. Even flicking though a glossy catalogue can stimulate a craving for something new and better— whether in the realm of security, sex, leisure or wealth. We can covet by lusting after anything or anyone that does not, cannot, or must not belong to us. A pastor met two of his church members in the high street who told him that the husband had just received a wage rise and they were out looking for something to spend it on. That mind-set of spend and get is coveting.

The apostle James was an uninhibited writer who never pulled his punches: 'Each one of us is tempted when, by his own evil desire he is dragged away and enticed. Then, after desire has conceived, it gives birth to sin; and sin, when it is full-grown, gives birth to death' (1:14–15). Notice the way James refers to conception and birth. To change the imagery only a little, coveting is the incubation of greedy desire until an embryo of an evil thought hatches into godless action. We are all familiar with the cruel results of those whose coveting 'gives birth to death'. Daily we hear of brutal rape and murder committed solely because someone was 'dragged away and enticed' into sin by the insatiable desire for forbidden fruit. Incredibly, in our society people are mugged and even killed all for the sake of a mobile phone!

But I am afraid the tenth Commandment does not let the rest of us off so lightly with the congratulatory comment that we have neither raped nor murdered.

Debt is a national disease, and it is almost always the result of covetousness. I see, I want, I buy—and I spend too much. In 1986 more than half a million debt cases reached the courts in the United Kingdom averaging four and a half thousand pounds, excluding the mortgage. Millions more families are in arrears in their repayments, and some loan sharks are scooping a cool one thousand per cent annual percentage repayment. Well-tuned advertisements and plastic cards are responsible for most of the debt disease.

Christmas 2001 was, against all expectation, a bumper season for the stores. The tills beeped, the managers smiled broadly, and the card companies waited for the fallout. Everyone knew that the nation's Christmas revellers were massively in debt. The simple rule never to spend beyond what can easily be covered by the next month's pay cheque is apparently too straightforward for many to follow. But not one of us is immune to the powerful pull of the enticing poster or the television or radio suggestion that we will be boringly average if we do not have this particular product. Sadly, many Christians are sucked into the whirlpool of coveting. This is why Christians should budget carefully, 'peg' their standard of living and, if necessary, cut their credit card in half. One reason why we rob God in our giving, as we saw under the eighth Commandment, is because we are so busy chasing the objects of our wanting. Coveting takes us into the fantasy world of our fairy-tale castles. But fairy-tale castles often cost a lot of money.

Coveting will do nothing without reward. Captain Cook landed on Tahiti in 1769 and discovered that a previous expedition had left behind a wooden cross, but had made no attempt to bring Christianity to the natives. The great explorer speculated on the chances of a Christian mission in the area and concluded, 'It is very unlikely that any measure of this kind should ever be seriously thought of, as it can neither serve the purpose of public ambition nor private avarice; and, without such inducements, I may pronounce that it will never be undertaken.' That speaks eloquently of the captain's opinion of human nature. Little will be done without the proper 'inducements'. Coveting has a mean and grasping spirit that takes but rarely gives; and if it does give, the purpose is to fuel its own popularity and applause.

Coveting reveals itself in pride

Keeping up appearances may provide good copy for a popular television series, but it leads many into the blind alley of coveting. The only reason why we must keep up with the people next door is the shame felt by not doing so. Washing powder adverts play upon the housewife's need to have her children's clothes more sparkling than the other kids at school; motor manufacturers appeal to the husband's fear of being 'Mr Average' when the gleaming goddess is rolled out for its weekly polish; and the sportswear people know how important it is to have just the right labels on the sweat-shirt and trainers in order not to lose 'street-cred'. Advertising agencies would go out of business if the trait of covetous pride was suddenly removed from human nature. Tragically many Christians have forgotten the value of being radically different and so we are sucked into the protection of pride—at a cost.

However, we often think that coveting has to do only with things. But the very first act of coveting was not to do with things at all, it was to do with wisdom: 'When the woman saw that the fruit of the tree was good for food and pleasing to the eye and also *desirable* for gaining wisdom she took some and she ate it' (Genesis 3:6). Perhaps the only incredible part of this story is that Eve shared her discovery with Adam! Wisdom is good, and a longing to be wise is no bad thing in itself. Tragically the only knowledge Eve gained by her covetous action was a knowledge of her own nakedness (compare Genesis 2:25 with 3:7–8). It opened her eyes to the possibility of sin. The reason for her failure to benefit from that longing for wisdom was that she yielded to the temptation to 'be like God' (3:5). Wisdom is good, but a wisdom that makes a god of self is evil.

Rationalism, the belief that human reason is all-powerful, has dispensed with the need for God, and believes that it can eventually solve all humanity's problems. That is arrogant pride. It covets human wisdom above all else because without it the god of reason will never achieve its hoped-for Utopia.

The greatest goal and ambition for many is to be wise in the sight of the world. Academic success will provide knowledge, and knowledge will gain control over the lives of others. The longing for worldly wisdom drives some to constant study and research. There is nothing wrong with study, research or gaining knowledge—providing it does not consume our lives. It is not wrong to want to be successful in our work and in our business, but we must not fix our attention on it to the exclusion of everything else. We can admire others, and respect and honour them, but we should never envy the arrogant, either their prosperity or their wisdom. Asaph envied the arrogant when he saw 'the prosperity of the wicked', but later when he understood 'their final destiny' he wisely concluded that he was far better off simply to be 'near God' (Psalm 73:3,17,28).

True wisdom is found in a humble acceptance of Jesus Christ and his offer of salvation. It may be ridiculed by the world but it is the wisdom of God. To live as a Christian and to be a friend of God is more valuable than anything else the world can offer.

Coveting expresses itself in violence

Mike Storkey in his book *Born to Shop* believes that modern advertising does not encourage us to keep up with the Jones's but to keep 'upset with the Jones's'. Aggressive coveting will buy more than merely wanting.

Coveting is the big sister of twins: envy and jealousy. These two are hard to tell apart because they were born at the same time and are rarely separated. Coveting longs for something beyond its grasp, envy passionately begrudges anyone else possessing what it wants, and jealousy is apprehensive of losing what it already has. Fear and resentment flow from these three and they make formidable enemies, even among the best of friends.

The spirit that longs for more and more always begrudges others what they have. Coveting leads to jealousy and jealousy overflows in anger. Watching others in the hope that they will fall so that we can take their place is all part of coveting. Begrudging the success of others in business, marriage, sport, friendships, and even in spiritual progress, betrays a coveting heart. Envy is a born loser and always a bad loser; it can say little to the credit of others.

The Old Testament does not have different words to distinguish between envy and jealousy; only the context will help us decide, and sometimes the word *kana* can refer to the holy jealousy of God as in 1 Kings 14:22. At root it means to be full of zeal—which can be expressed in a good or a bad way. On the other hand the New Testament Greek does distinguish between envy *(phthonos)* and jealousy *(zelos)*. Envy is ill will or spite (Romans 1:29 and Philippians 1:15), whereas jealousy carries the same meaning as the Old Testament *kana*. Used in a positive sense Paul refers to his 'godly jealousy' for the Corinthians (2 Corinthians 11:2); negatively it is used in association with orgies, drunkenness, sexual immorality, debauchery, dissension and quarrelling (Romans 13:13 and 1 Corinthians 3:3).

Coveting, though not his own, cost Naboth his life. Jezebel plotted his death so that Ahab, the king, could have the vineyard he so covetously wanted (1 Kings 21). The vicious cruelty of a coveting mind is painted in its worst colours in this story.

Envy led to the first murder in history. Cain killed his brother because Abel's relationship with God was right and his own was wrong; Cain determined that relationship would not continue (Genesis 4). It was a spiritual envy. Perhaps this is the worst form of coveting, and it is especially a Christian experience. The evident growth of the church down the road, the joy of another Christian's relationship with God, the popularity of another preacher's ministry, these can lead either to a deeper hunger to know God, or to a bitter, resentful and angry spirit.

Jealousy lost Saul the reputation he was so eager to keep. He 'kept a jealous eye on David' because Saul hated the people's applause of David's great achievements (1 Samuel 18). For all his heated jealousy, Saul lost his throne, his life and his reputation in the final battle with the Philistines on Mount Gilboa.

Coveting can simmer in the mind for years, but, like a dormant volcano, it may erupt at any time into violent action. Ultimately it is always a loser. James writes, 'Where you have envy and selfish ambition, there you find disorder and every evil practice' (James 3:16). It is commonly accepted by psychologists that envy is a primary cause behind human aggression and destructiveness. It was out of envy that the Jews handed Christ over to Pilate (Matthew 27:18). Typical of Jeremiah's cutting humour is his comment on the end of the violent man: 'Like a partridge that hatches eggs it did not lay, is the man who gains riches by unjust means. When his life is half gone, they will desert him, and in the end he will prove to be a fool.' (Jeremiah 17:11) Perhaps the wise man in Proverbs puts it most succinctly of all: 'Envy rots the bones' (Proverbs 14:30).

When Radovan Karadzic ordered his artillery to pound the city of Sarajevo in 1992, few would have used the tenth Commandment to describe his action; but that is precisely what it was. The rise of Muslim and Croat national parties in Bosnia was just too much of a challenge to this inveterate gambler and psychologist. He wanted power—at any cost. Karadzic's artillery killed around ten thousand of his friends and neighbours in the city of Sarajevo. Tragically a high percentage of human suffering across the world is due to the desire for more power or wealth. As a result, millions of children die because of international, inter-state or inter-racial conflict.

In his New Testament letter, James writes of envy and greed on the national scale: 'What causes fights and quarrels among you? Don't they come from your desires that battle within you? You want something but don't get it. You kill and covet, but you cannot have what you want. You quarrel and fight' (4:1–2). That is certainly not extravagant language on the international scene. Just before the Gulf War, I was interested to hear someone interviewing a spokesman for Iraq and the interviewer was sufficiently bold to ask the question: 'This invasion, it wouldn't have anything to do with the fact that Kuwait is a very wealthy country and you are not, and that Iraq owes Kuwait large sums of money would it?' The response was immediate: 'No nothing at all, nothing at all.' Yet the whole world knew that in spite of all the religious chatter to find a cover story there was only one reason why Saddam Hussein of Iraq invaded Kuwait—greed for more power through more wealth.

That is no modern phenomenon, nor is it a foible of the east. In 1672 the English and the French declared war against the Dutch. After a disastrous defeat suffered by the allied fleet off the coast of Suffolk, John Evelyn, the diarist, described the folly of that war: 'Losing so many good men, for no provocation but that the Hollanders exceeded us in industry and in all things except envy.' That went to the heart of it. Why did the French and the English go to war against the Dutch? For one reason only: the Dutch were brilliant traders and we were not. Or, to put it another way, the English and French were envious. That was about the only thing that could have brought the English and French to the same side!

Whenever I read Philippians 1:15–18, I am amazed at Paul's total humility and lack of envy. Apparently there were some who preached the gospel partly with the motive of showing how good they were as preachers and, by contrast, how poor Paul was. Paul is nonchalantly dismissive of their 'envy and rivalry' by concluding, 'What does it matter? The important thing is that in every way, whether from false motives or true, Christ is preached. And because of this I rejoice.' Incredible man! How on earth did he manage it?

The cure for coveting

Coveting proves that my affection and attention is fixed primarily here in this life. It demonstrates where my real treasure is. That is exactly what Jesus was talking about when he warned, 'Do not store up for yourselves treasures on earth, where moth and rust destroy and where thieves break in and steal. But store up for yourselves treasures in heaven, where moth and rust do not destroy, and where thieves do not break in and steal. For where your treasure is, there your heart will be also' (Matthew 6:19–21). The cure for covetousness is to shift our sights. We must look up and beyond. It has been wisely said that when some people die they leave their treasure behind, whilst others go to receive it.

Why did Abraham leave one of the most modern cities of his day and go out into the wilderness? Because his eyes were upon God and he knew that what God had to offer was infinitely better than the best of Ur of the Chaldeans. Why did Moses turn his back upon all the riches and glitter of Egypt and lead a motley group of slaves, who gave him nothing but trouble, into a desert? Because he counted the treasures and riches of Christ far greater than the best this world had to offer. Why were the prophets in the Old Testament prepared to be ridiculed and killed, imprisoned and stoned, and still to go on preaching when nobody wanted to hear them? Because their eyes were upon the things that last for eternity and they realised that all the baubles of this world are not worth comparing with the glory that is to be revealed. Why were the apostles prepared to suffer so much? And why was Stephen willing to die for the gospel of Christ? Because they could all say with Paul: 'I consider that our present sufferings are not worth comparing with the glory that will be revealed in us' (Romans 8:18). These people all coveted the things that rightly belong to them. And what were they?

Covet a sound mind

Anyone involved in the world of computers is familiar with the phrase: 'Garbage in, garbage out'. It means that you cannot get sense out of your computer if you programme nonsense into it. I found this very discouraging when my printer insisted on pouring out pages of rubbish in spite of my carefully prepared work! Was it an intermittent fault, a virus, or just a quirk? The expert came in to resolve it for me. One thing soon became clear: my printer was perfectly OK, it was just receiving all the wrong messages from the PC. My carefully keyed information was somehow rubbished by the computer to fill the mind of my printer with nonsense. Garbage went in, so garbage came out.

We began this chapter with the reminder that what drains into our minds each day is far more important than what we eat or breathe, because as we think, so we act. The Creator gave us a sound mind in fellowship with himself. That first Fall into sin introduced the garbage that continues to twist our minds until rubbish too often comes out in our actions. For this reason Paul reminded the Christians at Rome that they needed to be 'transformed by the renewing of your mind' (Romans 12:2). They needed a new mind-set, a new way of thinking.

As I walked out of my local newsagent with a tube of mints, the man behind me was purchasing tickets for the National Lottery to the sum of nearly thirty pounds; I reflected that, statistically, if he did that each week for the next seven thousand years he could still not be certain of winning the Jackpot! But his mind-set, and that of some nineteen million like him, did not work to that logic. The covetous mind had taken reasoning out of his action.

So how did Paul expect his readers to have a renewed mind? There are two answers to this. In the first place a sincere commitment to Christ involves a 'new birth' that gives us a new mind-set and new values. Paul was positive when writing to the Corinthians: 'We have the mind of Christ' (1 Corinthians 2:16); that means the Christian can think as Christ thought. Just how that is possible we will see shortly. But secondly, Paul expected the Christians to guard their minds against the onslaught of the way the world thinks; and he sums that up in a striking statement in Romans 1:28, 'The world is given over to a depraved mind.' That means that the world can't think straight! If that seems to be 'over the top', remember that this is precisely why our nation is in such a muddle over morals, and why the man in the newsagents spent thirty pounds for less reward than I had from my tube of mints. Writing to the church at Philippi, Paul expressed it plainly: 'Let this mind be in you which was also in Christ Jesus' (Philippians 2:5).

Psychographics is the big science of VALS (values and life styles). The advertising barons draw pictures of the various target groups in society, and they give them names like DINKS (double income no kids) and OINKS (one income no kids). But an older generation is targeted as well. There are the GLAMS (greying leisured, affluent, middle aged), the BOBOS, the WOOPIES, and a whole lot more. The serious side of all this is that someone is after our mind. In a thousand ways everyday product messages are draining into our sub-conscious; and, like it or not, we all fall for it to one degree or another. To win in this battle for the mind demands firm discipline. So, how can anyone keep 'the mind of Christ' under the persistent barrage of the negative philosophy and aggressive advertising in today's world?

Covet the word of God

In Psalm 19:10 David described his love of 'the ordinances of the LORD'. They were to him 'more precious than gold, than much pure gold; they are sweeter than honey, than honey from the comb.' We have seen that the word 'precious' is the word for coveting. There are millions of people across the world today who love the word of God, the Bible, more than anything the world has to offer. If they were offered the choice of the riches of the world in exchange for the Bible, they would not need to think about it twice. They would turn down anything for the words of the living God. Long after this world has passed away the word of God will still be there.

In the autumn of 1536, William Tyndale was strangled in the market square of Vilvord in Belgium, and his body was burnt to ashes. His crime had been to translate the Bible into English so that even the ploughboy could read it. At that time the Bible in English was outlawed by the Church of Rome. Tyndale's love for the Bible and his conviction that it was the word of God led him to spurn a comfortable life and the public applause for his undoubted scholarship, and to take on the role of an outlaw, leading to his inevitable arrest and martyrdom. Today, thousands of Christian workers from every continent are working to translate the Bible into hundreds of the six thousand languages in the world.

The reason for this urgency in Bible translation is because this single book is the most powerful and popular book in the world. It is 'God-breathed' for 'teaching, rebuking, correcting, and training in righteousness' (2 Timothy 3:16). It is described also as 'living and active', judging 'the thoughts and attitudes of the heart' (Hebrews 4:12). That is precisely why the Bible is so valuable today: our moral dilemmas can be resolved only by the plain teaching of Scripture, and its relevance is appreciated by millions across the world in every kind of culture. The 'mind of Christ' is found, not in modern 'revelations' and 'prophesyings', but here in the Bible. We guard our mind best of all by the word of God.

Robert Hussein was thrown into prison in Kuwait and placed under the death sentence of an Islamic *fatwa*. His crime? In 1993 he read the New Testament and committed his life to Jesus Christ. Islamic intolerance took away his wife, his family and his job and threatened to rob him of his life also. But still Robert Hussein continued to read his Bible and pray to the true God who has given him freedom and peace. That example is repeated constantly across a fanatical world today.

This is the age of counselling. But we have lost the art of counselling ourselves through the problems of life. This is hardly surprising since we have no reliable guide. The purpose of these laws is to provide a framework for life; they show us the way to live (Exodus 18:20), and even in the 'difficult cases' of life (v 22) a mind-set that is controlled by the Bible will be capable of handling tough decisions.

Covet Christ himself

That love song in the Song of Solomon where we read of the girl describing her beloved as 'altogether lovely' (Song of Solomon 5:16) is expressive of the longing every true Christian should have for Christ. Paul's longing expressed in Philippians 3:10–11 is similar: 'I want to know Christ and the power of his resurrection and the fellowship of sharing in his sufferings, becoming like him in his death, and so, somehow, to attain to the resurrection from the dead.'

Just as there is a right kind of coveting, so there is a correct way of boasting. Through the prophet Jeremiah, God actually encourages boasting: 'Let not the wise man boast of his wisdom or the strong man boast of his strength or the rich man boast of his riches, but let him who boasts boast about this: that he understands and knows me, that I am the LORD, who exercises kindness, justice and righteousness on earth, so in these I delight' (Jeremiah 9:23–24). The wrong kind of boasting is when we boast about ourselves, but we can boast about knowing Christ in such a way that others are attracted to him. To boast of Christ must surely mean that we covet Christ, we long and desire to know him more. We are to long for him so much that we would give up anything, so long as we do not have to give up him. Paul considered everything a loss 'compared to the surpassing greatness of knowing Christ Jesus my Lord' (Philippians 3:8). That was a covetous heart.

Covet eternal life

In six powerful words in Romans 5:1–2 Paul describes the benefits of justification. One of the words he uses is translated 'we rejoice'. That can even more correctly read, '*we boast* in the hope of the glory of God'. That was Paul's priority and it was the one thing that he coveted as the ultimate prize. He tells us that he was like the athlete reaching with every muscle and nerve to the final tape 'straining towards what is ahead' and pressing on towards 'the goal to win the prize for which God has called me heavenwards in Christ Jesus' (Philippians 3:13–14).

Contrary to what it thinks, the world has trained us to think small. From the family firm to the multi-national corporation, goals are set on rising production and sales charts; billion dollar deals are a cause for extravagant celebration. Buy-outs, takeovers and monopolies are the only things worth striving for. All this is pathetically small by comparison with Paul's great goal. At one point on his journey to Rome, Paul arrived at a town called Miletus. He sent for the elders at Ephesus in order to teach them and remind them of his ministry among them. Before concluding, Paul left them with this thought: 'I commit you to God and to the word of his grace, which can build you up and give you an inheritance among all those who are sanctified.' The veteran church planter and evangelist continued, 'I have not coveted anyone's silver or gold or clothing' (Acts 20:32–33).

Have you ever wondered at the connection? Why does Paul lift them to the glorious inheritance among the saints and then drag them down to the earthly level of silver, gold and clothing? The answer is that Paul knew the Ephesians would remember his complete unworldliness whilst he was with them and that would be the best testimony to the reality of his eternal expectation. The man or woman with a firm and confident hope of a glorious future with God, demonstrates by his or her life that they have a small and passing interest in the possessions, achievements and applause of this world.

Commuters hurrying for the train home from the city are familiar with the sight of the 'vagrant' curled up in a bundle of rags over a restaurant grating. Even when he is awake he tramps the streets aimlessly, watches with empty eyes and an empty mind the world passing around him, or chatters meaninglessly with his can-swigging companions. Do you envy him? Have you ever found yourself thinking, 'I wouldn't mind changing clothes with him, I wish I could be drinking what he drinks. I wish I could look and talk like him'? Of course not. Why? Because you have something a thousand times better. You are going home to a family you love, friends you enjoy, clean clothes to wear and good food to eat.

In a similar way, but for a greater reason, Paul never coveted anything anybody had. Why should he? He was going home. He knew that he had something that made the riches and baubles of this world look like a tramp in the gutter. The big deal, fast-track promotion, rocketing into the boardroom, huge salaries, company perks, golden hand-shakes and rich dividends would mean little to Paul. He enjoyed forgiveness, peace with God and the anticipation of heaven. That enabled Paul to set an example to every Christian, everywhere: 'If we have food and clothing, we will be content with that...I have learned to be content whatever the circumstances... I have learned the secret of being content in any and every situation... Keep your lives free from the love of money and be content with what you have' (1 Timothy 6:8; Philippians 4:11–12 and Hebrews 13:5).

It is this approach to life that will enable us to walk through 'Vanity Fair' without being distracted by the glittering market stalls and entertainments all around us, to know what is right for us to possess and what is not, and to live in an affluent world without a covetous eye. It is this approach also that will enable us to be glad in the successes of others without envy, and to set our standard of living without jealousy. Obedience to the tenth Commandment will guard the other nine, create care in our churches, protect our marriages and make a holy people. Proverbs 14:30 says, 'A heart at peace gives life to the body.'

Back to the beginning

Exodus 20:18–26

When Gallup polled six hundred and one adults in more than sixty areas of Britain one day in the summer of 1996 the question was asked, 'Do you think schools should try to teach Christian values?' Just under three quarters said 'yes'. Ninety three percent believed that schools should teach respect for those in authority, and an even higher number wanted their children to be taught respect for the opinion of others; the same number wanted children to be taught not to drink and drive, and a few less that they should not tell lies. However, chastity before marriage came very low down the poll. What are we to make of all this? Although we want values, and we would like them to be Christian values, we clearly do not know what Christian values are; or else we prefer to choose the values we want (no drinking with driving) and reject those that are inconvenient (chastity before marriage).

There is nothing surprising in all this. There can hardly be a nation on earth that does not expect some kind of standard from the members of its society; but given the chance, each of those members would prefer to set the rules for themselves. The history of the human race is the story of mankind setting the rules and reaping the harvest— while all along God has given a standard that, as Creator and Sovereign, he knows is the best for the world that he has made.

Cauliflowers and duck eggs!

The Commandments are God's shorthand to make us think. They are brief and to the point. In the Old Testament Hebrew the Ten Commandments are covered in just 173 words, and our Lord's exposition of them in the Sermon on the Mount amounts to 1647 in the Greek. Less than two thousand words to provide us with the finest ground-plan for human relationships that the world will ever receive. This compares well with the European Common Market regulations on the importation of cauliflowers in what I am told are almost thirty thousand words, and a similar number for the export of duck eggs!

Of course there is more in the Old and New Testaments that applies the detail of these two lists—much more. But the value of the Ten Commandments is that they are brief and uncomplicated. In the past three and a half thousand years, those who have taken these laws as the Maker's ground-plan have had little controversy over what they actually mean. Right at the start of this book we established the important principles that these are the words of God, that they are relevant in every age and culture, and that they are intended both for the people of God and for unbelievers. God does not have one set of laws for the law-keeper and another set for the law-breaker. It is true that whilst God expected his chosen people to keep his Commandments, he knew that an unbelieving world could not. But God did not lower or change his standard. The world will be judged not by what it is capable of keeping, but by what God has commanded it to keep.

These laws are God's title page for morality. They set the agenda and establish the priorities. The first three refer directly to our relationship with God, the fourth is concerned with both our relationship with God and with others, and of the remaining six Commandments, four warn against harming people, one against harming their property, and the tenth is a warning against attitudes and desires that will inevitably, sooner or later, harm both ourselves and others. So the order in the ten commandments is very simple: it begins with God, moves to other people and ends with ourselves. God, others, ourselves. That is the biblical pattern. It is the order in which we must get things right in our lives. If we are not right with God and with other people, then we are wasting our lives whatever we are doing.

Some years ago whilst in South Africa, I tried out one of my few Zulu words on a group of young boys in a township outside Durban; I approached them with a cheery 'Sanibona'—which means 'hello'—only to be met with a muffled grunt; the boys hardly even looked at me! Coming from a society in which the person who refuses to look at you is either shifty, rude, or incredibly shy, I assumed either that they had not understood my fluent Zulu or that they were being downright insolent. I mentioned this to the people I was with and was firmly informed that, since I was the senior, the boys merely received my greeting but would not presume to give me a greeting in return. That is a matter of culture, and as such the rules are free to change as society wants them to. I just had to fit in with *their* rules.

However, the Ten Commandments are not culturally limited, they are timeless statements of what is acceptable to God and what is not. They are for the benefit of every society; they bring freedom and not slavery. Breaking these Commandments is not simply anti-social behaviour, it is sin, and sin is rebellion against God. Anti-social behaviour changes from society to society, from culture to culture. But the laws of God do not.

In fact it is the Ten Commandments that enable us to distinguish between culture and morality. Culture is amoral, but when it conflicts with the revelation of God it is immoral. We can never defend such things as disrespect, violence, immorality, theft, lying, or greed, as 'cultural'. They are sin wherever and by whoever.

At Sinai, God was not offering a few ideas for Moses to discuss with Israel at their next home-group study. On the contrary, God revealed his laws for the benefit of the whole human race. We know what God expects, and there is no doubt about it. We know also the kind of God who expects our obedience, and there is no doubt about that either. But there is another thing about which there is no doubt, and that is that we all fail to keep these laws.

Rubbernecking

Travelling home late one night on the M25 I heard a news-flash that there was a six mile tail-back because of an accident between junctions nine and seven *anti-clockwise*. I was between those two junctions at that precise moment and suddenly I found myself on the end of a queue. In order to discover whether I am travelling clockwise or anti-clockwise on this 110 mile motorway that encircles London, I have to imagine the M25 as a gigantic clock face and myself sitting on a cloud looking down on it! This rapid mental imagery assured me that I was in fact travelling *clockwise*. As we crawled along at two miles an hour I concluded that 'Road-watch' was wrong and that they really meant to say 'clockwise'. Within a few miles we came alongside the accident which *was* on the anti-clockwise carriageway—and there the traffic was not moving at all. The reason for my delay was what is known as 'rubbernecking'—drivers on my side slowed right down to take a good look at the failure in the lives of others. I have never noticed a tail-back as people admired the careful driving of those on the opposite carriageway who are obeying the rules.

Christ spoke of good works influencing the world (Matthew 5:16) and Paul writes of Christians as living letters 'known and read by everybody' (2 Corinthians 3:2). Those who profess to believe in the value of the law of God are being watched by an often sceptical and critical world. Many are just waiting for us to crash our family life and our integrity, to spoil our Christian testimony and to break the very laws we profess to uphold. They are ready to rubberneck our disaster. It is vital that Christians do not give a watching world such an opportunity. If *we* do not show just how valuable obedience to the Ten Commandments is, the world will surely learn it no other way.

First things first

The Bible does not always present narratives in the precise order in which they took place; and when things are out of sequence it is always for a reason. I believe that to be the case here in Exodus 19 and 20.

In chapter 19 we read that Moses went up to God on the mountain. Then came the thunder, lightning and the trumpet, and Moses was sent down to warn Israel that they must not come near to or touch the mountain (vs.21–22). Chapter 19 concludes at this point and the list of the Ten Commandments intervenes. In fact Exodus 20:18–26 naturally follow on from 19:25 and in these verses God warns against worshipping idols and he presents an outline plan of the altar and sacrifices. This is vital information because the arrangements for sacrifice actually come before the giving of the law. Details of the laws run from chapter 21 all the way through to chapter 31:18 with one break in chapter 24. Then Exodus 31:18 reads, 'When the LORD finished speaking to Moses on Mount Sinai he gave him the two tablets of the Testimony (the Ten Commandments), the tablets of stone inscribed by the finger of God.' So, the Ten Commandments were the *last* thing that Moses received.

In other words, whilst the Ten Commandments appear in our Bible before the details of the sacrifices, they were actually given afterwards. God's provision of forgiveness is no afterthought. It is not a rushed response to an unexpected failure of the law to keep the people in check. God knew that the Ten Commandments would be breached more than they would be obeyed, but they were still necessary so that the people would live with a standard and without excuse. However, God planned the way of forgiveness and revealed it first. An altar and a sacrifice was the way of substitution for sinners; the place where those who acknowledged their breach of the law could find forgiveness.

When governments make laws, they accompany them with penalties for breaking the law. Few people will keep a law if there are no penalties. However, it was the character of God to precede the law with the provision of forgiveness. That is the gospel. Throughout this commentary we have often closed a chapter with the statement that where there is law there is gospel.

No hope from Hammurabi

In the first chapter we saw that one of the most ancient law codes known to us is that of Hammurabi, a king of the Old Babylonian (Amorite) Dynasty who, on the current reckoning, reigned from 1792 to 1750 BC. We noted that the Hammurabi Code contains a long list of civil regulations, some of which are similar to the laws revealed to Moses and recorded in Exodus and Deuteronomy. However, what is more significant than any similarity is that in the two hundred and eighty-two codes, the name of god or Marduk appears only a dozen times—and there is not one single reference to a sacrifice for those who fail to keep the laws. In other words there are codes and penalties, but there is no word about forgiveness.

Added to this is another striking difference: in the epilogue that appears on the reverse of the stone 'stela' or column, all the attention is drawn to the great king. It was the king himself, admittedly with the wisdom given him by Enki and Marduk and Shamash, who gave these 'precious words' to his people. Hammurabi proudly declared, 'My words are choice; my deeds have no equal' (Epilogue line 100). There are many lines of curses upon the ruler who does not teach his people Hammurabi's laws, but not one word about repentance or forgiveness. So much for the ancient laws that some critics assume Moses copied! Where did the leader of Israel obtain his ideas of forgiveness so intimately bound in with the moral laws of his God? Certainly not from Hammurabi.

Manners, morality and magic

I studied Jane Austen for part of my English Literature course at school. As the years went by it was almost embarrassing to admit my knowledge of this eighteenth century writer. But no longer! A 'Jane Austen frenzy' on both sides of the Atlantic saw the film *Sense and Sensibility* grossing over $21 million in its first few weeks. Yet Jane Austen's novels hardly fit in with today's image: they are non-violent, non-sexy—though very sexist—and romantic to the point of being *bijou*. Her writing is reminiscent of the age that spawned such organizations as 'The Society for the Improvement of Manners'. Writing in *Perspective* early in 1996, Brent Vukmer suggests that the Americans (and he could have been speaking for the Brits as well) are not simply yearning after a society that had 'manners', but many are longing for one that has fixed moral principles. A survey by the Family Research Council in 1995 found that two-thirds of Americans believe society is 'on the wrong track'.

Books about traditional values are best sellers. Whatever your opinion of the writing of J K Rowling, no one can deny that the Harry Potter series is staggeringly successful, with millions of books in forty-nine languages. But apart from the brilliantly written stories, vivid descriptions and gripping plots, Harry Potter ought not to be popular! The boarding school setting should be as boringly old-fashioned as 'The Famous Five'. But there is something that probably attracts both children and adults more than they imagine: so far, in Harry Potter good is always good, and good wins out. As with Tolkein and Lewis it is a battle between good and evil. The stories are scattered with gems of instruction. Dumbledore in *The Philosopher's Stone:* 'The stone was really not such a wonderful thing. As much money and life as you could want! The two things most human beings would choose above all—the trouble is, human beings do have a knack of choosing precisely those things which are worst for them.' Dumbledore again in *The Chamber of Secrets:* 'It is our choices that show what we are, truly are, far more than our abilites.' And in *The Goblet of Fire:* 'It matters not what someone is born, but what they grow to be.' It is this emphasis upon good winning over bad that makes Lewis, Tolkein, Rowling and a host of others in this genre so appealing.

All this *may* provide some encouragement by pointing to the fact that it reveals a uniquely human longing for standards and for clear lines between right and wrong. Perhaps it is too much to hope that our nation is on the verge of a move back to a better morality; but we will never find it so long as we side-line the Maker and his instructions. However, we are standing at a dangerous cross-roads because there are many offers of morality all the way from religious prophets and gurus to the Humanists' 'Golden Rule of Morality'.

The con of consensus

We are inundated with rules and regulations from Westminster and Brussels. Whenever we drive our car onto the road we stand the possibility of breaking any one of hundreds of laws involved with insurance, tax, rules of the road and so on. It is all very complicated—like the cauliflowers and duck eggs. But it is tragic if we send our children into life equipped with degrees and certificates for everything from astro-physics to athletics, but ignorant of the straightforward laws of their Creator.

The idea that morality is a social consensus has been tried and has failed. The cacophony of voices demanding our attention has been unable to provide the nation with a serious and consistent standard to teach our children. We have more religions than ever before, but they have not provided a clear standard either. Tragically we have chosen to ignore our Christian heritage and we are lost in a moral maze.

These Commandments are not to be apologised for, hidden away, rubbished as old fashioned, or discreetly forgotten in the service of respecting other religions, they are to be believed and taught as the laws of a wise Creator. Then we will begin to realise how good and beneficial they are. The youngest children can learn the Ten Commandments which will make them wise for life, and the youngest children can also understand about the cross which will make them wise for salvation.

A signpost to Christ

In the Old Testament the altar, which was provided at the same time that the law was given, was a picture preparing for the coming of Christ. Throughout the long centuries of Israel's history, every sacrifice, every animal that was offered, every drop of blood that was shed, and the smoke of every burnt offering, was like a signpost or finger pointing on to the coming of Christ. He was the Lamb both chosen and slain from the creation of the world (1 Peter 1:20 and Revelation 13:8). He who was utterly without sin would carry to the cross our sin and become our 'propitiation', turning away God's just anger on our sin (Romans 3:25; 1 John 2:2; 1 John 4:10).

In this powerful set of laws given through Moses, the Sovereign Creator tells us the best way to live, not to put us in a straitjacket but to set us free. The law, rightly understood is liberating; it should be our delight, as David found it to be (Psalm 1:2; 119:70,97,163,174). The true Christian should be able to conclude, 'I love these Commandments. They may interfere with what I want to do, but that is precisely why I love them. They set me free from the shackles of sin.' These laws are the standard of holiness and they reveal the kind of God we serve. They show us how holy he is, and therefore how holy we must be.

However, we need far more than the law, because it is inevitable that we will break it. No one will ever earn salvation by obedience to the law (Romans 3:20). Hammurabi had nothing to offer his people except curses upon the leader who led the nation astray. Moses offered the gospel. Here is a God who delights in his people both then and now. A God who made a way of reconciliation then and now. Ours is a God who says, 'I command you, but I love you.' And his love is measured by the death of his Son at Calvary. At Sinai the presence of God and his holy laws caused the whole mountain to shake, but that can only drive us to the place of the sacrifice which was provided even before the law. Let the law of God and the anger of God drive us to the cross. There is nowhere else for a law-breaking sinner to find forgiveness. Here alone is found a righteousness to cover our sin: 'A righteousness from God, apart from law, has been made known, to which the Law and the Prophets testify. This righteousness from God comes through faith in Jesus Christ to all who believe. There is no difference. For all have sinned and fall short of the glory of God' (Romans 3:21–23).

We do not need moralizing, or a social consensus of what is right and wrong, or even escape into the dream-world of late Georgian England, Narnia, Middle Earth or the magic of Harry at Hogwarts to fill the moral void felt by millions. It is urgent that we return to the robust laws of a kind and holy Creator. Because he alone knows what is best. But a return to the Ten Commandments has to be matched by our commitment to live out these laws and to teach them to our children.

Our best attempts to keep God's laws will leave us in need of forgiveness for failure. But where there is law there is always grace. And grace is offered in the cross of Christ where alone certain forgiveness is to be found and where also we find the greatest incentive and strength to keep the Ten Commandments.

Genesis

Exodus

Index

Index

Published by Day One

No longer Two—A guide for Christian engagement and marriage
Co-authored by Brian and Barbara Edwards. First published 1994. Large format. A fully revised edition 1999. 159 pages.

AD. A booklet to celebrate the millennium.
32 pages. Illustrated. Co-authored with Dr Ian Shaw.

Horizons of Hope—reality in disability
Eight stories of living with disability including Brian and Barbara's own story. First published 2000. 243 pages. Illustrated.

DayOne Travel Guides
Series Editor. A series of biographical travel guides. Full colour illustrations and travel information. Approx. 130 pages.

In Conversation
A series of booklets (about 20 pages each) dealing with contemporary issues and written in an easy-to-read conversational style. Suitable for teenagers and above.

What's special about Sunday?
What is the New Age?
Is Hell for ever?
How do we get Guidance?
Tongues and all that
Baptism in the Spirit – What's that?
Where are the Apostles and Prophets?
Help! I'm Redundant
Why shouldn't we?—sex before marriage
Healing Today?
What's the Sense of Suffering?
How can I become a Christian?
Not under Law—the relationship of Old Testament law and the gospel.
The price of Life—eugenics, abortion and euthanasia.

Symposiums edited by Brian Edwards and published by Day One
The following two books form part of the *Facing the Issue* series in co-operation with the FIEC.

Men, Women and Authority
A response to the debate on the role of women in the church. First published in 1996. 259 pages including a Scripture index and a general index.

Homosexuality Today—the straight agenda
First published in 1998. 263 pages including two appendices.

Published by Evangelical Press

Through Many Dangers
The story of John Newton (1725-1807). First published 1975. Also available in Spanish 1981, Portuguese 1988, and French 1992. English edition fully revised and expanded 2001. Illustrated and including Scripture index, general index, bibliography and significant dates. 368 pages.

God's Outlaw
The story of William Tyndale (1494–1536) and the first printed English New Testament. First published 1976. Fifth impression 1999. 185 pages with full index. Illustrated. Also available in German 1981 and Norwegian 1989.

Nothing But the Truth
The inspiration and authority of the Bible and how we got our English Bible. First published 1978.

Illustrated. New and expanded edition 1993 with Scripture index and full index. 392 pages. Second impression 2000.

Not By Chance
How can we believe in God with all the suffering in the world? 123 pages. First published 1982. Third impression 1989. Also available in French 1991.

Shall We Dance?
An examination of the use of dance and drama in worship and evangelism. 153 pages. First published in 1984. Second impression 1991.

Revival—a people saturated with God
A study of spiritual revival in the Bible and history. 303 pages with full index. First published 1990. Fifth impression 1999. Also available in Spanish 2001.

Can we pray for revival?
A biblical theology of revival. First published 2001. 214 pages with Scripture index.

Also from Day One

The Edge of Life—

Dying, Death and Euthanasia

JOHN R LING

288 PAGES £8.99

1 903087 30 9

Author Dr Ling analyses infanticide, bereavement, eugenics, ageing, suicide, hospices, autonomy, living wills, and much more within the rugged ethical framework of the Judaeo-Christian doctrines and the Hippocratic oath. His conclusion is that modern medicine has lost its way because it has departed from its historic foundations. To counter this, the author calls for a return to the culture of life and the exercise of 'principled compassion'.

REFERENCE: EOL

Responding to the culture of death

JOHN R LING

128 PAGES £5.99

1 903087 26 0

People often don't know what to think about bioethical issues. Dr Ling's conviction is that we now live in a culture of death. Much of modern medicine has gone very wrong and has become a threat to all.This book develops a rugged bioethical framework, based on principles derived from the Bible, and supported by analyses of recent trends in medicine and science. A response from readers is called for.

REFERENCE: RCD

An excellent book...warmly recommended'
EVANGELICAL TIMES

Hallmarks of Design

Evidence of design in the natural world

STUART BURGESS

200 PAGES £7.99

1 903087 34 1

This book exposes the weakness of evolutionary philosophy by arguing that God has placed His hallmark on creation, and that this hallmark is clearly evident in the complexity and design of living beauty all around us. This book strengthens the argument against current scientific orthodoxy.

- ● **Six clear hallmarks of design**
- ● **Over 30 diagrams**
- ● **Description of how the earth is designed**
- ● **Description of the Creator's attributes**

REFERENCE: HALL

He made the stars also

What the Bible says about the stars

STUART BURGESS

192 PAGES £6.99

1 903087 13 9

This book teaches clearly and biblically the purpose of the stars and the question of extra-terrestrial life. Dr Burgess explains how the earth has a unique purpose in supporting life and how the stars have a singular purpose in shining light on it. He explains why the universe contains such natural beauty and how the stars reveal God's character. Illustrated.

REFERENCE: HMS

'Dr Burgess has a very clear style and his book brims with interesting material...greatly appreciated'
DR PETER MASTERS, METROPOLITAN TABERNACLE

Call or email us for a full catalogue—see the back cover for details